PENGUIN CANADA

THE FIRST MAN IN MY LIFE

SANDRA MARTIN, a senior feature writer with *The Globe and Mail*, has won the Atkinson and Canadian Journalism Fellowships and multiple National Magazine Awards. She was the co-editor of the annual *Oberon Best Short Stories* and *Coming Attractions* anthologies from 1984 through 1986 and is the co-author of three books, including *Rupert Brooke in Canada* and *Card Tricks: Bankers, Boomers and the Explosion of Plastic Credit,* which was shortlisted for the Canadian Business Book Award in 1993. A past president of PEN Canada, she is the mother of a grown son and daughter. She lives in Toronto with her husband and her cat, Alice.

The first man
in my life
Daughters write
about their
fathers

Edited by
Sandra Martin
With a foreword by
Margaret Atwood

PENGUIN
CANADA

PENGUIN CANADA

Published by the Penguin Group

Penguin Group (Canada), 90 Eglinton Avenue East, Suite 700, Toronto, Ontario, Canada M4P 2Y3
(a division of Pearson Canada Inc.)

Penguin Group (USA) Inc., 375 Hudson Street, New York, New York 10014, U.S.A.
Penguin Books Ltd, 80 Strand, London WC2R 0RL, England
Penguin Ireland, 25 St Stephen's Green, Dublin 2, Ireland (a division of Penguin Books Ltd)
Penguin Group (Australia), 250 Camberwell Road, Camberwell, Victoria 3124, Australia
(a division of Pearson Australia Group Pty Ltd)
Penguin Books India Pvt Ltd, 11 Community Centre, Panchsheel Park, New Delhi – 110 017, India
Penguin Group (NZ), 67 Apollo Drive, Rosedale, North Shore 0632, Auckland, New Zealand
(a division of Pearson New Zealand Ltd)
Penguin Books (South Africa) (Pty) Ltd, 24 Sturdee Avenue, Rosebank, Johannesburg 2196,
South Africa

Penguin Books Ltd, Registered Offices: 80 Strand, London WC2R 0RL, England

First published 2007

1 2 3 4 5 6 7 8 9 10   (WEB)

Introduction, contributor biographies and selection copyright © Sandra Martin, 2007
Foreword copyright © Margaret Atwood, 2007
The Copyright Acknowledgments on page 254 constitute an extension of this copyright page.

Manufactured in Canada.

LIBRARY AND ARCHIVES CANADA CATALOGUING IN PUBLICATION

The first man in my life : daughters write about their fathers / ed., Sandra Martin.

ISBN-13: 978-0-14-305117-6
ISBN-10: 0-14-305117-2

1. Fathers and daughters—Literary collections.
2. Canadian essays (English)—Women authors. 3. Canadian essays (English)—21st century.
4. Women authors, Canadian (English)—Family relationships. I. Martin, Sandra

PS8367.F3F57   2007   C814'.608035251   C2007-900057-6

Visit the Penguin Group (Canada) website at **www.penguin.ca**

Special and corporate bulk purchase rates available; please see
www.penguin.ca/corporatesales or call 1-800-810-3104, ext. 477 or 474

For W.M.M., 1919–2005

Contents

Foreword

by Margaret Atwood

W hen I was asked to write a contribution to this collection of pieces about fathers and daughters, I said I would try. It was after all an absorbing and important subject. For many women who have later come out with surprising accomplishments, their fathers have been crucial influences, for good or ill. Encouraging, malignant or violent, benign and loving, maddening or boring, or simply looming large through their absence—for every daughter there is a father-shaped space that must somehow be dealt with, however well or badly it may have been filled. Sometimes a stone idol to be toppled, sometimes a locked door to be opened, sometimes a plain-looking box that proves to be full of unexpected treasures, sometimes a labyrinthine knot to be unravelled: Fathers keep turning up like Hamlet Senior's ghost, insisting we remember.

Remember what? Like Hamlet, we seek to recall and substantiate things we don't quite know we know. All parents are enigmas, possessed of secrets and mysteries. It's always a shock to a child to discover that a parent has had an independent life, a life that took place before the advent of the centre of the universe that is the child itself; and that there has also been another life, one led separately but parallel to the child's own life. In one sense, how dare they, these wayward parents? In another, how could it have been otherwise, and why did it take us so long to find out?

I did try to write my piece for this book. I was in fact already engaged on a story that was to be an account of my father's own—unsuccessful—attempt to write something about his life, a life that had seen him move from a backwoods farm in Nova Scotia at the beginning of the twentieth century through a series of incarnations—square-dance fiddler, village schoolteacher, logging-camp worker, scholarship boy, northwoods researcher—that had landed him in Toronto, as an entomologist. But this story of mine has not yet been finished, so I had to remove myself from the list of contributors. The collection you are about to read contains many wonderful essays about fathers, but mine is not among them.

Possibly my failure with this story had something to do with a visit I paid to Nova Scotia while in the throes of writing it. I got too much extra input; it interfered somehow with the neat scheme of things I'd come up with.

I went to see two of my aunts—one on each side of the family. Aunts always know unexpected things about your parents. I also met, by chance, a descendant of a woman who'd been a neighbour of my father's as a child. This person had an old photograph of him, sitting on a split-rail fence with his brother and three sisters lined up beside him, in Huckleberry Finn–type garments for the boys and frilly white Victorian dresses for the girls, all feet bare. "Your father was like a god to the younger kids," said the owner of the photograph. "He was always teaching them things." (My father was indeed kind to children, and delighted in showing them things under logs, such as ants, and explaining their ways.) "Is it true that when he was seventeen he used to walk ten miles through the woods, on weekends, on trails he cut himself, back and forth to the village where he was teaching school?"

I asked my Aunt Ada about this. "Of course," she said, as if it were nothing at all to be marvelled at. As for my Aunt Joyce, she told me something my father had once said to her. He used to walk to primary school along the Clyde River, and one day he saw an enchanting blue butterfly drifting downstream on a log. This was the moment at which he knew he would devote himself to the study of insects. Such moments do not arrive through reason, and are not decisions coldly made. They come through love.

This story completed a circle, for me. When he was seventy-seven, I'd taken my father to a rain forest in Ecuador, where huge Blue Morpho butterflies were drifting among the trees. "I never thought I would see these," he said, as if he'd said he never thought he would see Heaven. For him, Nature and wonder never came unglued.

I wish I'd known the blue-butterfly-on-a-log story earlier. But what do we mean when we say things like this? Only, perhaps, that we ourselves might at times have been more understanding.

I haven't finished my Father story yet, but I did write a poem. Here it is:

Butterfly

My father, ninety years ago,
at the age of—my guess—ten,
walked three miles through the forest
on his way to school

along the sedgy wetfoot shore
of the brimming eel-filled rush-fringed
peat-brown river,
leaving a trail of jittering blackflies,
his hands already broad and deft
at the ends of his fraying sleeves.

Along this path he noticed
everything: mushroom and scat, wildbloom,
snail and iris, clubmoss, fern and cone.

It must have been an endless
breathing in: between
the wish to know and the need to praise
there was no seam.

One day he saw a drenched log floating
heavily down the stream,
and on it a butterfly, blue as eyes.
This was the moment (I later heard)
that shot him off on his tangent

into the abstruse world
of microscopes and numbers,
lapel pins, cars, and wanderings,

away from the ten square miles
of logged-out bushlots
he never named as poverty,
and the brown meandering river
he was always in some way after that
trying in vain to get back to.

Introduction

by Sandra Martin

We all have fathers, even if some of them are absent, anonymous or dead. The longing to connect with them is a constant in both life and literature. Mavis Gallant, the short story writer, whose fiction is about outsiders trying to insinuate themselves into alien situations and cultures, has always been haunted by the cold animosity of her mother and the disappearance of her father when she was ten. It was years before Gallant knew the truth, that he had died of lung disease, but that unrequited loss is reflected in stories that are full of children who are frightened, unloved or alone. Although she has always been an elusive quarry for interviewers, she did admit once, "I think it is true that in many, many of the things I write, someone has vanished. And it is often the father. And there is often a sense that nothing is very safe, and you're often walking on a very thin crust."

When I was working on this anthology, I talked with a young New Zealand woman named Rebecca Hamilton, who had been conceived with sperm from an anonymous donor. There are at least a million children who have been created this way. Ms. Hamilton loved her mother and the father who raised her, both of whom have already died, but that didn't erase her longing to meet her biological father. That desire came partly from wanting to know her genetic and medical history and partly from wanting to learn whether she, supposedly an only child, had half-siblings, but much of it emanated from an unquenchable urge to look at a masculine face and say, "Yes, that's where I come from."

Even daughters who grew up in intact nuclear families often find that our fathers are a mystery that puzzles and torments us. We know what they look like, but not why they behave the way they do. We recognize mothers as creatures like ourselves, no matter how fractious the umbilical connection. Fathers are "the other," caught somewhere between our husbands and our sons in the aspic of romance, heroics and disappointment with which we construct our view of the world. Where would the wicked stepmother be without a cowed father of motherless children to dominate? Or the angel/whore without a father figure to inspire worship or lust?

The role of fathers has changed drastically in the last generation. If they choose, today's fathers can be more hands-on in the raising of their children, elect to stay at home while their wives grasp at the elusive rungs of the corporate ladder, or claim paid parental leave in that first clamorous year of an offspring's life. That physical closeness, borne of intimacy, is largely a new dynamic.

Most of us, who are now adults, and even parents, had a more tenuous childhood connection to our fathers. Saints or bullies, providers or louts, heroes or tyrants, loving or repressed, and often a mesh of several types—our fathers traditionally worked away from home and came back flashing their paycheques and signalling their authority over our mothers to let us know, as though we had any doubt, who was really in charge. As Margaret Atwood wrote in her 1988 novel, *Cat's Eye*, "All fathers except mine are invisible in the daytime; daytime is ruled by mothers. But fathers come out at night. Darkness brings homes the fathers, with their real, unspeakable power. There is more to them than meets the eye."

Some of us feared that our fathers secretly longed to escape from the economic and emotional burdens of wives and children and the authoritarian role that was thrust upon them simply because of their sex. But back then, the kind of frank conversation I have with my own children about role models and the sharing of responsibilities was rare.

After my father died suddenly of a stroke in 2005, I agonized over the fact that I would never again be able to talk with him or smooth some of the rougher contours of our relationship. His death was the end of shared conversations, of answers to questions about family history, of watching his pride in his maturing grandchildren. In my grief, I found myself thinking about him and his life, trying to make sense of a pivotal and often contrary relationship. And that made me curious about other women and how they felt about their fathers— and whether they had experienced unbidden revelatory moments, as I had done while helping to prepare a funereal collage of snapshots and other memorabilia.

Fairy tales, novels and plays abound with female characters longing for, submitting to or challenging patriarchal relationships. Think of *Cinderella* or *Sleeping Beauty,* Cordelia in *King Lear,* Brünnhilde in Wagner's *Der Ring des Nibelungen.* While there is plenty of fictional and clinical writing about fathers and daughters, there is very little reportage from the emotional front lines of real life. We don't have many smart, gripping and fresh narratives about fathers as three-dimensional figures, in all their idiosyncratic variety, written by the daughters who have observed them since childhood.

Traditionally, full-length memoirs written about fathers by their daughters tended to be admiring portraits that often owed more to romance than to reality. In the last decade, several women have written deeper and often very disturbing books, such as *The Kiss: A Memoir*, by Kathryn Harrison, *My Father's House: A Memoir of Incest and Healing*, by Sylvia Fraser and *The Shadow Man*, by Mary Gordon, an account of how Gordon peeled back her fantasy about her dead father to uncover a man whose values and anti-Semitic beliefs clashed drastically with everything she believed she knew about him. These images are extremes within which most of us try to reconcile masculine stereotypes with our emotional and psychological bonds to the men we call Dad. (As an aside, finding a title for this collection of essays that didn't imply incest as an overarching theme was an onerous struggle.)

So, I set out to find Canadian women with distinctive voices and compelling stories that illuminated different aspects of the father–daughter relationship—the good as well as the bad. The contributors come from a variety of backgrounds and experiences, both culturally and ethnically, and range in age from their twenties to their nineties. I asked them to highlight a moment of truth, an insight or a revelation that enabled them to see their fathers anew, as men, no matter how frail and uncertain.

Their stories are sometimes sad, sometimes angry, sometimes funny, sometimes heroic, but I believe they are all loving and all driven by a desire to understand what Margaret Atwood in her foreword to this book has called "a father-shaped space that must somehow be dealt with, however well or badly it may have been filled." And speaking of Atwood, she was not alone in finding it difficult to write about her father. I had at least a dozen conversations with confident, well-published women who quaked at the idea of breaking the silence that slams down like a trap door to protect the reality of family life from outside scrutiny. One contributor withdrew her piece after many painful drafts because confronting the extent of her father's pedophilia was simply too hard to process in print.

"Why do you think we write fiction?" a prominent novelist asked me when I broached the subject of autobiographical writing and its difficulties. Fiction lets you slide away from pesky facts and uncomfortable truths and imagine bridges to carry you safely over cavernous fault-lines. I know that in the challenge of writing my own piece, I often wished to escape into an imaginary world where I could excise stuff that still hurt or eluded me, but that was not the purpose of the exercise. "Why don't you just write the piece and put it in a drawer?" a relative asked me. But that is not what writers do: We write about our experience to make sense of it and then we share it with as many people as care to read it, hoping that it might illuminate some aspect of their lives.

I didn't try to slot these narratives into categories. They are too varied and too rich in humour, revelation, pain and love for easy lumping together like products on a grocery store shelf. Besides, that is not the way I read anthologies. I skip around, reading in the order that pleases me. That's why I have organized the collection alphabetically, beginning with Katherine Ashenburg's discovery, when she was thirty-five, that her beloved father was Jewish not Catholic, and ending, some twenty stories later, with Pamela Wallin's sweetly spoken gratitude to her father for literally saving her life.

Along the way, we travel to Anita Rau Badami's India, experience the terror Marina Nemat survived in Ayatollah Khomeini's Iran and visit a Haisla community in British Columbia in Eden Robinson's zany tale about driving, which is really a love note to her father. We revert to chippy adolescence in Catherine Gildiner's hilarious memoir, observe a modern take on Brünnhilde's conflict with Woton in Mary Anne Brinckman's treatise on her environmentalist father, relive the immigrant experience with Tina Srebotnjak and meet the private sides of some very famous fathers, including Michael Manley, the former prime minister of Jamaica, novelist Mordecai Richler, painter

Tony Urquhart and broadcaster Peter Snow. And we share the interior perspectives of fathers who may well have inspired fiction and poetry in the reflections of well-known writers such as Camilla Gibb, P.K. Page and Susan Swan.

There does seem to me to be a generational difference in the way that younger women such as Rebecca Godfrey, Rebecca Snow and Emily Urquhart write so openly and easily about the contradictions and vulnerabilities they see in their fathers. I think it has something to do with the way, in recent decades, fathers generally have become so much more engaged with the physical and emotional nurturing of their children. This connection may have made them feel less remote from their families and consequently more willing to reveal their own feelings as parents and as men. And that in turn, perhaps, has provoked empathetic responses from their daughters.

Two of the contributors, Nancy Dorrance and Jane Finlay-Young, write eloquently about family tragedies that, in very different ways, traumatized them and put onerous demands on their fathers. Their stories, which provide evocative testimonies to the travails that can befall any of us, leave me with an unsettling question: How would I have responded in the same situation? And finally, as the pieces by Christie Blatchford and Sarah Murdoch show so unequivocally, there is no getting away from our mothers and their influence, no matter how hard we try.

Collateral Damage

by Katherine Ashenburg

I spent my childhood denying that my father was Jewish.

(No, that's not right. A typical exaggeration, and misleading.)

I was determined to have Kaddish said at my father's funeral. When the time came, I realized that that was my wish, not his.

(No. Begin at the beginning, and keep it simple. But keeping it simple is difficult. I know the outward events, but the characters' motivations are stubbornly mysterious. All the principals are dead, or have lost their memory. And, worse, I've been dining out on parts of the story for so many years that I no longer know what I've distorted for better effect.)

The main facts are indisputable. On June 13, 1942, Elsie Siegl and Norman Ashenburg were married in a Catholic ceremony in Norfolk, Virginia, near the naval base where the groom was stationed. Their wedding picture shows a joyful wartime couple, she in a short, white linen dress and a picture hat with a ruffled brim, he in a dazzlingly white

1

naval uniform. While studying for a Ph.D. in bacteriology at the University of Rochester, he had taught a course for nursing students that included Elsie, a tall, pretty brunette. After he gave her an A, he began courting her, methodically outstaying the other suitors who came calling at her parents' Rochester, N.Y., house. The only family member at their wedding was the bride's mother, who travelled to Virginia by train.

In 1945, while my father was in Guam with the U.S. Navy, I was born. Once the war was over, he returned to Rochester, abandoned his Ph.D. and went to medical school. He became an internist, and by the time I was ten my parents had five children. We children lived in a world that was largely Catholic and centred on Blessed Sacrament parish. (The date carved into the cornerstone of the Gothic Revival church, 19+11, worried me in the years before I learned to "carry over" in addition. I took the cross in the middle for a plus sign.) The big sand-stone church sat half-circled by the school, the convent and the rectory. Across the street was Murphy's Funeral Parlor, ensuring that all life's rites of passage could be accomplished on Oxford Street, just off Monroe Avenue. At Blessed Sacrament, we were all baptized in a long, white, embroidered dress that came from my father's family, made our First Communion and first confession, went to school and attended Mass with our parents every Sunday.

My maternal grandparents, Francis Xavier and Katie Siegl, also belonged to Blessed Sacrament. They too had a wartime wedding picture, from World War One in Bavaria—my grandmother in an ankle-length dress with real floral festoons on the skirt; my grand-father stern and tall, as befitted a member of the Kaiser's Guard, with a handlebar moustache. The two had grown up in neighbouring parishes, and met when my grandfather attended a flag-blessing ceremony at my grandmother's church. In the mid-1920s, with the

German mark spectacularly devalued, they emigrated with their little girl, Elsie, to Rochester.

I never saw a wedding picture of my Ashenburg grandparents. I would love to know if one ever existed. The only photograph of them in our family album was taken when they were probably in their sixties, a staged-looking affair in front of their barn in which my grandmother, Pearl, rather formally presents a platter of corn on the cob to her husband, Morris. My grandfather, who died when I was about five, is a benevolent-looking bald man. My grandmother looks uncharacteristically eager to please. She was a tiny, compelling character who wore my father's boyhood knickers as full-length, bloomer-like trousers. I was fascinated by her dark hair that wound around her head in braids, and the family story that, when unpinned and unbraided, it fell to her knees. She and my grandfather lived in a village outside Rochester, on land that included a farmhouse and two small barns. My grandfather travelled into town on the bus, to work as a cutter in a tailoring factory. I think I knew that their native language was also German, but their accents were different from those of my Siegl grandparents. What country they came from before they landed in New York City around 1910 was obscure. Sometimes, Vienna was mentioned in connection with my grandfather, but my father usually responded to my questions about them with vagueness or professed ignorance.

(Did I imagine that my grandmother's report cards, which we discovered in her attic, came from Krakow? Or did I make that up? Did I say "somewhere in the Austro-Hungarian Empire" when asked about my grandparents' birthplace because I'd been told that or because it sounded glamorous?)

I can still remember exactly where I was sitting—in the middle bedroom in our house on Dartmouth Street, on the twin bed closer to the window—when Grandma Siegl told me that my father had converted to Catholicism before he married my mother. I was about nine or ten, and why she told me escapes me, but I remember it as one of the most pure surprises of my life. The fact that my parents had never mentioned it was almost as surprising as the fact itself. When I asked them what Daddy had been before he became a Catholic, the answer was, "Nothing."

That marked another difference between my mother and my father. Partly because he was away for long hours when I was very young, at medical school, his internship and his residency, and my mother was home with the dirty diapers and mess and crying of babies and toddlers, she struck me as the visceral, earthbound, practical parent. He was the more sensitive one, outwardly at least—the one who saw pictures in clouds, who hated to hear about one of our classmates not invited to a birthday party, who taught me one morning while he shaved that by adding "ess," I could transform words from the masculine to the feminine. Princess, actress, poetess, huntress. I was about six, and I loved that kind of information. "Now," he said, in his calm, quiet way, putting away his razor, "you've learned something, and you haven't even been to school yet."

By the time I was ten, it was clear that my father's Catholicism was, if not marginal, by no means mainstream. He was unacquainted with most of the theological concepts I was learning in elementary school, and when I taxed him about this, he admitted that his Catholic instruction had been a speedy, wartime affair. He winced, on hygienic grounds, at the holy water fountain in which hundreds of hands were dipped before blessing themselves, and the Good Friday custom where we lined up in church to kiss a wooden crucifix. Once, he made us laugh helplessly by referring to the nuns as "priestesses." (Just add "ess" …) On a family vacation in Quebec, he horrified me by doubting that the crutches hung on the walls in the shrine of Sainte-Anne-de-Beaupré represented real cures. I was at my most pious, perhaps thirteen or fourteen, and when he saw my distress, he recanted. "No, you're right," he said, "of course they were miracles." But I knew he was only being kind.

That was a rare expression of skepticism. Catholicism for my father seemed like an inoculation that hadn't really taken, but he treated it and its priests and nuns the way he treated most things— gently and with a respectful interest. At the same time, I was gradually realizing that some people thought we were Jewish. Like most mistakes made by grownups, this one didn't strike me as particularly interesting, but there were a few instances that made good stories.

(Now comes one of the episodes that I have burnished over the years. I tell it like this:)

When my sister Beth was about six, she sat on the bus one day in front of two women in our parish, who didn't recognize her as an Ashenburg. One woman asked the other, "What is it about the Ashenburg kids? They're all so smart, so talented …" The other woman thought about it, and said, "Well, they all have the Jewish oomph." Beth didn't know what "Jewish" meant any more than she knew what "oomph" meant. That night at dinner, she said matter-of-factly, "A lady on the bus said we all have the Jewish oomph." It became a family joke, something between a minor distinction and an ethnically named disease, like the German measles. When my father would examine our sore throats, looking for signs of strep throat, he would sometimes tease us, "I see just a little Jewish oomph by your tonsils, nothing serious."

(Where is the truth in this anecdote? Beth has no memory of the bus incident, but she says she often forgets things. There must have been a germ of reality in it, because I didn't often make things up out of whole cloth, just prodded and padded an incident into something more shapely and entertaining. Something that made my family sound wittier and

more like a family in a book. Probably Beth did overhear a conversation about us and our "Jewish oomph," or a similar description, on the bus. But I doubt it became a family gag, since none of my siblings remember that. And it's not credible that my father joked about it, because in fact he avoided the subject.)

It didn't occur to me in those days to wonder what Grandma Ashenburg made of our Catholicism. She had no Christmas tree, but every Christmas she and our aunt Helen, my father's only sibling, gave us each a present—usually something that impressed me as very fine, like the child's biography of Audubon I received one year. Grandma Siegl, by contrast, arrived at our German Christmas Eve celebration with a big cardboard box for each of her twelve grandchildren, filled with handknit sweaters, flannel pyjamas and other hastily but skilfully homemade clothes. Her box full of unwrapped presents spoke of Germanic industry and practicality; the Ashenburgs' one, distinctive, store-bought gift seemed to hail from a more refined sensibility.

Grandma Ashenburg's real religion appeared to be the teachings of Bernarr McFadden and other early-twentieth-century health faddists, whose doctrines she followed devotedly—strict vegetarianism, no alcohol, no medicine, no doctors. When I was prescribed glasses for nearsightedness, she fed me curds and whey. If I ate them regularly, she told me, my myopia would disappear and I could throw away my glasses. I regarded Grandma's miracle cures much as my father did the crutches at Sainte-Anne-de-Beaupré. He, of course, had had a much more intense childhood experience of her convictions. Meat or fish had never touched his lips until he disobediently ate a hot dog at a Cub Scout picnic, and he remembered it as one of the most wonderful sensations he ever had. (His weekly letter to her, as a married man in the Navy, always had to include his weight. To the end of her life, she never knew that her son drank an occasional beer.) Long after the other boys had short hair, she refused to cut his golden curls, just as he had to keep on wearing his knickers while his friends graduated to long pants. We children loved laughing at a 1920s triptych of photographs in which, wearing chin-length curls and a sailor suit, our father danced and pretended to play a horn. Depending on his mood, he smiled wanly or hid it away.

Grandma Ashenburg was so eccentric that nothing she did surprised me. Unlike my Siegl grandparents, who offered little scope for a storytelling child's imagination, she and the mysteries that accumulated around her were a cloth I embroidered on, finishing a fragment here, highlighting a detail there, so that I no longer know what was woven into the fabric and what was a later embellishment. As children, we enjoyed believing that the ashes of our grandfather were kept in a small Grecian-style urn on top of her upright piano. *(Perhaps they were.)* As a teenager and later, I told my friends that her bookshelf held a published essay my grandfather had written about Neo-Platonism in Nazi Germany. *(I can hardly have known what Neo-Platonism was when I started telling this story, so perhaps it is true.)*

When my father *("the golden-haired Messiah," in my story)* was born, my grandmother moved across the hall from the bedroom she shared with her husband to the baby's room, and she slept in her son's room until he left to join the Navy. *(My sister Carole remembers a different version, that she banished her husband to the attic.)* I have a precise memory of visiting her with my father when I was a young woman and she was very old. One of us opened her fridge and saw with amazement bright heaps of orange-and-turquoise capsules. With her usual disregard for the medicine her doctor son brought her, but with some bizarre sense that it shouldn't be thrown out, she had emptied bottle after bottle of pills into round cake pans.

(How to separate the truth from the fanciful here is a conundrum. Mary Gordon wrote a fine memoir, The Shadow Man, *about her father, who converted from Judaism to Catholicism, and lied about most aspects of his life. First she had to give up the idea of memory as a trustworthy source: It soon seemed "as malleable as last week's gossip, and as undependable." Then "the silence of the grave" took over. "This is the curse the dead lay on the living," she writes. "It is their punitive, their cynical, hold over us: They will tell us nothing. They ensure that we will be, in relation to their lives, incapable of distinguishing fact from invention. They guarantee the falsity, the partiality, of our witness." I am doubly guilty. Not only did I decorate reality until memory became even more unreliable than usual, but I let my father and his sister die without asking them the necessary questions.)*

When I was fifteen and a sophomore at Our Lady of Mercy High School, I had the title role in the spring play, *The Diary of Anne Frank*. One day, the rehearsal did not go well, and Sister Pius, the director, spent some time with me explaining why. At the end, she said encouragingly, "I know the role means a lot to you, with your father being Jewish." As usual when this happened, I said, "No, Sister, he wasn't Jewish. He had no religion, and he converted when he married my mother." By then, I rather enjoyed the mistake: It gave me a tinge of something exotic, definitely a bit tragic. Certainly it was more interesting than being in the smallish numbers of German Catholics at my school, or the larger numbers of Italians, or in the largest group of all, the Irish. When I was still in elementary school, my friend from down the street, Barbara Sharcot, had taken me to the quaint old synagogue she attended in our neighbourhood. It looked like an ordinary wooden house outside, except for the black sign above the door, covered with beautiful gold letters in Hebrew. Inside, the chanting, the people walking about and talking, the old man who was charmed by two little girls and kept trying to show us where we were in the service—it was as different from the Mass as could be, and I liked it. Now, as a teenager, I had a thing for Jewish boys—they were smart, highly verbal, and they made me laugh. They had an energy I responded to—no doubt, the Jewish oomph.

But it was still a mistake. My father wasn't Jewish. What about the christening dress that came from the Ashenburgs? (Never mind that that was a puzzling artifact from a family that claimed to have no religion.) Sister Pius probably went back to the Motherhouse that night, shaking her head about the Ashenburg children, who didn't know where they came from. Sister Pius was a good director. She began the *Anne Frank* production with slides of the concentration camps being liberated, and had bought a tape with authentic World War Two–era European sound effects, including the siren of the Nazi police that ends the play. My parents came for both performances. I'm sure they complimented me on my acting, but made no other comment.

About two decades after I played Anne Frank, I was visiting my parents in Rochester while my father recovered from a heart attack. One day, while he rested upstairs, my sister Carole and I chatted with our aunt Helen. I lived in Vancouver with my husband and two daughters, working as a producer at the CBC. My sister was in her late twenties, in medical school. But "the Jewish question" was still alive. Imperceptibly over the years, I had begun to see it as a possibility that in the dim European past, hundreds of years ago in a strange town, my father's family had a Jewish connection. It was that nebulous. Carole—the one in the family who always broached the un-askable questions—had actually asked my father some time before this if his family were Jewish, and he said, "No." End of discussion.

Now, without warning, Carole was doing it again. She asked Helen, a high school math teacher who had always lived in her younger brother's shadow as the less beloved, less special child, "Don't you think that long ago, your family may have been Jewish?"

My aunt paused for a second, as if a regrettable but un-dodgeable subject had been raised.

Then she said four words that changed everything.

"Well, we never practised."

There it was. My parents' living room—the Oriental carpets, the window seat, the club chairs, the antique pub tables—looked the same, but everything had shifted. What may have been a dim possibility in eighteenth-century Krakow, or nineteenth-century Vienna, among people we would never know, was suddenly a live certainty. Carole had invited our aunt into a historical speculation, but for her the question was neither historical nor speculative.

(Carole thinks I was the one who asked Helen, but this isn't possible. Through the years that we had joked about our Jewish past, it became clear that my father didn't want to talk about it. I assumed, wrongly as it turned out, that Helen had the same aversion, and I would not have raised the subject. I shrink from confrontation and uncomfortable questions; I respect reluctance when I sense it. I inherited this from both of my parents.)

This was the key—the only—conversation we would ever have about our Jewish roots with an Ashenburg of that generation, and I wish I could remember better what we talked about next. Carole and I were amazed, and we asked why no one "practised," and why no one ever talked about it. Helen said they simply weren't interested. Then, she either added, or I extrapolated from what she had said, that religion and modern, educated people didn't mix. Because they didn't believe in the theology, they didn't consider themselves Jewish. From a Catholic point of view (but not necessarily a Jewish one), that made sense, but it didn't explain why they didn't talk about it. Actually, now that we were talking, Helen seemed perfectly willing but a bit bemused about why Carole and I found it so fascinating.

Eventually, Helen left, and my sister and I consulted. Strange as it seems now, we believed that we were the only ones who had been entrusted with this great secret. Our father didn't know it, we were sure, and we were not going to tell him while he convalesced from a heart attack. We decided that our imperturbable mother could stand the shock, and we went out to the kitchen where she was cutting radishes *(in my story, they are radishes)* for a salad. We couldn't wait for preliminaries.

"Mom," one of us said, "Helen told us that Daddy's family is Jewish!"

She kept on chopping.

"Yes," she said. "I know."

"You know. You know? How long have you known?"

"Well," she considered. "I told my parents before we got married."

(Another shock.)

"When did Daddy tell you?"

"He never told me. We've never discussed it."

This from one-half of the most compatible couple, a couple who could talk late into the night over their instant coffee about the doings of some family member or a chest they had spotted at one of their favourite antiques shops.

"Then, if he never told you" (now we were feeling our way through increasingly strange territory), "then how did you *know*?"

Finally *(or so my anecdote goes, but I think it's fairly accurate)*, finally, we succeeded in stopping the salad-making. She put down her knife *(probably an added touch)*, and looked with some surprise at her two supposedly smart, worldly daughters.

With some finality, she said, "It's pretty obvious, isn't it?"

Carole and I looked at each other, at a loss for words. This would take some thinking about. A tailor named Morris Ashenburg and his wife, Pearl, whose culinary specialities—honey cake and sponge cake—were staples of the Jewish kitchen. It was starting to be obvious, but it hadn't been, at least to his children. But *why,* we asked our mother—our refrain—why didn't anyone talk about it? If we'd lived through World War One and Two, our mother said, we would understand what terrible things happened when people emphasized their differences and categorized others as "them" or "us." When she first came to Rochester after World War One, an English mother on their street wouldn't let her children play with "the German girl." She'd never forgotten the sting of that. After World War Two, there was even more reason to downplay differences in country, religion and culture. True, and sobering, but it still didn't explain why she and her husband couldn't discuss it.

Nor did we ever discuss it with our father. For years, I held two contradictory convictions: Daddy doesn't know he's Jewish, and Daddy doesn't want to talk about being Jewish. The second belief, an unspoken but massively present prohibition, ensured that I never found out from him that he did know. After the revelation from Helen, I decided that his parents had never told their prized son about his origins, either because it was rarely a subject of conversation or because he was too precious to learn about his ancestors' superstitions and folk customs. Why didn't I want to think that he knew? Because it made the story more romantic, casting him in the role of the little prince raised with no knowledge of his kingdom? Perhaps, partly. But probably also because I didn't want to think that he rejected being Jewish. That wasn't at all the kind of thing my father would do.

Because we'd been edging closer and closer to the truth over the years, Helen's revelation might have been anti-climatic. But it wasn't. At the same time, I didn't quite know how to react. Carole says I joked that I suddenly felt much smarter. I remember thinking confusedly that the Jewish men I'd always found so attractive were off-limits—now that I knew they were my brothers, it felt vaguely incestuous. More seriously, I felt deprived. Something rich and many-coloured and profound that I'd seen from afar turned out to be an intimate part of who I was. But it was so fragmentary and late in arriving that it left me at a loss, in more ways than one. Only the last feeling has endured.

Helen died nine years ago, and my parents decided to have an informal memorial service in their living room, after her body was cremated. When I arrived in Rochester, I asked about the program. My father and the principal of the school where Helen had taught would speak, and everyone would be invited to reminisce. Then, my father said, Helen's daughter-in-law, Carol-Lynn, "wanted to say a prayer she had found in a funeral parlour." That afternoon, in the same room where Helen told us that her family never practised, we gathered—my parents, four of their children, my mother's sister, Helen's son Paul, Carol-Lynn, and their twin daughters, and a few friends and neighbours of Helen.

Carol-Lynn, who is Jewish, was sitting next to me on the couch. After the remarks, she stood up. She said, "I'd like everyone to stand now and say Kaddish for Helen." She passed out copies of the prayer. We all took a paper. It was another of those stunning moments. None of my siblings looked at each other, and certainly not at my father, who had wept during his talk about his sister. We said the Jewish prayer of mourning together for Helen. I wonder whether she would have considered this "practising." I hope that she would have found it touching. It's doubtful that Carol-Lynn described Kaddish to my father as "a prayer she found in a funeral parlour," although that was probably where she got the copies. At the family dinner afterward, as usual, no one discussed it. (Carole, who probably would have, was in Seattle.)

In the years since Helen's revelation, some familiar things have become puzzling. When did what must have been Aschenberg become Ashenburg: at Ellis Island, or later? We've never figured out the fancy infant dress we used for baptisms—perhaps it served for a naming party or a bris? Another familiar thing that might have been a clue—the fact that my father, born in 1917, was circumcised—now makes sense. As a young woman, I was hazy about the history of circumcision and since my brothers, like the majority of postwar American boys, were circumcised, my father's state seemed unremarkable.

Occasionally, we get a glimpse of what we've lost, as if a lens were suddenly adjusted and a world snaps into focus. Beth was the only one of us who attended our cousin Paul's wedding to Carol-Lynn. Since the bride was Jewish, the rabbi, the huppah and the yarmulkes didn't surprise her. But when the ceremony was over, and everyone danced the hora, Beth watched our shy, serious aunt dancing with joy and confidence. Here is a side of Helen I never saw, she thought—and a whole culture into which she slips with ease.

More often, in my own case, I have to work at my Jewish connection, because we were told so little. A few years ago, I spent most of a day going slowly through the Holocaust Museum in Washington, D.C. Deliberately, over and over, as I read descriptions of shops destroyed, parents separated from children and life in concentration camps, I told myself, you could have had family members in this town, maybe your great-grandparents or great-aunts and great-uncles were transported in this kind of cattle car. By the time I reached the museum's last room, where candles could be lit for those who had died in the Holocaust, I really *knew*, as opposed to an intellectual certainty, that I was lighting candles for my own family.

When I would tell the story of my father's family to Jewish friends and acquaintances, they often concluded, "They just wanted to assimilate." I denied this vehemently, because my grandparents were perfectly content to be the village oddballs, a family with more than their share of quirks, who kept to themselves. As for my mild, tolerant father, why would he want to—ugly word—"assimilate"? He had plenty of Jewish friends. Jewishness was no impediment to a medical career in his generation. His most beloved mentor in medicine, George Engel, was Jewish. So was his oldest friend, Morrie Secon, who played the French horn at his funeral.

In the last year or so of my father's life, as he grew more uncensored, I understood more sharply than I had before that he hadn't liked his parents much. In his eighties, he had taken a selective interest in health foods, subscribing to newsletters on the subject and faithfully grinding his flaxseed in a little machine. When I teased him that his mother would be proud of him, he always looked glum. He had been a dutiful son, particularly in her last decades, but in some way he never forgave her controlling eccentricity. She had been the dominant parent, and it sounded as if his father had not opposed her. My father wanted to be a regular American boy, playing sports, eating hot dogs, going out with girls, and his parents tried to thwart that.

Once, when my grandmother was old and bed-ridden, Carole went with our father to visit her. Looking even smaller than usual, she lay with her hair longer than she was, streaming out down to the footboard of the bed *(my sister insists this is true, but perhaps her memory is fanciful too)*. It sounds like an Arthur Rackham fairy tale illustration crossed with Roz Chast, or some other surrealist artist. Above her bed was a picture of my father that we knew well because it was on his Kodak business card ("Norman J. Ashenburg, M.D., Medical Director"). But the little head shot had been blown up to absurd dimensions, perhaps two by three feet. There was this tiny old woman in her bed, underneath a huge picture of her middle-aged son. It was such a comic/poignant expression of her obsessive love for him that even my father laughed to see it. He could afford to laugh, because he had gotten away.

He escaped, but at the cost of his Jewishness. That was the price he paid, the collateral damage of his fight for independence. Even though his parents declined, or mostly declined, to be Jewish, he knew it was part of them. I think I've only really accepted that obvious truth—another one—in the course of writing this essay. Unlike his parents, he did want to assimilate, in that he wanted a more conventional, less eccentric life. Judaism wouldn't have prevented that, but he couldn't disentangle it from his parents' other beliefs and foibles. It was part of his parents' package, and he didn't want the package.

On one level, he was an obedient son, in that he never espoused the theology and culture they dismissed. On another level, probably not one he was consciously aware of, he found an exquisite revenge on them, in that he married a Catholic, converted, had five children and became a doctor. All those things disappointed his mother. (If she ever heard a Jewish "my-son-the-doctor" joke, she must have been baffled by it. Why would you want your son to be a pill-pusher who didn't understand the medicinal qualities of plants?) But at the deepest level, his values were Jewish: Above all, he prized his wife and children, education and the work of mending a broken world, in his case through medicine. In that cultural sense at least, in spite of everything that he—and we—lost, he saw to it that his children had a Jewish upbringing.

Since Helen's memorial gathering, I'd had the idea of saying Kaddish at my father's funeral. When he died, a Catholic funeral seemed appropriate. Although both parents had given up going to Mass decades ago, when he had recently faced a risky medical proce-dure, he had joined the local parish and even gone to Mass a few times. I interpreted it as a willingness to strike any bargain that would keep him alive to continue caring for our mother, who has Alzheimer's. The funeral was going to be held at the University of Rochester, and when Carole and I met the Catholic chaplain, I asked about Kaddish. No problem, he said. The funeral Mass has two readings from the Jewish bible, and two from the Christian bible. I asked if all the readings could come from the Jewish bible, and he said, "Unorthodox, but why not?"

But when I read through the book of suggested readings and thought about it, I realized that we should have readings from both bibles. My father chose Christianity and although it didn't quite work, he never renounced it. And Kaddish was a sentimental idea of mine that would have displeased him. His true faith was medicine, and the university where he discovered it, which was why the university chapel was the correct venue. Rich in family history as Blessed Sacrament was, he had always stood a little apart from it. Even the university's bald, prosaic name for its house of worship—the Interfaith Chapel—was right for him.

Waiting for Mountains

by Anita Rau Badami

In 1991, nearly ten years after my father died, I was in a plane flying over the Pacific Ocean to Vancouver and from there to Calgary, our first stop in Canada. I gazed down at snow-covered mountains heaped in jumbled piles for miles around, at silvery ice-covered rivers threading through the solid bulk of rock, at flat glacial sheets, and thought of how much my father would have enjoyed this aerial view. And later, when I emerged shivering from the airport into the frigid Calgary air, cursing my husband for having dragged me away from warmth, wondering whether it would be a good idea to turn tail and catch the flight back to India, it occurred to me that Daddy would have been at home in this wintry landscape. He would have rubbed his hands together and said, "Hah! Cold is good, makes the brain work harder...."

1981. It was early December in Madras, or Chennai as it is now called, and the northwest monsoon was howling through the city, high winds making the tall, slender Ashoka trees in our garden thrash in the air like possessed beings. It had been raining continuously for almost a week and there were fears that a cyclone might be approaching over the Bay of Bengal. Tamil Nadu, the state in which Chennai is situated, is the only part of India that receives monsoon rains in winter. Winter, though, is rather an exaggerated term to describe the weather conditions in the city at this time of year, with the lowest temperature being twenty-two degrees centigrade. Hardly cold enough to warrant the woollen caps, mufflers, shawls and sweaters that emerge, redolent of mothballs, from cupboards and trunks.

My father, who was asleep on the couch in the living room, his breath a pain-filled rattle, used to find these preparations for Chennai winters hilarious. Now he too was shrouded in a shawl, his feet encased in thick socks, a muffler wound about his neck. He refused to wear a cap, though. To do so would be to admit defeat to Madam Winter, an inconceivable thing, since Daddy considered himself a child of mountains and cold places.

I could see the top of his head from where I sat, and a sharp sorrow cut through me at the sight of brown scalp visible through the still black hair. Chemotherapy and radiation had made him lose most of his handsome thatch of hair. I had a sudden urge to stroke that beloved head the way Daddy used to stroke mine when I was a child and had a fever. The touch of his big, slightly rough hand had always made me feel better. But I stayed where I was, fighting tears at the sight of my father reduced to a skeleton, terrified that if I moved, if I made a sound, it might disturb his rare sleep—for that was another comfort that pain had taken away from him.

Daddy was suffering from bone cancer, and in the past year he had been in hospital more than at home. Two days ago, fed up with the medicinal smell of hospital corridors and the starchy impersonality of the medical staff, he had decided to discharge himself from the hospital where he had been incarcerated for nearly a month. He had phoned my brother, Anand, and ordered him to pick him up. "Don't tell your mother you are coming to get me," he had insisted. Then Daddy had somehow managed to wheel the IV unit linked to his wrist past the duty nurse's office without being noticed by anyone and had waited shakily at the entrance for my brother to arrive.

I had watched as Anand drove our ancient car, a twenty-year-old Morris Minor, through our front gate on his way to the hospital. On its rear window was a sticker which an uncle had presented to Daddy: "When I grow up I want to be a Rolls Royce." The car was on its last legs, but my father would not dream of getting rid of it. He loved that car— more than he loved her, Mummy would say with amused resignation— and had christened it Black Beauty. Rainwater swirled around the tires, and I prayed that it would not break down somewhere along the way.

My mother, who was visiting a friend for a rare break, would have been furious if she knew that my father was heading home. It wasn't that she didn't want him with us. This would in fact have been far easier for her to manage, for she spent the nights with Daddy in his room at the hospital and the days making sure that the three of us children were okay. But the last time he had sneaked out, he had had a bad relapse the same night and had to be rushed back in an ambulance. My mother could not bear the tension. Daddy, on the other hand, could not bear the hospital. And so my brother had been summoned.

Now my father was lying on the couch in the drawing room while I sat in the dining room trying to write. The two rooms were separated by a divider in the form of an enormous two-sided oil painting framed in teak and set on a low bookcase. It was one of my father's creations— although he was an engineer by profession, his passion was art. On the side facing the drawing room, he had painted a brightly coloured land-scape dominated by a copperpod tree much like the one that flowered profusely over our garage every summer. The side facing me depicted another, completely different scene with dark-toned pines glowering down on a snowy, silent landscape which unrolled towards a distant range of hazy mountains. I did not like this side of the painting very much, could not relate to it as my life, so far, had been full of the flashy over-bright multi-coloured jumble that is India. I didn't understand my father's fascination with snow, which I'd never seen.

My father had spent his childhood in Shimla, a small town in the foothills of the Himalayan ranges. He loved mountains—preferring them to the sea. He had once said that those huge thrusting towers of earth calmed him in a way that the restless ocean never could. He painted them often, and our home was full of his memories of those mountains from his past. Naturally, Daddy also preferred the cold to the heat. For a few years we had lived in Lucknow in northern India, where winter temperatures went down to zero degrees, making the rest of us miserable. Only my father looked forward to this season when frost sometimes crackled on the grass and the garden was aglow with poppies and phlox, roses and delphiniums. He would spend Sunday afternoons basking in the mild afternoon sun eating roasted peanuts and staying out there until darkness had descended and the stars had begun to appear, coming indoors only when summoned for dinner. And then looking at us huddled gloomily around the electric heater in the dining room he would grin, rub his hands and exclaim, "Come on, you lot! Cold is good—makes the brain work harder to keep warm."

He always hoped, rather unrealistically, that the temperatures would go low enough to bring down some snow—a thing that only he had seen, in Shimla, the town of his childhood, and later, in England, where as an engineering student he had lived for some years. And he dreamed of retiring to Dharamshala, a small village which, like Shimla, nestled in the Himalayan foothills. He would give my mother a teasing look and ask, "What do you say? You can knit sweaters and I will look at the mountains."

I don't recall why Daddy had picked this particular village on which to fix his dreams of retirement, but he mentioned it often, even going so far as to write to the tourism office for information. My mother, a woman whose habitat was the city and who could not bear the thought of spending her old age in some benighted, frozen village, would shake her head and say, "You can go if you want, I am staying in Bangalore with my children."

"But the mountains," my father would argue. "Don't you want to see them? We can go for long walks. I will show you how beautiful snow is."

"Not for me," Mummy would say firmly. "Mountains can stay there," she would point a manicured finger towards the sky, "and I will stay here." Another finger aimed at the mosaic floor of our home.

After my father discovered that he had cancer, he mentioned Dharamshala less frequently, and in the last year, not at all. Now it was my mother who brought it up every other day. "Come on Daddy," she would beg. "Tell me about the house you are going to build for us, hanh? And what about a garden? What grows in those cold places? Roses? Can we transplant my roses to this place in Dharamshala? And the walks? What kind of shoes will we have to wear for snow-walks? Tell me. And the mountains. Will we be able to see Kanchenjunga from our house? And Mount Everest? And what language do the people there speak? Tell me, tell me, tell me. Please." Thus urged, and if he were in good spirits, Daddy would talk a little about his utopia, but wistfully and without much conviction, as if he knew that it was a dream not likely to be realized.

But he had been home for two nights now and he was still okay. There had been no panic in the middle of the night and no frantic phone calls for an ambulance. My mother's eyes, however, followed Daddy around fearfully. She was jumpy, and if she could, I knew she would have called for the ambulance and kept it parked in our driveway. My brother was not allowed to leave the house, in case the phone lines were down because of the cyclone and he was required to drive Daddy back to the hospital. My sister was on the balcony upstairs, aimlessly (or so I thought) chucking pebbles at the shadows beneath the Ashoka trees in the front garden. And I was sitting at the dining table urgently writing another article for a magazine. Childishly, I was convinced that if it were published my father would be well and would not have to return to the hospital. I did not share this belief with my siblings, for I felt that it was like one of those sealed cylindrical talismans that were tied around children's arms by holy men, its power annulled if it was opened. Years later, I discovered that each of us had resorted to similar desperate superstitions to keep our father alive: My brother insisted on walking to the hospital every evening to visit, my sister spent her time watching for and chasing a large black tomcat off our lawn, for she was sure that it was the harbinger of illness and death. So obsessed was she by that cat that I would sometimes wake at night and find her standing on the balcony, her thin child's pyjama-clad body trembling with rage as she chucked pebbles down at the cat which, she insisted, was sitting tantalizingly in the shadows pooling beneath the Ashoka trees.

And I believed that my writing was keeping my father alive. This conviction had arisen when Daddy had first been admitted to the hospital and then had been released the day after a piece of mine had been published. And then it happened again. Daddy was taken to the hospital, a week later I had another publication, and miracle of miracles, my father was discharged the next day, suddenly and unaccountably better. And again and again, until I knew that it *was* my writing that was making my father better.

After all, it was he who had encouraged me to send out my first short story when I was a freshman at university. And before that my writing apprenticeship had been with him, as the author of the speeches that he, a senior officer in the Indian Railways, had had to deliver on important occasions such as India's Independence Day celebrations. I had written that first short story in less than an hour. With some trepidation I had shown it to Daddy, who made a few comments and then suggested that I could perhaps send it off to a magazine.

"What if they don't want it?" I had asked, delighted that my father, my sternest critic, had liked my story.

"What if they don't?" Daddy had demanded. "Send it somewhere else. And if they don't take it either, send it to another place. If it comes back three times, then throw it away. Or rewrite it. At best it will be published, you will be paid and you won't have to ask your mother or me for money to buy more novels. At worst you will lose the cost of a few postage stamps and get a dent in your ego." He had knocked my head gently with his knuckles and added teasingly, "And this ego isn't going to dent very easily."

The writing had come in bursts, between my studies, term papers, class assignments, exams. Then my father had discovered that he had cancer and the trips to the hospital had begun. And the returns home every time a piece of mine was published. Or so it had seemed to me. I had written feverishly ever since, building up a store of articles, sending them out in quick succession, never sure when I might need one to get my father out of the hospital.

The last few times, though, something had gone wrong. The gods were weary of my writing. Piece after piece had been published. I had cycled over to the hospital as fast as I could go, triumphantly bearing my article, eager to show my father his Get Out of Jail card, his ticket back home, but his health had not responded to the dark print on paper, the byline with his daughter's name. The magic had turned rancid. It wasn't fair. It wasn't fair at all.

On that December morning, however, I had decided to change tactics. Fool the gods perhaps. Now that my father had taken himself out of the hospital without any help from me, I was writing to keep him at home. He stirred and sat up, looked around blearily and then his glance fell on me. His eyes were tired and his skin stretched tight across the bones of his face.

"Writing?" he asked, smiling. "What about?"

I don't know, really, I wanted to say. Tell me what will make you well, Daddy, and I will write about it every day if you wish.

"Mountains," I lied brightly. I wished that I had asked him more about his childhood, about those mysterious snow-covered peaks that he had seen from the windows of his home, about how snow felt in his hands. My father nodded and struggled to his feet. He swayed, and before I could get to him he had collapsed on the sofa. I should have written faster, I thought numbly. My mother was already in the room, already on the phone. The ambulance was on its way. My brother rattled the car keys nervously—he had probably slept with them clutched in his hand. My sister stood close beside me.

"I saw the wretched thing just this moment," she said fiercely. I gave her a blank look. I had no idea what she was talking about. Outside, the rain hit the ground like gunfire and in the distance we could hear the wail of the approaching ambulance.

My father died a month later on a cool, cloudy January morning, a day before his fifty-fourth birthday. I remember his eyes a few moments before his death. They were dilated and seemed to be gazing beyond us at something in the vast distance, perhaps a cottage at the foot of the Himalayas, and through the window of that cottage, a range of snow-capped mountains.

Twenty-five winters have gone by since my father's death, and fifteen of those have been spent in Canada. I have yet to grow fond of the soft, chill feathering of snow on my face, the sharp crunch of feet in the frozen silence of the night, or the absolute solitude that seems to wrap itself around each one of us. Every year, in January, on the anniversary of his death, I look out on a snowy landscape much like the one Daddy must have looked at from the windows of his childhood home and wonder why he had yearned so much for it. I wish that I had asked him more about that remote time in his life. There was no wife then, no son or daughters, no railway officer's life or attendant duties, no illness nor the stealthy, sure-footed approach of death. Only mountains crisp as starched napkins peaking up towards the sky, and fresh snowy mornings to delight a child. And *jalebis* fried hot by the vendor around the corner from his school and frothy milk served as soon as he came home, and whistles made of wood and the British Miss Henrietta's piano going plinketty-plink in the late afternoon. I wish that I had asked him the exact taste of those juice-laden *jalebis,* or who had made the whistle for him, and whether the British woman's piano playing was any good at all. I wish that I had asked him what fears churned within him that could be silenced only by those mountains looming in the distance. And I wish that I had reached out that day in December as he lay on the sofa and run my hand gently over his head.

Sometimes I try to imagine what it would have been like to have him here, in this country, visiting me. I see him walking down the road towards my small brick house in Montreal, an old man in a long jacket, negotiating the icy patches on the sidewalk, his glasses foggy from the cold, his knobbly artist's hands hidden in mitts, his thinning hair neat across his scalp, for naturally he would not deign to wear a cap, for to do so might be to admit to a fear of winter. I wait for him to come into the warmth of my home so that I can ask him about the things that a woman in her mid-forties might need to ask her elderly father—about life and memories and family history, everything that I never thought to ask about when he was alive. And most of all I would find out about winter and how one learns to love it.

Mother's Milk

by Christie Blatchford

I was in my second year at college when my father mentioned—for the first, last and only time—that he was thinking of leaving my mother.

I was by then out of the house, or, as I assumed my dad thought of it, safely out of the house, living on my own in a small, ramshackle basement apartment in downtown Toronto. My brother, almost a decade older than I am, had long since fled the nest. Our parents were alone with one another in a way they had not been since they were first married, and since I could not conceive of being trapped at home with the woman my mother had become, I wasn't surprised that he might not be able to stand it, either.

I had always imagined that my father stayed with her as long as he did only because of me. She was such an enormous presence that even in a story supposedly about my dad, my mother figures as large in my memory as she did in our lives.

My mother was an alcoholic who started drinking as a teenager to allay her social nervousness. At first it worked and she was able to function—a cigarette in one hand and a drink in the other. Pictures from those days show a striking and confident-looking young woman, hair glamorously upswept in one of those big-shouldered, nipped-waist 1940s suits that so flattered her athletic frame. But as the years wore on, it was as though the booze, once a lubricant that allowed her to beat her acute self-consciousness into submission, thickened as soon as it hit her bloodstream, becoming so viscous that it all but paralyzed her.

Her drinking would not have been so noticeable, probably not even to my father, in the small northwestern Quebec town where I was born and raised and where my folks lived for about twenty years. Rouyn-Noranda was a hard-drinking mining town with a frontier mentality as rough as the wooden sidewalks that were in place when my parents and my brother, then just a little boy, moved there after the Second World War.

My parents' social life centred around bridge games at our house and their friends' homes, casual parties at the local curling or golf club and nights out at the Canadian Corps or the Moose Lodge. In this milieu, where it seemed everyone drank a lot, my mother's drinking would not have drawn any particular scrutiny, and indeed, perhaps it didn't warrant any then.

Her natural athleticism and competitiveness would have masked her incipient alcoholism, and the time she devoted to sports would have placed arbitrary limits on how much she could drink and still play the games she loved, at a high level. I am not the best reporter here, for obvious reasons. My story is pieced together from my parents' recollections, and my own observations, once I was old enough to make them.

Certainly, in Noranda, my mother was still playing badminton—she was once nationally ranked—tennis and golf, clobbering the ball off the tee as far as most men, and showing the same trademark impatience on the greens as she did on the rare occasions when she lost a badminton match and she'd throw herself onto the gym floor and beat her fists in frustration. My brother told a story at her funeral about the time when, as she was walking by the field where he and his friends were playing baseball, she picked a long ball out of the air and, without breaking stride, casually hurled it right to home plate, just about tearing off the recipient's arm—and impressing the hell out of my brother's friends.

No accident she was known as "Babe" in her heyday.

But at some point after I was born—a surprise, relatively late-in-life child—her drinking changed, or rather, she began to do more of it. I was still small, maybe in grade one or two, when I first picked up the glass that was always by the kitchen sink, filled it with water and spat it out because of the yechy taste. It was my mother's rye glass. It was the glass she used when I was at school and my father at work; it was the glass she kept at the ready when she made dinner; it was the glass she took to bed every single night until she was about eighty, when she finally quit booze because it had become clear to her that if she didn't, she would die. Frequently, in the last years of drinking, her potassium levels would plummet dangerously, and she would end up hospitalized for a week or so. Finally, she was scared straight.

But long before then, she morphed from party drinker to stealth drinker, sipping at that damn little glass all day long so that by dinnertime, she was, as they said in those days, well-oiled, keeping mickeys of rye in her lingerie drawer, under the kitchen sink, and in her bedside table. I'm not sure who would have noticed except my father, or how long it took him to notice. It was the kind of town where kids went home for lunch, and so did fathers. My mom was still fine at lunch, cheerful and functional: Egg-salad sandwiches would be waiting for me; toasted cheese for my father; big glasses of milk for us both. I don't remember what, if anything, my mother had.

My suspicion is that even this far back, she may not have been eating much. I wonder now if she also had an eating disorder, or if her appetite loss and vomiting was part and parcel of her alcoholism. By the time I was in high school, she was vomiting after almost every meal. I have no memory of ever seeing her eat, but vivid ones of the acrid smell of vomit in the bathroom after she used it. Is it even possible that she could have been throwing up what I don't remember ever seeing her swallow?

The awful alchemy, for that's what it was, would happen in the afternoons.

By dinner—and dinner was always served at five-thirty sharp—the woman from lunch had disappeared, and in her place was this sharp-tongued, sometimes vicious, almost unrecognizable person. I remember always being very worried if my dad was even five minutes late getting home for dinner, because my mother would turn on him and berate him, such that it was almost unbearable to watch; I remember knowing it was better to talk about anything important with my mom at lunch; I remember being nervous about having my friends over at night.

Like many children of alcoholics, I knew far too much about my parents' married life. One story alone will illustrate that. One Christmas Eve, when I was maybe thirteen, I heard my mother crying for help, and ran to the bedroom where they had their separate single beds. I can't remember what she said when I got there, but I knew my dad had gone in search of some intimacy or comfort, that she had used me to avoid it, and that he was mortified with shame by my presence. Not long after that, he moved into his own small room.

Still, had we never left Noranda, her decline probably would have been slower, or less remarkable. But, in 1967, when I was about fifteen, we moved to Toronto because my father thought life would be better there for all of us after the political situation changed in Quebec. My mother had lived in Toronto as a teenager with her own family, but this turned out to be an adjustment beyond her diminishing abilities.

My dad was a hockey rink manager, so my folks were never rich, though they spent—particularly on me—as though they were. In Toronto, they couldn't afford to join a golf or tennis club, as they had done in Noranda, so my mother's sporting outlet was effectively gone, and where my father and I made friends at work and school respectively, my mother in the main remained at home, alone. She only ever worked part-time, as a typist or secretary, and her shyness and insecurities would have rendered her difficult to get to know. Her drinking grew heavier, or at least its effects became more pronounced, and so did her neuroses.

In Noranda, though an immensely capable driver, she was always a nervous passenger; in Toronto, she drove only within a six-block area of our apartment (mostly to the Dominion store and the liquor store, and back) and refused to go on the expressways, no matter who was behind the wheel. In Noranda, she had avoided big crowds, but there, that meant only the local movie theatre; in Toronto, it meant she hardly left the house. In Noranda, she was afraid of elevators, but there were almost none because the buildings were all one or two storeys tall. In Toronto, the dentist's office was on a high floor, as was the doctor's, so she just stopped going.

And where in Noranda, she was afraid of bugs, in Toronto, it seemed she was frightened of people, and the places they went—shopping malls, public squares, business functions, baby showers. Even staying with family, on my parents' occasional out-of-town trips, was unsettling for her: Was it only that she was afraid that, at my brother's house in Montreal for instance, she wouldn't be able to bring her mickeys, or get enough to drink? Or was she, as it sometimes seemed, no longer able to be comfortable with her own family? Instead my parents stayed at motels, where at least my mom could be assured of having a ready supply and unrestricted access to it.

Periodically, we began having little family talks, our own version of an intervention, where my dad and I would broach the problems her drinking was creating, or the idea of her joining Alcoholics Anonymous, or even having her go to a treatment centre. No, no, no, she'd say; I don't need that; I can quit any time.

And she would, too, cold turkey, all on her own, bringing her still tremendous will to bear. The storm clouds that seemed perpetually to hang over the house would lift, day by day, and soon enough she'd be back, healthy-seeming, happier, sober. She would gain weight; the red in her eyes would clear up; even her hair seemed shinier, though perhaps that was my imagination. And there would be no more of that terrible meanness, no more of the small cruelties from the razor blades she seemed to take in with each sip from her rye glass and then hide in her mouth.

During one of these phases, my father even had her convinced to try going on the subway, which encapsulated so many of her fears—it was underground; it was enclosed; it was often crowded and busy. I remember the day they set off, hand in hand, for Eglinton station, and how they returned, not long after, failure written on my mother's face and disappointment on my dad's. A few times, they'd go to a matinee showing of a film—the theatre would be almost empty, he figured—but my mom would flee halfway through the show.

Once, we drove her to an AA meeting; when we picked her up, she was full of faux-scorn for the people there, who needed this crutch. "It's not for me," she said. "I can do it on my own." At least twice, my dad arranged for her to attend a thirty-day program at a rehab centre, but the problem with that was, when push came to shove, my mom had to sign the forms herself and agree to go. She never would.

These sober periods never lasted longer than a month. We always knew she was drinking again long before she would tearfully confess to having "just one," or before we found the evidence in one of her drawers.

The clue was always the same: the viciousness would return. Once, I remember, my father had volunteered to let Angelo, one of his nice young staffers from the rink, then newly married and with a baby and no money, use our cottage (the only piece of property my parents ever owned) for a week when my folks weren't planning to go.

"You don't mind, do you?" my dad asked, "if Angelo uses it?"

"Fuck Angelo," snapped my mother. "I don't want them there."

Where she once reserved her sharpest comments for my dad, constantly belittling him, with me her next-favourite target, she now broadened the circle to include her grandchildren, my brother's two kids, on their increasingly infrequent visits. She would be outright drunk by eight o'clock at night, and wander about the cottage in her nightie, demanding that the children, who were then just little, be still, or quiet. An ordinary card game, the very kind she used to love, if it went any later than that, would have her stumble into the main room in a rage and demand that everyone go to bed.

Were my father and I enablers, as AA calls those who inadvertently, or deliberately, make it easy for drinkers to keep on drinking, or at least difficult for them to stop? I don't think so, though I've worried the point for years. My gentle, generous father's life would have been so immeasurably better if his wife had just been kinder to him. I can't imagine him sabotaging her efforts to stop drinking.

But at some point, I suppose, my dad and I gave up: There seemed little we could do to make her want to stop drinking, and the drinker who doesn't want to stop can't be made to stop.

It was easier for me, because I moved out, and was of that age where for a few fleeting years, you strike out on your own and barely pay attention to your parents. But I remained close to them both always, and saw them frequently even during this period.

I believe that for the rest of their life together, things remained much the same, or worse. The woman who in her twenties was physically so strong, and vibrant, became increasingly neurotic and it seemed to me that her alcoholism had turned her into a gaping maw of exposed needs—imagined and insatiable.

And yet, after that one remark about leaving her—he told me in the car, as we were returning to their apartment for dinner, and selfishly, I remember thinking that this was bad news for me, as I would now have to bear more of the load he shouldered on his own—nothing happened.

He would have been fifty-six or fifty-seven then. He would have had time to meet someone new, or at least try. Even so, a life alone would not have loomed as a terrifying possibility, but rather, I imagine, as a relief. My dad was still working. He had many friends. He was a voracious reader, of newspapers, novels and non-fiction. As ever, he enjoyed the occasional drink, and he could still pound down a few at a party, but he never needed booze the way my mother did. He had always quit drinking whenever she tried to stop.

I didn't wonder why he never left her. I was just relieved, I suppose, that he didn't, because it meant less worry and work for me. I don't think I ever asked him about it; he just stayed, and I was glad, less for my mother, I'm ashamed to say, than for myself.

I used to think he had stayed with her because of me, afraid that if he left, I would be exposed to too much of that relentless criticism and have my confidence permanently undermined, the very way that hers had been. I always thought he saved my life.

But then, even when I was an adult, establishing a career and married, he stayed.

Now, I believe, he stayed because he loved her. He may not have loved what was left of her, but he loved the essence of who she still was, and he could see that person still; he could see past the alcoholism and the years of damage it had done to them both.

Their final years together were quiet. I know because I saw them at least once a week—I could no more abandon my dad to the un-tender mercies of my mother than he could abandon me to them. And perhaps he knew, too, that I would have my turn looking after her. His lung cancer was discovered when, feeling perfectly healthy and bullet-proof, he asked his doctor what his life expectancy was, and to answer the question, the doctor took X-rays of his chest and they found the shadow there. My dad always joked that he would live forever, but I think he knew in his bones he would die sooner rather than later, and sooner than she.

They had the cottage in summer, where my father would count the trees on his property and tend his garden (he knew them all by their Latin names), and my mother would sit in the sun. They played cards or Scrabble, went out for dinner occasionally and took little day trips in the country. In the winters, he worked part-time until just a few years before his death. Aside from me and my ex-husband, they had few visitors, and went out infrequently.

Every Christmas, he bought her something red to wear, because he loved her in red. He always beamed when she got dressed up, told her she was still beautiful, that her legs still went all the way up. He told great, warm stories about her as a young woman, throwing a tantrum whenever she lost a badminton game, throwing her golf clubs when she blew a shot. He bragged of her long-gone athleticism as though she were still able to throw a baseball the way she had that day when my brother saw her in action.

When he entered hospital for the final time, my mother was drinking a lot. His room was on an upper floor, and she could neither force herself into the elevator nor take the stairs with any ease, so she hardly came to see him. The night he died, my ex and I were with him, and at the behest of a nurse, erring on the side of caution, I took her advice and called my mother and told her to come.

She was drunk when she arrived with my brother, and belligerent. Restless, she stayed perhaps twenty minutes, and furiously insisted that they leave. She complained in the hall that I had called her there needlessly. "If Daddy dies tonight," she said, and I will never forget either the words or the inflection, "don't call me again. The morning will do."

He did die, a few hours later.

I thought I'd never forgive her for that, and for a time, I didn't, though I always took care of her. But over the next fifteen or so years, for she lived that much longer than he did, I got at least most of the way to forgiveness. And in the last months of her own life, as she battled illness and her own enormous fear, my mother was as brave and as tough as my dad had been, and I too could see past the glass of rye, to the girl she had once been.

The Inheritance

by Mary Anne Brinckman

One sunny afternoon, almost sixty years ago, when I was just a child, my father Arnold Cook passed on to me a sense of responsibility for the natural world and a way of looking at the role we humans play in it. Even now, a lifetime later, I don't know if it was a blessing or a burden. But I do know that, whichever it is, it became mine and I cannot escape from it.

Man, my father could paddle. Most people would not say that paddling a canoe is an art, but if they had seen my father doing so, they might have changed their minds. He sat upright—I never remember him kneeling—a man with a smooth thin muscular body that always seemed brown from the sun. Even now, thirty years after his death, whenever a canoe passes, I observe how proficient the paddlers are. I'm not impressed by show. I know that serious canoeing is for distance, so I note if the paddlers are using their body strength correctly, and if the strokes are long enough to keep the canoe gliding smoothly, and yet not so long that precious energy will be wasted. He taught me to paddle on weeklong canoe trips with him when I was a child. When I went to a summer camp, I was taught to paddle with a longer draw, and my father laughed when he saw it. "If you paddle like that," he said, "you'll be completely worn out in three hours," and it was true.

He didn't tolerate dilettante paddlers. Two of my now-grown-up children tell tales of him shouting at them. "Don't lily-dip. Bloody well put some effort into your paddle." (They were only six and seven, but he made no concessions.) Fifteen years ago, my younger sister, Wendy, and I continued our father's tradition of canoe tripping with her son, Simon, who was seven, and we too shouted at him to put some muscle into it as the three of us battled a strong wind on our way to our next camping spot. And a few weeks ago at our cottage in Georgian Bay, my younger son, Nick, took his six-year-old son, Dashiel, on a three-kilometre paddle to buy an ice-cream cone. On the way, there was a headwind. Nick shouted at Dashiel, "Paddle harder. Don't lily-dip. Put your back into it," and Dashiel returned glowing with pride. Now he wants to do it every weekend.

Nothing made my father happier than going on a canoe trip in "the bush," which was what he called our northern Canadian wilderness; and during the winter, he would plan his next route. Then, long before the ice was off the lakes, he took over a room and spread his gear all over it. "Arnold's camping list" was famous in the days before freeze-dried dinners. Serious canoe-trippers passed it from hand to hand, and neophyte trippers were told that they had to get a copy. The items on the list included everything from needles and thread to just the right amount of Scotch so that everyone could have a slow drink before supper after the campfire was lit.

He always had a cedar-strip canoe. It was broader-beamed than most canoes as it had been especially commissioned to carry his heavily laden khaki canvas packs. This canoe, or perhaps it was one of a series of canoes, was always painted blue-grey so that it would blend with the changing colours of our Canadian lakes and streams; and when one spotted them, my father and his canoe, gliding across the water, they looked indigenous. The Canadian environmentalist John Livingston wrote in his book *Rogue Primate* that he thinks wild animals feel as one with their environment, and I think that for short times my father did also, as he moved smoothly across the water.

His strong sense of family made him physically very affectionate. He loved doing things with Wendy and me. In the summer he took us birdwatching and in the winter he took us skating on small creeks outside Toronto. On these chilly days, he would always build a little fire, and then heat a tin of soup in a small black saucepan, both of which he would produce out of his ever-present packsack. It was all such fun, unless one of us complained about being too cold or hot or tired. This was simply not allowed; and now, I, too, have no tolerance for whiners.

My father passed on to me the burden, or the blessing, when I was ten. He had taken me, just me and no one else, on a weeklong canoe trip in Algonquin Park. It was wonderful. We paddled, chose camp-sites, set up our tent, gathered wood and lit campfires between rocks upon which we balanced our black-bottomed, soot-covered pots to cook our suppers. Sometimes we went fishing, and we even caught some that we cleaned and fried. We took turns at throwing a rope over a branch (I have to admit that he was better at this than I was, but it was fun trying) and tying one end to the pack, and then together we hauled on the rope until our food pack hung high so that a bear couldn't reach it. When we went for a walk on an unmarked trail to find a secret lake where we could have a secret swim, he taught me how to bend twigs along our path so that we could find our way back to our canoe.

The sun was bright and we were paddling slowly through a meandering stream that wound its way though a wetland. There were tall grasses on either side, and the rushes under the canoe formed soft, pale, incomprehensible patterns. The dragonflies were blue, and we were paddling slowly and quietly. I chattered endlessly in my happiness. Then he spoke a very few, not particularly original words, but nevertheless words that changed my life.

Daddy said, "Do not talk here, Mary Anne. This is God's country." And suddenly, and very oddly, because these words alone did not convey any passing on of responsibility, my understanding of this earth and my place in it changed. What I suddenly understood was that I was not so important. I was just one amongst the many living things that deserved care—including the swamp with its meandering stream and dragonflies. And that anything I did might affect it, including my voice that might frighten animals from coming to the swamp. From then on, I knew that this natural world was something that I must respect, and that, also, I had to try to look after it just as I had to try to look after my family and friends. I understood then that humans are just one amongst a multitude of species and that each one, animal or plant, must be respected and never harmed for any unnecessary or frivolous reason.

Since that moment, I have not been able to rid myself of this understanding, and the accompanying feeling of responsibility, for more than short periods of time. And despite the great pleasure that I have received from being in, and loving, natural places, there are more times than I would like to admit that I want to put down this heavy responsibility with a shout of exultation. It is too often an unrelenting burden for me, especially in today's world where we now understand how our actions are affecting the health of the earth.

I know that my father's words alone could not have been the sole reason for this new perception. I must have already partly absorbed

my father's spiritual conviction that we humans have a moral responsibility to look after and respect the natural world, but it was those
words telling me to be silent in the swamp that clinched it.

Why he felt like this was a mystery. He came from a prosperous
United Empire Loyalist family that had made its money in mining and
in cutting down trees (which my sister and I have always thought was
ironic). Members of his family had lived straight, godly, conventional
lives—in short, they were good people, but not particularly original.
Then along came my father. He saw most things differently from the
rest of his family and the fathers of my friends; and he dressed and
acted differently, but I was never embarrassed by him. I thought he
was a bit weird, but just great.

When my friends came over to our house, he would sometimes
rant at them about his latest obsession. One was about goats. In a
passionate voice, he would tell my seven-year-old friends how herds of
"bloody" goats were being taken to graze on land where no other
domesticated animals could survive. These herds were eating all the
prickly plants and spiky grasses on the edges of deserts. He was very
angry about this and said that these goats should not be allowed to
graze on this poor land. As a child, all I understood was that he, myste-
riously, preferred spiky plants that hurt people's feet to sand that one
could run on, but I filed away this preference as another vaguely interesting fact about some of the perplexing likes and dislikes of my
father. It was many years before I understood that these desert plants
are the stitches that hold down soil and stop it from turning into a
desert that will become even less productive for the people who live
there. Sometimes I wonder if my friends ever understood why he
hated so many of the tame goats of this world.

In some ways, he was conventional. He worked hard at his job as a
stock market analyst in Toronto and was considered a very clever, if
eccentric, financial guru who had a real feel for the stock market. He

refused to wear a suit to work as he thought that people who were impressed by clothes were probably people who were not interesting to him. Off he went each day, often on a bicycle, dressed in a dilapidated brown tweed jacket, usually with a tired narrow tie woven in diagonal stripes of different shades of dreary brown. On weekends, he would wear the oldest tramp-like clothes he could find.

He also worked hard at the family farm at Rice Lake, near Cobourg, Ontario. He loved the place. I remember him perpetually cutting the grass, tending the vegetable garden and repairing fences. He loved making a delicious jam from his own gooseberries, and he would joyfully jump about the kitchen in cut-off khaki shorts, stirring a vast cauldron of the boiling mess with a broken-off branch. He even dug the deep well that supplied our drinking water for our new cottage at the farm, and I remember his voice coming out of the six-metre-deep hole, shouting at the man at the top to haul up another bucket that dripped wet mud on him all the way up. Even some of his lighter pleasures looked like hard work to me. He read mostly history and reread Edward Gibbon's *Decline and Fall of the Roman Empire* several times. As he thought that the Western world was heading for another decline, I think he found some comfort in reading about Rome's fall, and he was certainly fond of pointing out lots of parallels.

My father made me feel that I was loved and valued. I adored him, although he was not an easy man. And God, he could be tough. My son Jonathan tells a story of being at the farm with some school friends in November. The swimming pool was full of dead, rotting leaves and had a thin film of ice. They were standing looking at this mess when my father arrived and asked them if they would like to swim. They thought he was joking, but then he stripped to the buff and plunged in. After swimming several lengths, breaking the ice as he swam, he emerged covered with slime and sprinkled with rotting leaves. He grabbed a towel, said, "Bracing," and disappeared into the house, leaving the group of schoolboys gaping in amazement.

He did not seem to care for most of the trappings that money can buy—except for skiing in the Alps. My French/Belgian, born-and-raised-in-Cairo mother, Zita Hansval, was the one who cared about chic clothes, good food and a well-decorated house with flowers and antiques, and he went along with it. He grumbled at the expenses, but I think he was secretly very proud of the style she imprinted on everything she touched. He certainly was proud of her beauty and wit. We lived well. We had a large house and the farm, and Mummy had lovely clothes and furs. We went frequently to Europe to see her family or to ski. It would seem that life was good, but it wasn't. My father worried terribly about two things. He worried about my mother's depressions, and he worried about how humans were harming the earth.

He predicted that as populations grew, more people would farm marginal land—places like the edges of desert or the steep slopes of mountains—with the result that this land would become even more barren and less able to feed people. He even worried about the destruction of the rain forests, and would rant about how these living forests were being turned into plains of a baked infertile eroded soil called laterite that would take centuries to recover. While many of our friends heard about golf and hockey players from their fathers, my sister and I listened to our father raving about laterite. I know he bored our childhood friends by telling them about soil depletion, but although he chose a strange audience, many of his theories were right. According to the November 2006 *Wikipedia*, more than ten thousand kilometres of arable land are being lost each year, and our populations are still growing; and, to top all this off, the devastation of climate change is only beginning.

He was also frantically apprehensive that we would run out of natural resources, so much so that he feared that there would not be enough left for his grandchildren and great-grandchildren. Again, he was right, if a bit premature. It was only in the autumn of 2006 that the World Wildlife Fund announced that we are using the earth's resources at such a rate that if we continue as we are, we will need two earths by 2050 to supply our needs.

My father grieved constantly about the destruction of his beloved forests and marshes and other beautiful wild places by lumbering, the filling in of wetlands for farming and housing, and the destruction of wilderness by mining and its wastes. Once, he told me in a sad voice that a rich man whom he knew slightly was going to lumber his large patch of old growth white pine near Algonquin Park. He was totally mystified why anyone who did not need the money would destroy such an irreplaceable place of beauty. He was often upset when we drove through the Ontario countryside because there were almost no large, old trees left, and the odd big tree in the towns or beside the farmhouses only made him sadder as they represented all that we had destroyed. He contrasted our countryside to that of England and France, where stands of ancient trees still stood. (By the way, depending on the estimates, only between .07 and two percent of old white and red pine forests remain in Ontario today.)

Despite his worries about what humans were doing to his beloved earth, I'm sure that it never occurred to my father that he and his family should live in a more environmentally responsible way. You see, he found the perfect answer to all his concerns. It was simple and self-evident to him: If everyone had only two children, then everything would be fine. Even though this may sound a bit nutty, one must realize that he was thinking about this in the thirties, forties and fifties, years before most people were even aware of the problems that concerned him. His solution of *fewer* footprints rather than *less heavy and better* footprints was a bold attempt to grapple with what was then beginning to happen. And even if his solution was unworkable, his foresight was impressive

His opinions were altruistic, and he did not hesitate to speak out. This led, as you might imagine, to some unpleasant conversations with some of his friends, and one very funny scene. Like many men of his period and background, he disliked male homosexuals. When I reached my teens, I was appalled by this incomprehensible intolerance. We argued a lot, but nothing I said seemed to change his views. One day, in desperation, I said, "Daddy, you are making no sense. Not only are you disliking people for no good reason but you are disliking people who will not be having children. He stared at me, and slowly nodded. Then he sat very still and nodded again. Shortly after that conversation, we—me wearing blue jeans and he in his brown tweed jacket with one of his drab brown ties—were walking in a park and we passed two men holding hands. He looked at them for a long moment, and then said quite loudly, "Good for you." And we continued along the path.

I understood his views about the dangers of population growth and each person's individual responsibility completely, and I agreed with him; but despite this, a moral clash was about to happen between the beliefs we shared and my own desires.

After I married, I gave birth to a boy, Jonathan, in 1960, and a girl, Sophie, three years later. My father was pleased. But then I became pregnant again. I was living in England and I wrote him with much trepidation, as I knew that he would be disappointed that his beloved daughter, who agreed with him about the need to limit population growth, was having a third child. (I was disappointed in me, too, but in spite of my own conviction that any responsible and aware couple should produce only enough children to replace themselves, I wanted this child and I was going to have it!) His letter back was generous, given the circumstances that we both understood so well.

Darling Mary Anne,

   Of course, I will love any child of yours, but I have to tell you
that I am surprised. You know that children like yours will
probably grow up to use more than their share of the earth's
diminishing resources, and you know that you should not have
had more than two.

   The letter was both a nod to our mutual belief and an acceptance
of my actions. It went on to other things, and he never made another
allusion to how I had disappointed him.

   As I have said, I understood that my third child, Nicholas, was an
indulgence, but then he was one that I have never regretted. And my
father, as he said in his letter, loved him too, although he died when
Nick was only seven.

   Although I agreed with him, as I still do, that our growing populations are harming the earth, I think that it is not enough to simply
curb the growth of populations, as the Chinese authorities have
decreed with their one-child policy, or as my father thought we
should by agreeing to have only two; we must look at the way each of
us uses or abuses the earth's resources in our daily lives. We know
now how our lifestyles are polluting the water and air, and that the
changing climate is endangering the earth's balance. My father didn't
know about these things, so despite his own fears about the future, I
think that, in a way, he was lucky. He could live his own life as he
liked, guilt free.

   For me and people today, it's different. I know that my choice of
which car, toilet paper, meat, fish, washing powder and many other
products makes a difference, and I am puzzled why anyone with a
few extra pennies would buy toilet paper made with trees cut from
forests rather than recycled paper fibres. (Perhaps I am, *au fond*, as
intolerant as my father, but I hope not.) I wonder if my father would

have thought like this, too, if he had lived longer. Would he, too, buy organic, shade-grown coffee so that there is more bird habitat for our migrating warblers in South America? Would he have kept his air conditioner turned off on hot days so that its emissions did not add to the smog? He was lucky because he could do so many things with a freer heart than I can. He could drive across the United States on birding holidays with the unencumbered pleasure of anticipating a wonderful adventure or fly off for a glorious holiday. I drive and fly to far-off places, too, but I always have some guilt when I know the voyage is not necessary. He didn't know, as I do, that a person travelling on a one-way trip from Toronto to Vancouver is responsible for the release of approximately one tonne of carbon dioxide into the air and that flying is a large cause of global warming. As George Monbiot, columnist for *The Guardian* and author of the best-selling book *Heat: How to Stop the Planet from Burning*, says, "Perhaps the most intractable cause of global warming is 'love miles': the distance you must travel to visit friends and partners and relatives on the other side of the planet. The world could be destroyed by love." I know this, but I still fly 'love miles' to see my son who lives in Oregon, and my daughter, who lives in England—and I continue on with side trips to Europe too. These feelings of guilt are mine, though I hate them fiercely, and I envy my father, for even though he was so worried about the earth's and humankind's future, his life was environmentally guilt free. I so wish mine was.

Life became particularly difficult for him during his late 50s and early 60s. My mother, who had had periodic depressions, had been suffering from a bad one for more than five years. My father took her to various clinics in Canada, the States and Switzerland, but to no avail. Also, he watched incredulously as more and more harm was done to his beloved earth. He was very sad.

He died in 1971, eighteen months after Mummy, and is buried, where he chose to die, in a small graveyard amongst the stony drumlins of Northumberland County, near the family farm. His tombstone is a round boulder from the lawn above Rice Lake. It has a brass plaque that starts out with generally accepted phrasing: *Arnold Elliot Cook, 1908–1971, much loved by his family*. Then comes the sting, the words my father chose to express his despair about how we humans are thoughtlessly fouling the planet that he so loved: *Blessed are the dead and unborn for neither destroys God's world.*

I think my father was a man born before his time, an intolerant but lovably flawed and rather zany prophet. He saw the harm that humans were doing to the planet seventy years before most people were even aware of the problem, and he cast around for a means to protect the next generations and the wild places that he loved so much. His sole solution, limiting population growth, sounds too simplistic to our ears, but he saw the situation as urgent and he grappled with it as best he could, using the information of his time. Because he often spoke out with such vehemence and his opinions were so unacceptable to most people, he was often seen as a hard, uncaring man, but I think the opposite was true. I think he spoke out because he cared so much. It would have been easier to be quiet, but his strong sense of moral responsibility did not allow him this choice.

I still miss him, although I'm a grandmother now. It is really hard being as conscious as I am of how our human actions affect the environment. I judge myself and I know how badly I fail. As I inherited this feeling of responsibility from him, I would love to talk to him about the way I'm handling it.

I argued with him, laughed with him, loved him and admired him. I am lucky to have had such a father, but, in a way, I'm glad that he did not live long enough to see what has happened, and is happening, to his beloved earth. Aldous Huxley said, "The most distressing thing that can happen to a prophet is to be proved wrong. The next most distressing thing is to be proved right." I know my father would have seen this the other way around. Unfortunately, most of the things he feared have happened, or are happening. I know how joyful he would have been to have been proven wrong.

Consequences

by Nancy Dorrance

My father came home for lunch at the usual time that muggy spring day, rumpled tweed jacket slung over one arm and a stack of exam papers tucked under the other. At the front door my mother was waiting for him, looking pale and agitated.

"Something's wrong, Russ. I'm scared," she said and crumpled to the floor. Those were the last words she would ever speak to him in her normal voice. Alone in the house with their three-month-old daughter, she must have been clinging to consciousness until his arrival.

That horrific scene, which my father only shared with us years later, has haunted me ever since. Learning about it helped me make sense of events that at the time were too overwhelming to process.

What I do remember vividly is a tense family dinner two days after my mother's collapse. My father, at the head of the table, cleared his throat and told us the unthinkable. "Your mother has a cancerous tumour growing in her brain, and the doctors can't take it out," he said in his measured, professorial tones. "They don't expect her to wake up from her coma."

Coma? Tumour? Brain cancer? At the age of six I could comprehend only that something serious was happening and that like most other mysteries of the adult world, it was beyond my control.

More shocking than my father's words was the sight of his mother, sitting across the dinner table with swollen, red-rimmed eyes. My grandmother's sudden arrival from Ottawa and her tears—she never cried—indicated more than words ever could how our lives were about to change.

Two days earlier, while my older brothers and I were at school, an ambulance had rushed our mother, Shirley, to the hospital emergency ward, where X-rays had revealed a massive brain tumour and the doctors had presented my father with two options. They could operate and temporarily reduce her discomfort, possibly prolonging an intolerable life. Or they could do nothing and she would almost certainly die—in pain, but perhaps mercifully soon.

It was the first of several critical choices that my father, a decorated war veteran and a university professor, would have to make, quickly and under duress. Just as he had done in the war with soldiers under his command, my father gathered what information he could, carefully assessed each alternative, and then acted decisively.

But this wasn't an intellectual decision involving troops, he realized: The life now hanging in the balance was his wife's. Even though a rational response might be to withhold consent and let her die quickly, there was no way he could do that. He told them to go ahead with the surgery. Then he summoned his mother from the family farm to help restore order in our chaotic household. Four active youngsters aged ten and under could be a handful at the best of times, and this was far from that. Suddenly, with both our parents out of commission, what had been "normal" for us only two days ago was now just a memory.

When he came home from the hospital after the operation, my father had another wrenching decision to make: whether to let us know the truth about our mother's condition. The surgeon still held little hope that she would come out of the coma. In the end, although his own mother was against the idea—thinking it would be too much for young children to absorb—he had decided to tell us.

Despite the doctors' grim prognosis, my mother did wake up. But it wasn't the kind of miracle we heard about in Sunday school or watched Dr. Kildare perform on TV. The damage to her brain had left her physically and mentally impaired, and she was never able to care for her baby, or the rest of us, again.

It was on our first visit to see her in hospital that we realized our mother had left us forever. Propped up with pillows in the narrow, steel-framed bed, a flowered pink scarf covering the stubble of her new hair growth, she was painfully thin and pale.

"Come and say hello," my father invited us, but we were shy of this frightening-looking stranger. Dressed in our Sunday best (we had come from church), my brothers and I slowly approached the bed clutching a fragrant bouquet of lily of the valley, her favourite flower, plucked from the garden that morning.

When she smiled, there was a flash of recognition, but her words were hesitant and slurred: not at all the voice we remembered. After several stilted attempts at conversation, the much-anticipated reunion with our mother was over. Confused and disappointed, we raced across the hospital parking lot, wanting only to get home and shed our good clothes before escaping outdoors.

As he did most days, my father returned to the hospital that afternoon. Between visits to my mother and his work at the university—

where in addition to teaching he had just taken on a major research project—we saw him only at suppertime now.

What must have been my father's biggest worry—how to care for his infant daughter, Barbara—was resolved almost immediately when his brother and sister-in-law offered to take her into their home. With three boys already it was no small commitment, but they lived on a farm, with my grandmother nearby, and they had always wanted a little girl. I felt cheated because I'd wanted a little girl too. My father promised us that we would visit her regularly, however, and as always he was true to his word.

But who could have predicted the situation would last so long? That our baby sister would be almost five before she came back, or that our mother would live, on a roller coaster of small triumphs, frequent pain and increasing depression, for seven more years? That the consequences of my father's decisions, made hurriedly in a time of crisis, would continue to affect us for the rest of our lives?

My memories of those years, though hazy, are tinged with sadness and guilt. Embarrassed by my mother's uncertain speech, shuffling walk and difficulty following conversations, I constructed a carefully preserved wall between my lives at home and at the school downtown, where no one knew about her condition.

Although occasionally invited to sleepovers and after-school visits with girls from my class, I never returned the favour. As a result, I found myself spending more and more time on my own. Our house-keeper, an old friend of the family who prepared meals and looked after my mother during the daytime, became my after-school confidante. She and the boy next door—a free-spirited type untroubled by the stigma of befriending a girl—were the extent of my social circle for almost seven years while I grew from a child into a teenager.

Perhaps because we saw my father so little during this period when work and my mother's illness consumed him, he took on a mythical quality in my childish eyes. Other adults in his family seemed to share this perception as well. He was, after all, the revered oldest brother, cousin and favourite son upon whom the sun had always seemed to shine.

A clean-shaven farm boy fresh out of university, he'd come home from the Second World War with a moustache and a Military Cross from King George VI for his role in a desperate mission rescuing British paratroopers at Arnhem. As kids, we considered that neatly trimmed black moustache an integral part of who he was. I can still remember the way it tickled my cheek when he kissed me—all the more memorable because those occasions were so rare.

My father's family had never subscribed to public kissing or hugging. Although close in many ways, they shied away from both physical and vocal expressions of affection, preferring to convey their feelings through writing or not at all. Rumour has it that my grandmother—who had a special bond with her oldest child—shook my father's hand when he went off to war. That may not have been true, but everyone conceded it was possible.

Even the tragedy of my mother's illness could not disrupt the pattern of my father's model behaviour. Instead of becoming morose, taking to drink or bailing out of a bad situation, he did what everyone expected of him. He rose to the occasion without complaint. To me, he possessed the same exalted status as my comic book superheroes. Strong and brave, he was the fount of all knowledge worth knowing and had an answer for every question we asked.

What we didn't receive from him were outward displays of affection or the sense that he cared about the minutiae of our daily lives. This gave us a degree of freedom that was the envy of our friends, whose parents seemed to track their every move. But it also brought loneliness, for me anyway, and I secretly wished he would interfere more in my life.

My brothers at least had each other to fight with, which they frequently did. They also played church league hockey—the only outside activity in my father's busy schedule. Those were the days when girls either learned to figure skate or sat, bored and shivering, in the arena stands. An avowed tomboy, I had no interest in wearing pointed white skates and sequined outfits sewn by someone else's mother. Instead I tagged after my brothers, cajoling for membership in their secret clubs and the chance to play hockey with them in pickup games against neighbourhood teams.

Being smaller and not very athletic, I was usually the last to be chosen, or ended up as referee. At the age of nine I took early retirement and for the next few winters ran a profitable skate-unlacing service—a penny a skate—for my brothers and their friends. Since that business venture was located in our basement, just steps from the neighbourhood rink, my father certainly knew of it. As for our other leisure activities, so long as we didn't get into trouble, few questions were asked.

Rather than punishment for our transgressions, we worried about not living up to his expectations. And that was the tricky part since we knew that those standards, although unspoken, were high.

Two years after my mother's tumour had turned our world upside down, my father wanted to provide a diversion for us as well as a break for our grandmother, who was now in her seventies. While he divided his time between the university and the family farm where she lived, we spent our entire summer holiday in her sprawling red brick house with its overflowing bookshelves and steamer trunks full of treasures. We "helped" bring in the hay, cadged rides to go swimming in the nearby river and made daily treks to the general store for candy and soft drinks.

This arrangement worked well from our point of view since my little sister, Barb, now lived in our aunt and uncle's bungalow across the yard, with cousins who had become more like brothers to her than her own siblings. And the baby sister I'd so eagerly awaited as a six-year-old—planning to initiate her into all our childhood games and secrets—was like another cousin to me instead. We had to become reacquainted at the start of each new visit.

Adding three more children to the mix every summer was a strain for my asthmatic grandmother, whose attempts to divert us with exercises from her school-teaching days usually fell flat. Hence my father's plan to build the "cat": a motorized catamaran houseboat that became a focal point for us and all the other city relatives who descended on the farm each summer.

Like most of his building projects, this one started as a boys-only exercise, with me on the sidelines as usual. After school and on weekends he and my brothers worked together in his basement lab at the university, constructing it in sections from his precise engineering drawings. Once the cabin was transported to the farm, however, we all had a hand in its painting and furnishing. Even my grandmother joined in, unearthing an old wooden high chair from her cellar that, minus its tray and with a fresh coat of varnish, served nicely as the captain's chair.

Although the finished product was far from elegant—a sky blue plywood box perched on canary yellow pontoons that looked like elongated oil drums—we were all proud of our ugly duckling creation. Christened the *Sea Shanty*, she plied the choppy waters of the Ottawa River, patrolling the rocky shoreline of the riverfront farm.

As they grew older and more self-reliant, my brothers, now in their early teens (with me, as always, in tow) were given increasing responsibility for running the boat on its annual excursions. Too young to be allowed on the *Sea Shanty* alone with us, our sister never became part of the crew.

We reached the peak of our nautical adventures when, after much pleading and under my father's supervision, we were allowed to take the boat from Ottawa to Kingston along the Rideau Canal system. He spent several days aboard, ensuring that we could manoeuvre through the locks, then he left us on our own for the last part of the trip, checking in each night at pre-arranged docking sites. We all revelled in our newfound responsibility and even I—now truly one of the guys— took my turn at the wheel wearing the coveted captain's hat.

The only near-catastrophe occurred when we rammed into shore one evening at dusk. The impact knocked out all our lights and sent my brother Rob flying face-first into a pot of spaghetti sauce he'd been carrying to the table. He slithered across the floor, bouncing off my other brother, Ian, at the wheel, who unwittingly turned the boat around in the commotion. Still sitting at the table in near darkness, I screamed as Rob's dripping red face rose up at my feet, convinced it was covered in blood.

By the time order was restored, we were headed at full speed— about eight kilometres an hour—in the wrong direction. My father, waiting in vain at the rendezvous, had to use his army reconnaissance skills to track us down. Instead of being angry as we'd feared, he laughed with relief and then genuine amusement at the sight of our spaghetti-strewn cabin and spattered faces. The story remained a family favourite for years, and our shared experience of boating, one of the few things we could all enjoy together, brought my brothers and me closer to our father than anything else had done.

Memories of those long-ago summers drifted through my mind again recently when Rob and I drove with our father to the farm near Ottawa where our aunt and uncle still live. Thick, wet snow swirled against the windshield, but the weather didn't deter Rob, a seasoned driver, who seemed oblivious to the wind squalls and whiteouts that surrounded us. Inside, the car was a cocoon of warmth and intimacy.

I snuggled down further into my parka, idly watching the backs of their heads as Rob and my father droned on about the details of their latest building project. Once a defiant and headstrong youngster who categorically rejected my father's value system, Rob has discovered in middle age that he's very much like Russ.

That drive reminded me of the many times we had travelled this same route as kids, to see our little sister. If we were leaving Kingston on a Friday, it meant hurrying home from school to change into regular clothes and double check that we'd packed enough comics for the two-hour journey. Supper would be cheeseburgers and milk shakes at a restaurant in Smiths Falls: A rare treat that we anticipated as much as the trip itself.

My father at eighty-nine is still remarkably robust, despite brushes with several kinds of cancer and the usual afflictions of aging. His posture remains erect, his mind as sharp as ever, and he works out regularly at the Kingston YMCA. He and his siblings have inherited their grandparents' longevity genes; these days, they enjoy nothing more than a chance to reconnect with each other.

Just past Carleton Place, as the storm's intensity increased, the conversation between my brother and my father shifted abruptly. Instead of drills and routers, they were now talking about the period when my mother was at home after her partial recovery in hospital. It's a topic that, although not taboo, is rarely discussed in the family.

I listened intently as my father described his dilemma when the tumour in my mother's brain began to grow again. Her doctor recommended that she be moved to an institution with round-the-clock nursing and a structured routine. "But I was afraid it would destroy her to be taken away from the family," he said sadly, looking over his shoulder and addressing me for the first time. "I couldn't bring myself to do that."

The decision was made for him when she had an attack of pneumonia that put her back in hospital, five years after the tumour had first struck. From there, she was transferred to a long-term care facility, where she lived another two years. Surprisingly, this move restored something that illness had robbed from her: a sense of purpose. During our evening visits, when we played records in her room, the music began to attract other residents, many in wheelchairs. As the audience grew, we relocated in the hospital lounge, and for almost a year she took great pleasure in hosting these mini-concerts.

My father's next words truly shocked me. Again, turning around to look directly at me, he said, "The biggest change resulting from that move was in you." My personality had altered "drastically" during my mother's illness, he continued: from an outgoing, happy little girl to one who was quiet and withdrawn, never bringing friends home. "It was wonderful to see you becoming your old self again when that stress was removed."

The fact that he'd noticed my isolation and, even more, that it had caused him concern was an amazing revelation to me. Although he hadn't said anything back then, it made me realize now that he'd been more in tune with our needs than any of us had imagined.

Shortly after the car trip, he showed me a large, brown envelope filled with papers he had saved for almost half a century. One was a letter he'd written to the local director of education when my sister, Barb, was approaching school age.

I hadn't thought about the impact on him of sending his three-month-old daughter away, even to a brother with whom he'd always been close and whom he trusted completely. The extent of his loss was only brought home to me when I read the letter. Four and a half then, Barb wasn't old enough to qualify for kindergarten by the board's strict regulations, but he argued in his letter that she was "a bright and sturdy little girl" who could handle the program successfully. He said he was anxious to reunite his family and felt that she could make the adjustment more easily with an outside interest like school.

The director granted his request "in view of the very special circumstances," and my sister came back to live with us that fall. But the wounds inflicted by that five-year separation failed to heal. Never bonding as closely with us as with her other family, she continued to call our aunt "Mom" and to consider the farm her real home. In her early teens, Barb moved back to the farm, and today lives in another part of the country where she has built a life totally separate from both families. My mother's death was tragic but inevitable; the schism with my little sister, which has been just as painful, is a loss that is still raw.

Among the items my father had saved—all labelled and dated—were birthday and Father's Day cards from each of us, containing crudely drawn pictures and silly but affectionate poems. He'd also kept a mysterious batch of valentine cut-outs marked, "To Daddy from Me" and a crayoned note from my sister: "Dad. Am eating lunch at the fort. Back soon."

Who knew that this seemingly unsentimental Calvinist/Presbyterian academic would value and preserve the inconsequential trivia from his children's lives? Or that he took note of and worried about our social development?

All these years, I had pictured myself as the forgotten one in the family. My oldest brother, Ian, who was a star academically and athletically, physically resembled our father. Rob, also brainy but in a different way, received even more attention—much of it nega-tive—from his frequent acts of rebellion. And my sister, in her early years especially, was a cute and precocious youngster surrounded by adoring relatives.

As a middle child who didn't stand out in any discernible way—or so I thought—I seemed to excel only at making myself invisible. Now I knew that wasn't true. Quiet and shy, I had still been seen, and my unhappiness had mattered to him.

I also knew that my father, though not the swashbuckling super-hero I'd once imagined, had heroic qualities nonetheless. Faced with a medical assault on his family as deadly in its own way as bullets or mortar fire, he fought back with the best strategy he could.

In some ways, his choices brought us closer together, while in others they created lasting rifts. But at the time he had no way of fore-seeing this. All he knew was that he couldn't have lived with himself, or us, if he'd allowed his wife to die without a struggle on his part.

An adult with my own family now, I can only imagine the courage it took to make those decisions and deal with the consequences. I wonder if, in a similar situation, I would be as heroic.

Ten Million Atoms
Fit on the Head of a Pin

by Jane Finlay-Young

His shoes; that's what I remember about my dad coming back to get us.

There, on the Seascale Station train platform, in Northwest England with the heavy September sky pressing down on us and the salty suggestion of the nearby Irish Sea, it is his shoes I remember; not his eyes, not his voice, not the hope he brought us or the feeling of safety. All that came later.

The first thing I noticed was his shoes: their polished, well-worn, shiny blackness. The gentle, creaking, longing sound they made as he bent his long body down and crouched in front of us. His shoes crinkled as he lowered himself. Crinkled like a smiling face.

I didn't look up at his actual face; my head was fallen forward and looked only at the ground.

Close to his shoes, lolling casually off the ends of his bent knees, were his fingers. Long and soft and opening carefully, turning so the palms were up and we could see the criss-crossing tiny lines that tell a fortune, that predict long life or early death. Our mother believed in such things: the powers beyond, the invisible. She sat in the dark, smoking her cigarillos and drinking her sherry and talking to the walls, to the invisible creatures, to God. But we were trying to shut all that away, along with her wild, bulging tiger's eyes and her hair that lifted up above her in a tangle of snakes. There, on the train platform, we were hoping that now that he had come, all of that would be gone.

His fingers were not reaching or grasping, but steady, hesitating. They were fingers that wondered, just like we did, what was next.

And so we waited, along with his fingers and the beautiful black shoes, there on the train platform with the conductor calling out and doors slamming shut and the engine growling and hissing until no one was left around us.

Our legs were bare; we wore our best dresses.

He shifted his body and we tensed. Had he changed his mind? Was he going to jump back on the train? Were we that … were we that unlovable, that bad, that ugly, that he would take one look at us and run?

The damp air on our bare legs made us shiver.

But he didn't run. Instead, his fingers bent and made a bowl. In that damp and heavy air, those hands looked warm. They looked like something we could climb into and go to sleep in. We'd dreamed about such things for that whole year of waiting for him.

The last doors slammed shut, the whistle screeched and the train began to slide past us, scraping along the tracks, crying and complaining. And then there was nothing but the faint, muffled huff, huff, huff. And our own breathing.

Even the fells in the distance were gone; hidden behind the heavy fallen sky.

His fingers curled and then uncurled again.

Well, he said into the silence, his voice wobbling in the thick air. Well, aren't you three beauties.

We raised our heads then and lifted our eyes towards him. First to his lips that spoke the words and then to his eyes. Pale blue like ours. And wet.

A small smile crept onto his face, wrinkling it like his shoes had wrinkled, and we felt the same smile creep across our own.

Beauties, he repeated, and opened his arms like two great wings.

We three moved then, like one being, towards him, and he scooped his arms around us and lifted us from the ground.

That was 1965. I was seven and my sisters were five and three. The details of that moment are no doubt not quite as I have written them, but I can vouch for the feelings and for their truth. I can still feel the damp on my bare legs, I can still feel the stillness as I stared at his shoes, not daring to look up, in case …

In case what, I wonder now. In case he didn't want us? In case he had changed? In case he wasn't the person I had remembered, the person I had held in my mind to get me through the terrifying times of being alone with our mother?

Our mother had tried to kill someone and was put in prison. That's what brought our dad back to England from Canada. Our aunt, his sister, called him with the news.

I can imagine the transatlantic hum on the line, her hollow voice cracking with disbelief: Joan's in jail. Joan tried to kill someone; a stranger at a boarding house they were staying in. Yes, yes, the girls are fine.

I can imagine my father standing in his quiet, empty house looking out the window at the brilliant fall leaves spinning lazily from the trees. The sky, empty of clouds, blazing impossibly blue.

There was a trial. There were headlines in the newspapers: Nuclear Scientist's Wife! And her picture, with a caption underneath: "I wholly intended to do it." She was given a diagnosis: paranoid schizophrenic. She was locked away in Broadmoor, an institution for the criminally insane.

We were told none of this. And we didn't ask. Not once did we ask: Where's Mummy? It was enough that she was gone.

Why were three little girls left alone with such a woman? Why were we left in her care when she couldn't even care for herself? Why was he not with us when everything was falling apart?

These are painful questions and I hesitate even to type them.

I hesitate because the desire to protect my father is terribly strong. The desire to protect him from himself, I suppose, from his actions, from his past. And from the opinions of others. And the desire, as soon as the questions are set down on paper, to shout out: No! That's not it. His actions then are not *all* of who my father is. Not at all.

Twenty minutes ago, I walked away from the computer, from those difficult questions, and went downstairs to make myself a cup of tea. I turned on the kettle and looked out the kitchen window at the bright spring sunshine and shivering bare trees.

There was a familiar blankness inside my head. An airy tingling in my limbs.

How could I write about the intense love and old hurt that I feel concerning my dad? Perhaps what I have to say is too complicated to put down on paper. Perhaps I don't have the courage to say what I have to say.

Outside the window, a brilliant cardinal sat on a curling yellow branch of the corkscrew willow in my backyard, the first cardinal of the season. An astonishingly urgent splash of red amidst a dulled-down world.

I closed my eyes against the harshness of the colour, and saw instead the image of my dad's polished and well-looked-after shoes. They are a symbol of his solidity, his constancy. They are a symbol of his ability to hold, to contain, to cope. It was that essence of him that I wanted to capture as I sat down to write.

There are many images that I have of his shoes: his two pairs of proper shoes for work: black and brown. His hiking boots for our walking holidays in England. His Nike waffle trainers from the days when he and I used to jog together. But none of these images are as strong as his shoes at the train station. And, unfortunately, that image prompts the questions that I don't want sitting on the page.

The truth is I have much to say about my dad, but it's a high-wire act. There's the bigger part of me that only wants to write about the good stuff, the fun stuff. However, there's more to my dad and me than that. Of course. Between every parent and child there is, no doubt, more than just the good stuff.

The kettle hit full boil. Ah, life's odd synchronicities. It came to a full boil and then it shut itself off. There is a similar switch in my own head; things get too hot and it all turns off. That familiar blankness.

The seven-year-old me at the train station might have been at full boil. If she'd had the guts she might have screamed and kicked with outrage. If she'd felt safe enough she might have returned his smile with accusations: Where were you? Where were you when everything was falling apart?

But a child at full boil switches off, too. A child at full boil disappears through her eyes into the lace-holes of shoes, or into an electrical socket on the wall, or gets lost amongst the crazy zigzag patterns of the tiles on the kitchen floor. She leaves her weary, shivering body. And she's grateful for whatever she's offered. She knows there's a line drawn close by and if she crosses it, she might die.

A child knows, instinctively, that she cannot survive alone. And so she keeps quiet.

I poured boiling water over a tea bag and went back to staring out the window, waiting for my tea to steep.

My dad would have been thirty-five in 1965, beginning his career in nuclear research and development. He had his Ph.D. and had risen well above his shopkeeper father—a seller of shoes, in fact.

We had left civilized England in 1963 to come to Canada, to the bush in Manitoba, seventy-five miles north of Winnipeg. We were among the first fifty families to live in Pinawa, a new community built by Atomic Energy of Canada Limited.

One straight, narrow dirt road led into the half-built town. I can imagine the silence in the car as we drove mile after mile with nothing but untouched bush on either side of us and a vivid blue streak of sky above. The snap and spit of the car's tires on the dirt road. My sisters and I rendered speechless, our noses pressed to the window glass, looking at the endless miles of trees crowding in at us.

Our mother, already unstable and often unable to focus on the everyday tasks of raising her children, would, I imagine, have felt like she was being driven into the heart of darkness, her own mind beginning to scramble.

And my dad? I imagine him elated. I imagine that he would have been humming and singing and beating his long, lithe fingers on the steering wheel. I imagine him ready for adventure. I imagine him liberated, released from the world of his parents, from the soggy, dark and depressed place that was postwar England. This was 1963. This was the beginning of the rest of our lives.

But, as my dad played in the lab with his atoms and pencils and like-minded pals, and as my youngest sister perfected walking, my mother began to tip. Her inner conversations became more real than the outer ones with the ladies she would have over for tea. The bush and rock and silence outside the picture window in the living room would have offered no comfort, no direction. Her young children would have been demanding, would have needed food and naps and attention. And her head would have been full of noise and chatter.

She hung on for a year or so and then she cracked. She believed a visiting scientist had been sent to kill her. One Sunday morning, she walked down the street to where the scientist was staying and handed him a note. It said, approximately: I know you're here to kill me. I'm ready to go. I'll give you no trouble.

She was waiting to be taken.

She spent a few weeks in a hospital in Winnipeg for what was diagnosed as a nervous breakdown, but was, in fact, something far more sinister.

Once discharged, she took my sisters and me back to England.

Was there a plan? Was it meant to be just a bit of a break? Were we supposed to come back?

I don't know.

I imagine there would have been a part of my dad that would have been relieved to see her go. She must have been impossible to live with.

I imagine Dad would have driven us to the airport. I imagine he would have waved us off and then got back in the car and driven himself home. Seventy-five miles across all that flatness and through all those trees, through all that silence beneath a prairie sky that went on and on and on.

I remember hearing, either from him or someone else, that once he got home, he collapsed. He lay on the couch, stared at the ceiling and couldn't move for hours.

My dad was young; he'd had no training for life on the edge; he'd developed no antennae for the possibility that life might take a turn, might throw him a curve. There are many places that the logical, rational mind has no knowledge of, or interest in. I imagine he was attracted to the atomic and subatomic world because he was drawn to the beauty and order of nature, because it is a cleaner, clearer world, less ambiguous than the world of human interactions and emotions.

My mother was not just a crazy woman. She was a painter, a writer, a reader, a thinker. She was, no doubt, a complement to my dad in many ways. Her mind was messy and chaotic, while his was orderly. Her way of being in the world was loud, bold, brash, while his way was quiet, deliberate. Her feelings were huge, her visions vivid, while my father's were contained.

Opposites attract. She was a compelling woman. I imagine the unstated promise that my mother would have offered my father was: I'll bring you to life! We'll have an adventure!

For all the quiet my dad exudes, he is an adventurer. He loves the wilderness, camping, canoeing, hiking. He loves to venture down unknown dirt roads. He loves to laugh.

Perhaps my mother offered a freedom that my father couldn't reach on his own.

So, why would my dad have suspected that the woman he got into bed with night after night, the woman who was his wife and mother of his children, who was, yes, perhaps a tad eccentric, was actually mentally ill, was unfit to be a mother, was delusional and could, in fact, be violent? She'd been hospitalized, yes, but the doctors had written that off as a little bit of nerves.

It would have been difficult to imagine, there in that cozy community in the bush full of rational, fun-loving, highly educated folk, that a mother of three children would not be able to cope.

Perhaps we could say: Those three girls were left alone with that woman because of a failure of imagination. Because in the 1960s, when the world was exploding with hope and prosperity, who could have imagined that such a strong-looking woman as my mother was crumbling inside?

Perhaps it was ignorance and lack of information. Perhaps he thought that once she got back to England she'd get over her "little bit of nerves." Perhaps it was hope. Perhaps it was a belief that everything would work out in the end.

My dad is an optimist. Throughout my childhood, there's one saying of his that sticks out more clearly than the rest: *Don't worry, Janie, the sun always comes up in the morning.* I can see him sitting on the edge of my bed, in the dark, listening to me cry. I can feel his steady, certain presence as he spoke those comforting words.

Perhaps it was inconceivable to him that a mother couldn't mother her own children. Perhaps the whole world conspired to keep those girls with their mother because the whole world believed that only mothers could do what was needed to be done for their children.

I don't know.

Ten million atoms can be lined up on the head of a pin. Why could a scientist like my dad believe in that—in something he could not even see—and yet the possibility that his wife couldn't cope was inconceivable?

I don't know. I find I am staring into the face of a mystery. I find I am trying to hold two totally different images in my mind: the father who abandoned us and the father who saved us.

There's something I've thought about a lot since hearing the stories of people killed in the Twin Towers, and I think it relates to this dilemma of mine. I think it helps me understand my dad.

I remember thinking at the time that I would have been one of the ones who died. I would have been one of the ones doing what she was told: *Stay put, stay at your desk, someone will be there to get you.*

I would have waited to be saved. I would have trusted the authorities. And I suspect that my dad would have done the same. I suspect that if we'd been there, together, we would have sat quite still and gone thundering down in that massive, screeching collapse.

The thought is unbearable, but it sheds a clear light for me on this question: *Where was he when everything was falling apart?*

He was waiting. He was sitting still and waiting for instructions.

Is it hereditary, that passivity? Is it learned? Is it in our bones? Would most of us have done the same?

Most of us would never have conceived that those massive buildings were that vulnerable. And, likewise, I imagine that my father couldn't conceive that motherhood was either.

Why would my dad and I have sat still and not fought our way down the stairwells? Is it lack of passion? Does it mean we want to live less? Does it mean we love less?

I don't think so.

I can say with certainty that it wasn't through lack of caring that my sisters and I were left alone with our mother. I can say with certainty that our father loves us deeply.

He had to be both a father and a mother to my sisters and me after our mother was locked away, and he did it gracefully and firmly and with deep love and commitment. He did it without any role model. What man in the sixties was a single parent of three little girls? What man could be as comfortable in an apron at the kitchen sink as he was at the office? Very few, I think, could take on this enormous task and love it, have fun doing it, *want* to be doing it.

Somehow he managed to turn the everyday world that we had to get through into fun. All those small but essential details that need to be attended to, he made into a game. That was the amazing thing. And we knew, we could feel, that he was enjoying himself as much as we were.

After our cleaning jobs on Saturday morning, he'd make pancakes in the shapes of the letters of our names.

He warned us of bones in the Jell-O and so we ate it slowly, meticulously.

He made treacle toffee for our birthday parties so, he said, he could have a few minutes peace and quiet when he handed it out and all of our mouths were glued shut with the stuff.

We sang songs from *Oklahoma* at the top of our lungs as he drove us across the never-ending flatness of the prairies.

We took honey to the dump and lured the bears to our car; our own, terrifyingly huge, Paddington Bear.

He read us bedtime stories every night. We crowded into one bed and he read: *Kidnapped, Wind in the Willows, The Lion, the Witch and the Wardrobe*. Every pirate and witch, every four-legged creature and every child had a different voice, a different facial expression. We watched his face as much as we looked at the pictures in the books; the stories seemed to be as real for him as they were for us.

We invented scary ways to slide down the stairs on pillows and blankets, and he was there to cheer us on and catch us at the bottom.

He was there to catch us. He was then, and still is now.

When my dad was sixty, he reconnected with his grammar school sweetheart. They hadn't seen each other for forty years. When he was sixty-one, he married her.

I consider this one of the great miracles of my life; that he found someone so wonderful who loves and appreciates and respects him. And, that he is happy.

I was thirty-three. For most of my life, I had taken on the self-appointed role of taking care of Daddy. And suddenly I was replaced. Suddenly I no longer needed to feel responsible for his happiness, for his well-being.

Within a short period of time, everything under the surface bubbled up. My dad and his new wife announced they would be making England their new home, not Canada. It was a reasonable enough decision, of course; the three of us "girls" were adults with our own independent lives. But, in a neighbourhood restaurant in down-town Toronto, as my dad and sisters and I sat down to talk about the move, I opened my mouth and couldn't shut it, couldn't stop what came rushing out … all the why didn't yous and how could yous. All the disappointment and hurt.

Where were you when everything was falling apart? That was the essence of what I said that afternoon. I don't remember now in what guise that question presented itself, but I do remember, quite vividly, that the feelings were ancient, the feelings were old companions.

I blurted out all sorts of angry accusations and he sat there stunned, listening, not defending himself, or making justifications. And then I ran.

I didn't answer his phone calls for days. I lay on my bed and cried—overwhelmed and afraid and full of rage and hurt. The lid had come off. My sense of responsibility towards him had been causing me to protect him, and now that I was no longer protecting him … I feared I might have destroyed him.

A week later, I answered his call and agreed to meet him for a walk.

It was a beautiful fall day. Not damp and heavy like that September day at the train station so many years before. I walked up my dad's street and there he was walking towards me. I slowed my pace and looked at the sidewalk below my feet. It was littered with brilliant fallen leaves.

He was afraid, no doubt, and uncertain about what would happen next. The unspeakable had been spoken. *You abandoned us. You failed us.* But the unspeakable, once spoken, had not destroyed us.

Ten million atoms can fit on the head of a pin: such an inconceivable statement. How do we hold such things in our minds? How do we contain the hugeness of our existence? How do we contain the opposites within ourselves: abandonment and embrace; fear and joy; the chaos and the stillness.

How do we deal with the unanswerable? If our mother had not gone to such an extreme, if she had not been taken away, would he have come back to us? Or was he beginning his life anew without us?

The only answer I have, or perhaps the only answer I care to entertain, is the only answer that matters: He was there.

He was there, walking towards me.

I raised my eyes to meet his steady gaze. He was wearing a pale blue jacket that matched the colour of his eyes. He was not a destroyed man; he was strong, flushed with life. He was uncurling his hands and lifting his arms from his sides. They opened like wings and I took that last step towards him and folded myself inside.

A Character Walks Off the Page

by Camilla Gibb

In 2001, I hired a private detective. I had a novel to finish and I needed a professional to give me my ending. For five hundred dollars I got the news that my father, who had been missing for twelve years, was alive and living three thousand kilometres away. And so, at the end of my second novel, the father, who has disappeared, is killed.

If I hadn't known the truth, I would have been superstitious about mowing my character down on a lonely highway. I had taken all sorts of other imaginative liberties—filled in that twelve years with all manner of crimes—but I could not, somehow, manage to kill him. Once I had the truth, I was free to rewrite it. And with that ending, I rewrote the rest of my life as well.

My father was always—to be rather British about it—somewhat peculiar. He was never "diagnosed" as having anything more than an over-inflated ego and a ruthlessly competitive spirit, and that assessment was made not by a mental health professional but by his employer at his first (and last) job in Canada. After that, he declared himself an inventor. And my mother decided she'd had enough.

He was wildly enthusiastic about grand schemes that neither money could nor logic would support. In the mornings, he would draw up plans and make lists before the ritual visit to Canadian Tire— all this, a prelude to the massive destruction that would take place in the afternoons. He tore down a wall in the apartment he was renting. Then he tore down the ceiling as well. When the landlord tossed him out he moved to the country, where he bought a rundown farm and promptly ripped into a hillside with a backhoe, felled (illegally) a good number of trees in a government pine plantation and tore down three of the farmhouse's exterior walls. He lived behind tarpaulin, he lived without plumbing or heat, as did we, his children, on divorce-decreed weekends and holidays, because nothing he tore down was ever rebuilt—least of all his relationships.

Throughout all of this, my father drank a litre of gin every day, turning grimmer with each sip, mutating into a mass of bitterness and paranoia. By nightfall, his transformation was complete. And we were trapped. He seethed: skewering us with profanity and insult, taking perverse pleasure in amputating any growing limbs. The more upset we became, the crueller he would get, so we learned to shrink, becoming shrivelled remnants of ourselves, hiding in cobwebbed corners with spiders and imaginary friends. We took a vow of silence. As families do.

At ten, I "diagnosed" him as an alcoholic, but even then, I knew it wasn't simply the bottle. As I got older, I read in search of answers. I seemed to need to label it/him—to contain it, perhaps depersonalize it—in order to believe that I was more than a shell that might have once had the potential to house a person. And what if it was contagious or I inherited it, as I inevitably believed I would? I needed to name an illness in the hope that there was a cure.

I read about manic depression, which, somewhere in my years of reading about it became bipolar disorder, but no wording, politically correct or otherwise, seemed to capture it/him entirely. I needed a great deal many more words and a big canvas over which to splatter them.

And so I wrote a novel: *Mouthing the Words*. And then another: *The Petty Details of So-and-so's Life*—both stories of what happens to wounded children. In each case, I took what I knew and embellished and developed it for narrative purposes. And I took what I didn't know and found answers—fictional albeit, but answers nevertheless. Except for that question of what happens to the father in the end of *The Petty Details*. I could mess with the character's life but not his mortality, it seemed; at least not until I had the assurance that the man whose absence inspired the story was still alive.

Why? Because the guilt is always there, hovering on the threshold, threatening to walk through the door. Because for all the bad, I remember how beautifully he played the violin, and the guitar as well; how he made elegant cabinets and carved things out of wood; how he painted and quoted Shakespeare, taught me how to use the dictionary, bought me pencil crayons and goggles and took me swimming. For all the bad, I wouldn't want *that* person dead. And so I added a postscript at the end of *The Petty Details*: Oliver sends a postcard from Hell. From the grave, he gets the final word.

Just in case.

Fast forward to October 2002. I'm reading from my second novel at a writers' festival—a passage about a father who tears down every-thing around him in the name of "invention" and then promptly disappears. After the reading, I spy a weather-beaten man in the lineup clutching a book, my book, between his hands. He looks hunted.

Haunted. I burn. Guilt and an anxiety manifest in the form of an old and familiar feeling: separating from my surroundings, everything in front of me becoming pixellated, as if I am in the middle of a dense swarm of bees. What has it cost him, I wonder (as I implode), to appear?

The agony of that moment leads us, the following morning, to the cafeteria in City Hall, where the coffee is only sixty-five cents a cup and smoking is still allowed.

It's his teeth I fixate on. Black nubs like charred kernels of corn. He rolls a cigarette between sepia-stained fingers, pours coffee between cracked lips and spits out burnt, blackened words. He's telling me about a blind rage that once, long ago, led him to run over a flowerbed and drive his car into a stone wall. The car he used to drive to the train station in order to commute into London to do the job he hated, only to return home to the house he hated, where he was forced to resume his role as the husband and father he neither wanted to nor could be.

"I hated myself for doing that," he says. "I abhor violence. It sickens me; it makes me physically ill."

And so, although the car was still operable, he crashed it again so that it would die and be taken from his sight.

A character from one of my novels has walked off the page, but he's saying things far more surprising than anything I could have put into his mouth; he speaks of things that make me question the fertility of my imagination.

He carries on, a man without a filter, without any sense at all of what is appropriate to tell a daughter, or even, for that matter, a stranger. I now have him pegged as a sociopath (because "psychopath" seems to have gone the way of "manic depression")—unable to form attachments, unaware of his impact on others.

"The world terrifies me," he confides, clarifying: "I mean, the people in it."

"But you assume everyone is hostile," I say.

On this, he completely agrees.

"It must be very painful to move in the world," I say, as if my therapist has replaced me at the table. I imagine having to navigate a landscape carved up by electric fences.

And it is painful, so he doesn't move. He hides, ekes out, scams, squeaks by and drinks himself to sleep every night. He describes himself as asocial—"Not antisocial," he tells me, "but asocial." He calls himself "the world's ultimate loner." He says he cannot have relationships, that he has never actually loved anyone, except his daughter, because she loved him unconditionally, at least she did once, when she was small.

He is introspective enough to ask tough questions, recognizing that it is something in him that makes him this way, rather than blaming others. He wonders if it was because he was dropped on his head as a baby, or because he was put in an orphanage temporarily as a toddler, where he was punished by being tied to a banister. He wonders if it is because he was sent off to boarding school at such a young age, molested by the head master, bullied by other boys. He wonders if it was the army.

I think: How difficult it is to be a British man; how gruesome these rites of passage must be for even the most capable and equipped.

I ask if he feels he is "missing" something that other people have, meaning whatever that "thing" is that connects people to others.

"Yes," he says, nodding.

"Is it the capacity for empathy?" I ask.

"That's part of it," he says.

He does not offer the rest.

He tells me my first novel devastated him when he read it, but that he understands where it comes from now. *Mouthing the Words* is about a secret, he tells me, a family secret. To him, that secret is about him having run over our precious flowerbed and driven into the garden wall. He says I must have known, I was old enough, there is no way I could not have known.

But I don't have any memory of it.

"You've repressed it," he tells me, insisting this is what the book is about. Analogy, metaphor, therapy.

And irony. Some of my relatives choose not to, or refuse to read my work, some have been advised not to and some have refused to speak to me ever again, but my father, the one person most implicated and demonized and fictionalized in my work, has read every single word.

Every day he goes to the same bar and drinks two beers, he tells me, before going home to drink a great deal more. The waitress there is kind to him—talks to him, lets him linger. He tells her he has a daughter who is a writer and that she has written a book that has devastated him. Perhaps this woman reads the book, I cannot remember, but what she says in reply shifts his thinking. "But it's not really about you," she says. "It's about her."

He thinks she is wise, this twenty-year-old waitress, and he is able to sleep again at night.

To me, he says: "You must have had a very rough time."

I have no response to this. I don't know quite what to think—nor does the therapist who has replaced me at the table. Is this empathy? Remorse? Part of me will admit no vulnerability to him, will not offer him any way in, but it's also that I'm not entirely sure this story is my own. Ultimately it is fiction that owns the majority share. And what of the truth that, to whatever extent, has informed the fiction? Even that, apparently, is open to interpretation. A stone wall it is.

There are one hundred and eighty thousand words between us now. One hundred and eighty thousand of my words. I left him sitting in the cafeteria and walked away, rather stunned to realize that even if he had

come out with the most destructive invectives that morning, they
wouldn't have even chipped the fortress of words that surround me.

That week in 2001, when I heard from the private detective that my father was alive, I killed off the father at the end of *The Petty Details.* And then everything about my life changed. I abruptly left a relationship in a lifetime of relationships that had been polluted by the ghost of him within me. I dared to leave everything and almost everyone I knew. I was homeless and hated for my abrupt departure—my stuff in storage, renting a grotty room by the week in a building full of grotty rooms rented by the week, I had lost almost everyone I knew. It needed to be ugly for a time, and it was. I rode the elevator with careening boozy men who had just left or been thrown out by their wives. I hid in that room, violence bounding down the hallway on the other side of the door, and finished working on the novel.

And eventually I was done.

I would leave my place of exile but never return to the streets I'd abruptly left, literally or metaphorically, again. I found new streets, necessarily, and fortunately, better ground. I dug a borehole thirty-five metres in that new ground and drank new water. And it tasted clean.

When I began a new novel, *Sweetness in the Belly,* I found that the parents, although selfish and irresponsible, were actually quite affectionate and well intentioned. Admittedly, I killed them off right at the beginning of the book and replaced them with a cast of loving surrogates, but still, this seemed like some measure of progress. As did subsequently throwing away the entire story of my protagonist's childhood—forcing her to grow up.

I have wondered if my father will, ironically, be disappointed by this book; there is nothing in it, after all, that suggests he exists. No analogy, no metaphor, no therapy. No stone wall.

The Loafers

by Catherine Gildiner

1965 AGE 16

On Tuesdays, my mother had her Ladies' Alliance Club, so my father and I always dined at the Your Host Restaurant in the Harlem Plaza. There was a shoe store in the same strip mall as the restaurant, which was fortunate since on this particular Tuesday I had a desperate yen to spend my babysitting money. I popped in and bought some Bass Weejun penny loafers on my way to meet my dad.

As I listened to the constant whining of the New York State Thruway, which was almost overhead, I walked along the cracked sidewalk with a feeling of dread. I prayed no one I knew came in. Who had dinner alone with her father in a chain restaurant dive? No one—that's who. He was a total embarrassment. Teenagers went to greasy spoons to smoke and meet boys, not to have the daily special with their fathers.

He was already ensconced in his favourite booth when I arrived. He took a drag on his Camel, put down the *U.S. News & World*

Report, stood as though I was some kind of date and said, "Hi, Peaches."

I just scowled, flopped down in the opposite booth and opened my new shoebox and perused my loafers, picturing how great they would look with my new green Adler knee socks with matching sweater and dickey. He admired them as well, saying that it can get "monotonous" (he loved words like that) wearing saddle shoes.

Like he hadn't been wearing wing tips for maybe forty years straight in a size fourteen? He could have been mistaken for Clarabell in a dark alley.

The waitress ambled over wearing a tan uniform with dark brown trim, with an insignia across her chest that read, *Relax! We're your host this evening.* She stood leaning on one hip holding her order pad, and lifted one eyebrow. My father beamed a tobacco-stained smile and said, "Well angel, where do you hail from?"

I longed to drop through a trap door in the floor and fall into the pit where all teenagers go whose parents give the word *humiliation* a new meaning. He still thought he was the big cheese in the small town of Lewiston where he had been the pharmacist who owned the drugstore. He really didn't get that he was now a tiny cog in a huge drug company in the big boring city of Buffalo, and that we were in a greasy food chain in a suburban strip plaza. He didn't seem to be remotely aware that no one knew him or wanted to know him—let alone give him her family tree. He didn't sound friendly, he sounded like a stalker.

Before the waitress could answer, I quickly ordered a burger and my father had the Salisbury steak special. After she left, I looked across at him for the first time. I guess he was wearing Jed Clampett suspenders just to torture me. After a few minutes of silence he said, "Well, I understand there have been a few new developments on the road to higher learning." (He used the same tone you would use if you were going to say, "I heard you won the Nobel Prize.")

I assumed he'd seen my report card. "So?" I demanded.

"So?" He answered shrugging his shoulders.

"I got a D in French—so sue me. I have no idea why that tiny country has any clout. I'm never going there. In the vocabulary film strip, all they do is eat mouldy cheese and let their kids drink alcohol. What's with the Eiffel Tower? I could build that with a lousy erector set."

"I have no intention of discussing your report card. It's your affair. You're the one who has to get into college. I've already been there."

Thankfully, our food arrived and we ate in silence. While we were having our coffee, he tried the what-happened-in-your-day grating drivel. Since I said "nothing," he told me about his—like I cared. He said that his company was introducing a new drug next month called Valium.

"Well *that* name is never going to catch on," I informed him.

"Cathy," he took a drag on his cigarette and a deep breath, "It strikes me that you are angry for some reason."

"I am not *angry,* and I wish you would stop saying that or I'm really going to get angry!"

"Actually, it is the first time I've said it. Bear with me. I was young once as well. I know what it is to be a teenager and I know what it is like to be angry."

"That was years ago. I'm not talking about *Our Town* and *Oklahoma* (two plays I'd seen at Melody Fair that summer). You know nothing about life. Everything is different now." I looked at his old, bald head and realized there was no point in saying any more.

"Believe it or not, I was prom king and captain of the football team—just to show you how the mighty can fall," he said smiling.

"Prom king? Where did you go, Braille High?"

Ignoring me, he leaned across the table and picked up my shoebox, opened it, and carefully unfolded the tissue paper. He lifted out each loafer, and in the slit where the penny belonged he crammed in a dime, saying, "It isn't easy to be young. It's hard to learn the ropes. Sometimes teenagers do stupid things. I know I did. I am putting two dimes in here—the price of two phone calls. If you ever get in over your head, call me. I will come and get you—no questions asked—ever."

As if he could help me?

He then paid the bill and we rode home in silence. He attempted to make conversation. I guess he assumed that because we'd worked side by side in the drugstore since I was four, I was still thrilled to be, as he used to say, "his right-hand man." The truth is he hadn't seemed so bad then. It was only in the last few years he'd become so annoying.

We used to share an interest in Cassius Clay, and together we'd watched him move through the ranks. My father and I used to do imitations of the TV interviews. I'd be Cassius Clay and he'd be Howard Cosell.

As we pulled into the driveway, my father pulled out his last conversation card. "Now that the Liston fight is over, Cassius has changed his name, get *this,* to Muhammad Ali."

"Even Rapunzel knows that."

"Howard Cosell has even started to call him Muhammad."

"So? That's his name."

"Little strange don't you think?"

"No."

"Well, then I think I'll change mine to Pope Pius X."

"Better than Jim McClure."

1966 AGE 17

I wrote the junior class skit for the March of Dimes drive. I had to have a business meeting with Rhonda Levit, the class treasurer, in order to find out how much of the class's till I could spend on set design.

Rhonda was a math wiz and was in all advanced classes. She had a notebook labelled for each class and she underlined possible test items in coloured pencils. I barely knew her other than that she was in my geometry class. When I arrived with all of my stage design storyboards, she said she couldn't start the meeting until she'd solved some dumb proof. She seemed really riled up and asked me if I'd solved it. I told her I never took the geometry book home. It was far too heavy. Besides, I worked at The Donut Hole at night. In an attempt to calm her down, I assured her that if she ever needed an angle measured or something built she could call a carpenter, unless she was Robinson Crusoe.

I had the feeling I was not reassuring her, as she wound her thick, black, curly hair around her green pencil. She looked genuinely worried and said, "I worked on it for three hours last night until my father finally had to call Mr. Eagleson at home. He told my father not to worry about it. He said we would go over the solution in class because it involved some ideas we haven't even learned yet."

"Your father called Mr. Eagleson over a geometry problem?" My father would no more have called the teacher at home over a math problem than he would have called President Johnson over a pothole.

"He goes over my homework every night and corrects it."

Finally, I had her calmed down enough to get her to focus on the class accounts. After working for hours on a Friday night, I offered to drive her home.

As we walked through the parking lot that muggy June evening, I decided I'd stop off at Brunner's, the neighbourhood bar where everyone-who-was-anyone congregated. I thought it only polite to ask Rhonda if she wanted to come with me for a nightcap. After all, Buffalo was a bar town. Everyone had a neighbourhood bar where they hung out. If you were underage, you had fake ID in the form of a Sheriff's Card. Everyone in my school who wasn't hopeless bought fake IDs from Jackie Holmes, the best artist in our school. His brother took the pictures and did the laminating. This counterfeit business paid for them both to go to Parsons School of Design in New York City.

Rhonda looked appalled when I asked her if she wanted to go to Brunner's. She said she didn't drink alcohol except on Passover. I said I didn't drink it even then. I just had a Tab—but I liked seeing every-one—chatting for half an hour and then heading home. She said. "No, thanks, I have work to do—just drop me off."

Schoolwork on a Friday night?

She stopped dead in the parking lot. "Wow, is this your car?" She placed her hand on my robin's-egg-blue 1964 Impala convertible with a 409 engine. (Actually, it was my mother's. I made her tell my father she needed it.) Since the top was down, I jumped in without opening the door, which was one of the only benefits of being a washed-up high jumper. As she got in the tedious way, by opening the door, I pushed in the lighter, blared the radio and then sped out of the school parking lot on two wheels as I did every day, singing in perfect Beach Boy cadence, *"She's real fine, my 4-0-9."*

As we approached the signal at the corner, I saw a friend hitchhik-ing. Rhonda said, "Look! It's Tony Maglionno. *Oh my God!*"

"Stop! In the Name of Love" blasted over the radio. Tony had a great voice and sang at high school dances. I sped up to the light and then slammed on the brakes. I stood up, held up my hand to indicate a stop motion and he and I sang, *"Stop, in the name of love."* He laughed his head off at the perfect timing—jumped in the back seat and said, "I'm going to Brunner's."

"Me too. I'm just dropping Rhonda off. Then we can phantom together." We continued singing as loud as we could and held up our hands like Diana Ross at all stop signs. Rhonda was clearly over-whelmed, but she was laughing more than I'd ever seen her laugh. At the end of the song, she said shyly, "Tony, I remember when you sang 'The Wanderer' at the grade-nine mixers and then at the end of the song you opened your shirt and had a rose on your chest."

"Wow that was junior high. You have a good memory." He then regaled us with an updated, jazzier version of "The Wanderer."

I pulled in Rhonda's driveway and faced her mock Tudor home with its tiny black leaded-glass windows. "Have fun at Brunner's," she said while getting out of the car. Hugging her advanced-class books close to her chest, she stared up at the heavy barred dormers. She hesitated, "I've heard about Brunner's, but I wouldn't know anyone there."

Tony, unlike most of the boys I'd ever met, actually talked and he was kind. "You'll know Cathy and me," he said. She still looked hesitant, so Tony continued, "Rhonda, you are still going to get into Wellesley even if you take a Friday night off."

"I have to get into Cornell. It's cheaper," she said as she started to walk up her gravel drive. One of my favourites by The Animals, "We Gotta Get Out of This Place," came on and we sang at the top of our lungs as we peeled out of the driveway.

She waved at us from her front stoop and then called out to us, "Would you mind if I came for an hour or two? Sorry I had you drive me all the way home."

Studly was the first person we saw at the entrance to Brunner's. He was perched on a bar stool by the door checking Sheriff's Cards for proof of age. In exchange for this, Doc, the bartender, gave him free drinks. He never really checked the proof, but only held it in his hand and greeted everyone as though he was host of the Inaugural Ball and their Sheriff's Card was an engraved invitation.

He was the most handsome boy in the school. Years ago, someone put the caption *Studly* under his picture in the school paper. The name stuck and was written on his football uniform and now even the teachers called him Studly. He always had extra money and drove a

British-racing-green Triumph TR3. He was clearly limping to the finish line in his sixth year of high school and was, therefore, older than the rest of us. Although he denied responsibility, it was rumoured that he had gotten Arlene Nickeerbaum into trouble. She left school, went to an unwed mother's home and no one ever saw her again.

Studly was accompanied, as always, by Shaky. Frank Metz had been born with a bit of palsy. One side of his body was slightly weaker than the other and one arm shook involuntarily. His mind was also palsied in a way that no one could ever quite put a finger on. People just said he had a screw loose. His look was one of constant derision. His rage focused on the very few who were physically weaker than he was. No one could predict what would set him off, but when he was on a cruel streak, his mind was as bent and shaken as his arm.

Studly and Shaky were a study in contrasts, both physically and emotionally. For some unknown reason, they went everywhere together. Shaky basked in the glory of the friendship and Studly didn't mind a jester in his court.

It was hot, humid and crowded and all the doors and windows were flung open and the crowds lined up outside having their friends hand them a beer through the casement windows. Some girls sat perched up on the beer fridge, letting their legs hang over the glass doors. Doc, the bartender, parted his way through dangling calves, muttering "Ladies, you are not making my job any easier."

I introduced Rhonda to Studly and, knowing he could hold his own in conversation, I parted my way through the multitude to get a Tab from the bar. While waiting for my drink, I ran into Tony at the bar. We watched from afar as Studly leaned against the wall chatting with Rhonda. Shaky stood there pretending to be part of the conversation. Studly laughed easily and touched Rhonda's arm, gently reeling her in. Tony looked at me, shook his head and said, "Poor old Rhonda has no idea what hit her."

Rhonda was rather plain, but she had a head of long, beautiful curly hair. She was petite and had a large bust line. It never ceased to amaze me how important breast size was to boys. Odd since large testicles made no impact on me.

By the time I got back with my drink, Studly and Shaky were all excited about going out to the Idle Hour, a roadside tavern out in the middle of nowhere. It was an hour away on the thruway, and then you had to wind around a series of dark roads and then somehow you wound up on some rocks by Lake Erie. It was a cave-like place that smelled stale no matter how long the windows were open. It was furnished in old picnic tables that were carved up with defunct declarations of love. However, in the summer it was cool and they had a huge patio for dancing, decorated with faded paper lanterns that had been ripped by the wind. In the summer, they occasionally enticed big entertainment acts to come out there.

"Guess what? Chuck Berry is coming to the Idle Hour next week. We ought to go out there now and check it out with your friend Rhonda," Studly said.

"If we went now we would be a little early for Chuck Berry," I said.

"Come on. It's hot in the city."

"No, Master Studly. I have to get Rhonda home."

Rhonda was sipping a Singapore Sling through a straw while staring up at the statuesque Studly.

"It's going to be ten degrees cooler out there. Lake hasn't warmed up yet. *Come on,*" he wheedled.

"That place is a dump, and when no one is performing there it's depressing and full of drunks—not the interesting kind of drunks, the boring lifers. Besides, it's minimum an hour's drive and it's already late."

Shaky said, "You never want to do anything. We got to case the place for Chuck."

Rhonda agreed with Shaky on this one, saying she would love to case it out.

While having another drink, Rhonda, Shaky and Studly really got on to this Idle Hour rant. Finally, I agreed just to shut them up. Besides, I didn't know if Rhonda would ever get out of her house again.

Studly headed out on to the New York State Thruway in the two-seater Triumph with the top down, Shaky in the passenger seat and Rhonda and I perched up on the back boot, like the girls who lie on cars as decoration at the auto show.

We had a harrowing ride out there since Studly had already been drinking and Shaky always encouraged any wild behaviour that he didn't have to take the rap for. We came upon the exit suddenly, so Studly crossed three lanes to make it off on time and Rhonda and I almost flew out the side. All four of us were partaking in Rhonda's first walk on the wild side. We laughed so hard we were crying when Studly made the car jerk to the beat of "Help Me Rhonda," which blasted on the radio.

When we walked into the Idle Hour, she didn't see the drunks slumped over the bar in a seedy old beach tavern that was full of townies drinking cheap beer off-season. Having just finished *The Old Man and the Sea* in our English class, Rhonda saw the Idle Hour as a haunt of the Hemingway Lost Generation. All I saw was the bullshit.

I had been around bars long enough to know full-blown losers when I saw them, so I just went out to the patio by myself to get away from the stale beer smell. I hung out at an old, cigarette-burned picnic table listening to the waves hit the rocks and watching the ugly plastic coloured lights strung up around the periphery pick up the moonlight off the waves. Amazingly enough, nature could dress up even the Idle Hour.

By the time I went back inside, all three of them were hammered. They had ordered french fries, which they hadn't even eaten. I told Studly I had to get home.

He told me to "cool my jets" as he barely crept around the empty dance floor to "You've Lost That Loving Feeling," by The Righteous Brothers, with both arms clenched around the tiny Rhonda. Shaky and I sat morosely looking at each other. Shaky chewed on his coaster that said *Schlitz, the beer that made Milwaukee famous* and, between bites, said, "We were lining up shots with beer chasers. We challenged those guys over there from Bethlehem Steel, to see who could drink the most in a five-minute span. We drank them under the table."

Christ. Shaky was slurring and Studly was weaving around the dance floor, staggering and laughing with Rhonda who was tipsy but not nearly as drunk.

"Guys, we have to get going. It's amazingly late and we have a forty-five-minute drive ahead. Studly, I'm driving your car and you're sitting up on the back boot."

"No way, you can't drive stick shift. Don't worry, my car knows the way home."

I knew we were in trouble.

I went to the ladies' room, which was labelled *mermaids,* and looked in a grimy full-length mirror. There I was with my blonde hair pulled back in a long ponytail with a blue grosgrain ribbon tying it. I had on my John Meyer of Norwich sleeveless flowered blue blouse with the pleats down the front with a matching powder blue A-line skirt and my Bass Weejun loafers. I stared down at the dimes shining in the loafers. I remembered that my father had said to use the dimes to make a call if I was in trouble. I had driven home with many a drunken driver, but never dead-drunk drivers who couldn't even walk.

Studly could probably get home, but it wasn't worth the risk on the busy New York State Thruway at ninety miles an hour in a two-seater convertible. I took the dime out of my shoe and marched down the hall that stank of Pine-Sol, which failed to camouflage twenty years of old beer, urine and regret. I made the call.

"Hi, Dad."

"Mmmm." He'd been asleep.

"Remember when you gave me those dimes for phone calls and put them in my loafers?"

"Yup."

"I'm calling in the right foot tonight."

"Everything okay?"

"Yeah, I don't want to go home with a dead-drunk driver. Would you pick me up and then I have to get the 409 at Brunner's."

"Where are you?"

"The Idle Hour out in Lakeview, about an hour out of town on the lake."

"I'm on my way."

"Don't come in. I'd die of humiliation. I'll wait on the outskirts of the parking lot."

"I'm leaving now."

I went in to get Rhonda, who was leaning on the bar giggling. I pried her away from Studly and led her to the *mermaids* room. I told her we couldn't go home with those drunks. I said I'd called my father and he was on his way. She looked stricken. I had never seen the colour drain from someone's face like that. "You can't be serious." She covered her face and leaned over the sink as though she was going to be sick. "Oh my God. Did you tell your parents I was here?"

"No." What was her problem? "I know it's embarrassing, but there is no way around it. We are in the middle of nowhere."

She let out a sigh of relief. "Thank God. You didn't tell I was here. I can't go home with your father. He would tell my father we were here. He thinks we are working very late on the class books. It terrifies me to even think what he would do if he ever knew I was here."

"My father won't tell him. He'll just drop you off and watch to make sure you get in safely."

She looked genuinely terrified—more frightened than I'd ever seen anyone look. "I can't take that risk. My father cannot know I was here."

"He won't find out. Even if he did, it isn't the worst thing in the world. It's the weekend on a hot night. You're a teenager who came to a raunchy Lakeview bar. Some guys got drunk. You called for a ride. Worse things have happened."

"You're sure you never mentioned my name?"

She wasn't listening to me.

"Positive."

"You should have told me you were calling *your father*. Now he'll see me."

"First of all, he doesn't know you and second, he isn't coming in. Lastly, he really doesn't care."

"I have to go home with Studly and Shaky."

"They're drunk. Remember how they drove out here after only a few beers? They've downed a dozen whisky shots—not to mention the chasers—since then. They don't give a fig what happens to themselves or anyone else."

"I don't care. They'll sober up in the air. My father can't know I've been here. Do you swear you won't tell your father? You have no idea what my father would do."

"I swear."

She walked out of the *mermaids* and returned to the bar.

I walked into the parking lot and waited on the edge of the woods. A raccoon sat on some rocks and looked at me. We exchanged glances. Yes, I really am this stupid teenager waiting for my father to pick me up.

The headlights of my father's beige Lark appeared. (Maybe the least cool car in the world. I guess I shouldn't complain since I got the Impala.)

I got in the car, slammed the door, never saying a word. We drove through the back roads near Lake Erie and made Tobacco Road turns. We heard the constant lap of the waves, providing a heartbeat for the forest. I turned on the radio, blaring it. Danny Neaverth, the DJ of WKBW, announced it was the hottest day in June in New York State since 1936. He said people do strange things in the heat. I thought my father might say something at that point, but he didn't. In fact he never once mentioned the whole Idle Hour Affair.

As we hit the New York State Thruway, "Stand by Me" came on. My father sang along as he smoked his cigarette. I looked at him like he was mental. Then "I've Got You, Babe," by Sonny and Cher, came on as we were a few blocks from Brunner's, where I had to pick up my car. I ignored him completely, looking out the passenger window and clinging to the armrest. As we made the turn into St. Benedict's Church parking lot across from Brunner's at three-thirty in the morning, the last stanza was blasting and I felt him pause as he sang Sonny's part, waiting for me to sing Cher's part. I looked at him and could feel how much he wanted me to sing the duet, but I remained silent. He paused and then belted out the last line alone, *"I've got you, babe."*

I never had to use the other dime. One was enough. Rhonda made it back that night without her father finding out where she'd been. But when she made the same trip three weeks later, she wasn't as lucky. They flew off the road on a thruway exit and hit an embankment. Studly and Shaky walked away without a scratch while Rhonda became a paraplegic.

2006 AGE 57

My relationship with my father was frozen in teenage time. While I was entrenched in adolescent rage and never once gave him a break, he developed a brain tumour and died.

I didn't thank him for that dime. Sometimes I wish that I could use the other dime to call him wherever he is and say one kind word, or at least do my Muhammad Ali imitation and hope that he would still answer me as Howard Cosell.

The other day, I heard Cher interviewed on the radio for her latest farewell tour. She said it's been forty years since "I've Got You, Babe" was recorded. Cher says that whenever she sings that song, she feels overwhelmed. I know what she means.

The Stubborn Heart

by Rebecca Godfrey

The night I saw my father die, we were gathered around the dinner table, my younger brother, my mother, my father and I. My father, at the head of the table, was in the middle of a sentence when he made a piercing, choking sound, his skin paled, his chair fell backwards and he collapsed on the floor. We thought he might be joking, for the moment seemed almost slapstick, so exaggerated and comical. *Ha, ha. Dad's kidding around. He's fallen to the floor.* Because I was sitting across from him, I was the only one to have seen the strange colour of his skin and perhaps that was why, even before he fell, I sensed he was in some true peril.

My father lay still on the carpet for several seconds. My mother bent over him, one hand on his heart, one hand on his forehead. My younger brother, ten years old, with a cherub's curls and full smile, knelt down as well, silent and unsure. We stood there as if in a frozen tableau: my father on the floor, my mother's hand on his heart. Our house in Victoria was perched high on a cliff, above a strand of the

Pacific Ocean, and below us, the waters seemed to turn greyer, as did the sky.

And then my father sat up; he blinked his eyes, and he seemed disoriented, unaware of the reason for his fall. He's fine, my mother said. I'm okay, he said. I ran to hold him, and then, before reaching him, a terrible panic seized me. "Take him to the hospital!" I screamed, for I felt a kind of tremor of warning in my own body.

My father and I were close, and shared a bond that often felt like some unspoken telepathy. Yet, now he didn't seem to share my sense that he was in danger. He agreed with my mother that he was fine, and he went to lie down on his bed. I considered calling an ambulance, but what could I say to the dispatcher when my father was upright and appeared healthy?

I was fourteen, and stubborn; I kept yelling about the hospital in the dramatic manner of an overly sensitive teenage girl. Take him to the hospital; we *have to* take him to the hospital. Though he was not fainting or weak, my father must have wanted to assuage my panic, or he respected my raised voice. Whatever the reason, he agreed to go to the hospital, and together we drove to the emergency room.

At the hospital, my father was taken in for observation while we sat in the waiting room with other worried families. A girl in purple eye shadow began to talk to me in a rapid, frenetic way. "He just flew off the roof," she said of her boyfriend. "I don't know what he was on. He thought he had wings or something." I tried to listen, but her fluttering voice unnerved me and I didn't disclose that my father had not flown towards the sky but instead had fallen limply. An alarm went off like some crude wail. Nurses rushed by, another alarm rang loudly. In the sterile room, away from his family, my father died. His heart, as the experts explained, beat so quickly it lost all shape, and only their electroshock brought him back to life and his heart to normality. If he had not been in the hospital, this quick beating of the heart would have been fatal.

When we were brought into his room, my father looked out of place on the dull cot, with the yellowed pillow and the mass of tangled wires attaching him to stacks of machinery. His dark hair lay across his forehead. His long, slim face seemed not to have changed but in repose looked different. He was a man with the sharp, vivid features of a slim hunter—high cheekbones, a long jaw, bright blue eyes which seemed alternatively observant and amused. But now, his features seemed soft and blurry, as if he was lying under the weight of moving water. His eyes were closed. He seemed unaware of the presence of his family.

The doctor then told us his heart had beaten in this wrong, dangerous way once before, and that was the reason for the collapse in our dining room. He must have died then and his resurrection mystified them. They'd never heard of a person surviving symptoms that were always fatal. How had he revived without an electric shock to kick-start him back to life? I wished the girl with the flying boyfriend had been in the room because I might have been able to tell her what I could not tell the doctors: I'd known he was in danger without the benefit of wires and machinery. I might even have kept him alive by the force of my own will. I kept this notion to myself while they talked about ventricular fibrillation, for I knew the doctors wouldn't believe a daughter's love could be some kind of remedy.

Though the hospital in Victoria was like all hospitals, with that particular scent of stale carnations and disinfectant and skin, and a generic cinder-block design, outside there was a sudden and surprising sight of pink petals all over the pavement, fallen from the clusters of cherry blossom trees. The trees reminded me of the chrysanthemum bush my father had planted outside of my bedroom window when we first moved to Victoria, as if he'd known I'd want some hopeful colours to bloom in the new home where the wild trees were gnarled and grave, and where the sky was so often full of fog. I wanted to sweep up the wet petals and bring them back to my father's room where he lay, sedated, under observation, while the doctors kept watch on his unruly heart.

At home, I went to his closet and I pulled his plaid shirts from the hangers, ignoring the tweed blazers and ties. The shirts were from our time living on a farm in Ontario, and I thought he might want to have them, for he'd loved the roughness of the country, where he was surrounded by wild horses, winter storms, and field after field of gold, uneven wheat. He'd known little about farming, but had taken to the challenge with a kind of determination which only increased with every difficulty. I'd spent most of my time avoiding the dirt and chores, choosing instead to wear dresses and daydream under the refuge of a lilting willow tree.

One day, two men had come from the electric company and cut down the tree because it wasn't orderly. It was in the wires. It was interfering with the transference of electricity. As though he were already gone, I remembered how my father had never minded my escape to the willow tree, and how he'd comforted me when the tree was felled so unexpectedly. I planned to bring the shirts to my father the next morning in the hospital so he wouldn't have to wear the depressing gown, but before I could find a suitcase, I collapsed into the pile of flannel shirts, sobbing and terrified. Six months before, my older brother had died in a drowning accident and it seemed to me that my father would die as well. It seemed suddenly like the most natural outcome, and I clutched all the plaid shirts to my chest, as if the fabric could provide some safety.

My mother returned to the hospital but came back, alone, later that evening. It might have been much later, perhaps three in the morning. I was awake when she returned, as I had been all evening, keeping watch on my own heart to see if the tremor would return, as if I carried some vessel of connective warning. For ten minutes or so, I lay down beside her, too afraid to be alone. The rise and fall of her breath reassured me, and yet I remained awake.

I wandered through our house, which was full of books that might have been a map to the paths of my family. My mother favoured stories of stoic detectives who solved the secrets of locked rooms and other mysteries. My brothers liked science fiction and tales of faraway planets and rings of power. My tastes were more romantic and girlish, stories of feisty, orphaned girls in boarding schools. My father's books included many he'd written, others he'd published, all the words he'd forced into the world no matter if others found the stories or language strange or difficult.

As I walked through the house, in a nervous, floating panic, it seemed as if one of the characters from my brothers' books, some deformed villain with a dark cape and sharp talons, might have swept into our home carrying off the men I loved. I walked past my older brother's room, feeling the familiar rending in my heart. I could still not believe he was gone, when he'd been so vivid and towering, sixteen, with braces on his crooked, knowing grin. The panic kept rising and only subsided when I pushed open the door to my younger brother's room, and saw him, still there, asleep, with several comic books beside him like paper blankets.

It might have been the next morning that they taught us more about my father's heart. The words they used were scientific, clinical, and made no sense to me at all. He had not suffered from something as common as a heart attack. His heartbeat was just quivering and wavering in a way they said was disorganized and chaotic. My mother seemed to understand the mystery. She nodded patiently, while clutching my hand. She'd met my father in San Francisco when she was just eighteen. They'd gone to Africa to teach and had taken a journey together soon after their marriage, in a cramped boat down the Niger River on the way to Timbuktu. The heat from the sky and crowding passengers caused them both to faint. Some rowdy American had knocked the last bottle of water into the river and, as my dad told the story, my mother had never lost her nerve, even when the boat tilted and he became dizzy and faint. The boat had dropped them off miles from Timbuktu because over many years the river had drifted far from the city, but they had reached the city they had dreamed of and loved telling of the adventure.

What was the heart? A symbol of love? Or blood and oxygen, ventricles and atria. Chambers and routes. Impulses, transmissions. We looked at drawings in a room where the walls were full of certificates with calligraphy. The heart was depicted as a black cavern rather than as I'd always imagined it: red and perfectly formed as a sweet candy given on Valentine's Day.

There were polite but insistent questions. *Did your husband smoke? Was he ever obese?* No, my mother answered, he never smoked; he's been skinny since he was a boy. *Did he ever complain of chest pain? Has this happened to his father or grandfather?* No, my mother said, they're all very healthy. *Has he been under any stress lately?* My brother and I exchanged glances. We never spoke of my brother's death to strangers. It seemed something too painful to say out loud. It surprised me that the doctors weren't speaking of cures. *Here's the medicine,* I thought they'd say, *Here's how we'll fix this in surgery.*

I wandered back to the room where my dad lay still, attached to a monitor and other machinery. He seemed to be awake but sleeping, and his skin was very pale, paler than it had ever been. "Hey, Dad," I said loudly, in a jovial way, as if I was rousing him to go off to help me find a new tree. I willed him back again, as I had in the moment when he'd fallen on the floor. *Get up, wake up, live!, come on, let's go.* The whole place seemed so antiseptic and grim. He liked being in gardens,

in fields, in Africa, anywhere but offices or shopping malls or hospital
rooms. If he'd been awake, we might have joked about the doctors.
They say your heart is chaotic. And he would refuse to accept the
doctor's interpretation. He'd understand me, as he often did, as
though he could finish my sentence. *Everyone's heart is chaotic,* he'd
agree, *there's nothing wrong with me.*

A few days later, my father was airlifted in a government jet to the
University of Western Ontario. Two young researchers there, who
were said to be specialists in hearts that had gone awry, would try to
find a medicine which might, perhaps, regulate his heart so that the
beats were ordinary. My mother went with him, and I couldn't
imagine what those uncertain days were like for her, having just lost
her first son, now possibly about to lose her first love. My brother and
I stayed in school, and learned about stars and Ecuador. We may have
been looked after by my father's sister, or our Israeli babysitter—that
part of it I don't recall. Like most children facing some unknown fate,
we were dazed and stoic and sometimes stubbornly carefree.

We taped ourselves in fits of giggles, created musical performances
to send to my father. I played piano and my brother played my dad's
trumpet. We knew somehow that we were supposed to create some
gift that would be cheering. We mocked the deep, earnest sounds of an
announcer: "Here's a song you might enjoy." We sent tapes and little
booklets we'd made to the hospital, and waited for my father's return.

It was not going well. My aunt did not tell us that, but children know
how to interpret silence. We were sent off to Ontario, and the hospital seemed more foreboding than the one in Victoria—a maze of
levels and hallways. Instead of cherry blossoms, the trees outside held

ordinary leaves. The younger doctor wore a pinstriped suit and smelled like lavender. "You must be the daughter; you have your dad's blue eyes." I nodded, not sure if he was merely being polite or trying to say something kind before he gave us the bad news. I had become convinced that if I stood close to my dad, close enough, long enough, I would revive him once again. I knew I must have looked strange to the nurses, a skinny girl in blue overalls, standing by her father, refusing to move when they brought in his trays of food, but I did not move.

He recognized me, but often slurred my name, and his eyes filled with tears while his smile seemed alarming and almost feminine. He spoke in long, sudden sentences, but not as he used to speak, in that professor's manner, with a kind of certainty and indisputable logic. "There's a man," he once whispered nonsensically, "who might see on the mountains."

Slowly we worked it out—what it was that the pair of doctors were doing to his body. They had found the particular electrical message that sent his heart awry, so they could imitate it at will. They tried one bit of magic pill and then worked their way to his heart and sent it the hard message that caused fibrillation. My father could watch his heartbeat fade and rise and stop on the overhead monitors. His beats looked like waves. If the pill didn't work, they'd revive him with a shock, and try another one. *Live,* I thought when waiting in his room, as I'd thought when he'd first fallen to the floor. Then two nurses came and told us we had to leave, for they were about to send the message to his heart. I knew this was the seventh and last of the medicines.

My brother and I waited for an hour or so, played cards on the plastic table, played war and solitaire. I worried, but the worry was less for some reason. I might have chosen to see my father as some type of brave, strong hero as daughters often do, pushing away any doubt as I'd once wanted to push away the wires and machinery. If something terrible was going to happen again, I would have sensed it. I believed

I would have felt the clutching tremor inside. I flipped cards and talked to a lady wearing a cameo brooch. She said her husband fought in the war, fought for the Queen, and she was sure the Almighty would take care of him.

When the lavender-smelling doctor appeared, his voice was less aloof than it had previously been. "I have some very good news," he said. "The medicine's been successful. I'm sure we've found the one." He spoke some words of science, maybe Latin, some words that may have been a more formal way of saying luck and hope. The other doctor was beside him, also smiling. My little brother rushed from his chair and ran down the hallway towards my father's room.

My father was sitting up, straight-backed and restless. "I'd really like to get out of here," he announced, impatiently, before holding us to his warm chest.

Perhaps it was the medicine, or the deaths that he'd endured, but in the years following this incident, my father became calmer, less prone to sudden rages and impossible plans. He spent more time in the garden, whacking a path through the blackberry bushes which grew tangled and intertwined. We didn't drift apart, but spent less time together as I became more interested in the things he knew nothing about—gossip, movie stars, punk rock, secret downtown parties. But, one day, I returned from a warm afternoon of suntanning on the dark sand, and wandered near to him, pushing back the branches of thorns. There were piles everywhere.

He told me he'd seen the doctor that day, and everything was fine. "I don't think I need that medicine any more."

"You're just going to stop?"

He shrugged his shoulders. "I don't need it any more." He cleared a space of debris and we sat on the mossy rock and had lemonade from a thermos, like a normal family. "Why do you think it happened that day?" I asked him, not sure if I was asking about the fall or his surprising survival.

"My heart was broken," he said, "I see that now." And I knew it was the only answer, something I'd always known even when they'd tried to explain it away with diagrams and words like *fibrillation*. In truth, and simply, his heart had been broken by the death of his son, and how could it not have been?

The rest of us had buried or muffled our tears, but my father had wept for my brother in a vicious roar of grief. The house had shaken from the force of his sobs, so how could his heart not have trembled from something so unwieldy and immense? In the moment when I'd sat across from him at the table, watching death linger and rise, I'd known his heart had lost its being.

Now, he was sunburnt and calloused, with dirt under his nails, procrastinating, putting off marking papers while his daughter plucked early, reddish blackberries and put off her own homework. "I saw a white light," he said, softly, "just like people say they do. Not when they knocked me out, but that first time, I could see the light, and I knew I was dying; the time you saved me." That was more than he'd ever said about the incident, and I wasn't sure how to reply.

I asked him why he thought he hadn't died, and he answered, with no great flourish, but in a manner rather matter of fact: "I just decided I wasn't ready to leave." And then he shrugged his shoulders, and returned to the purpose at hand. And I helped him for a while, while the sun was still warm and before the late afternoon chill came in off the strait. Some of the oaks were stunted by winter storms, but the blackberries were enormous sprawls and tangles. He chopped at them with an axe and it rang against the old rocks that edged down to the quiet ocean. I wore his gloves and made piles of the slash and told him what I had learned about the stars and Ecuador.

The Mirror's Shadow

by Rachel Manley

Casually walking into a room full of strangers always makes me anxious unless I am expected to play some leading role … to teach, to make a speech, to do a reading. Nowadays I have resorted to humming a little tune in my head, a well-known song, "Don't worry, *da da*, be happy." This helps. It took me years to find out why I felt such pangs of shyness. And it was my father who inadvertently provided the answer.

In 1989, he came to visit me in Switzerland, where my journalist husband had been posted for an eighteen-month stint. I knew no one in Berne when we arrived there. After a frustrating search, we found a fifth-floor penthouse with no elevator on a quiet avenue. It had recently been renovated by a young couple. Though just a loft, it was quite an exotic apartment, tucked under the low eaves with dormer windows looking out through the tops of endlessly muttering trees, and, inconceivable to me, a bathroom decorated by Balenciaga.

But the best thing I got from the rental arrangement was a weekly

107

game of bridge with my landlady, who wished, along with two friends, to learn English. That is why somewhere in Berne there are now three ladies peppering their conversation with Rastafarian "irie," usually spoken only in Jamaica.

Otherwise, I would never have left my apartment during the week. As in Montreal, where I had lived for six years, I could never pluck up the courage to shop by myself or go sightseeing. Even picking up a take-away sandwich, much less sitting in a restaurant eating alone, was an agonizing experience in self-consciousness. I would feel clumsy and ridiculous, not knowing what to do with myself. My husband found it perplexing.

"But, why? No one's even looking at you?"

But that was the point. My insecurity was about being anonymous.

You can't really be anonymous in Jamaica. Growing up in any family is growing up in full view of siblings, cousins, aunts, uncles and grandparents. But growing up in the Shearer/Manley family was like swimming in the proverbial fishbowl.

Jamaica was always a powerful mistress whose whims sucked my family's men in and spat them back out like some wilful goddess of Caribbean tides. We had already had a total of five politicians in the extended Shearer family, four of them heads of state. There are two political parties in Jamaica, both of them founded by men who were cousins, one of whom was my grandfather.

As a child, I knew we were either out of power or in; my grandfather was either chief minister or premier or "in the forty-day wilderness," which meant he was leader of the Opposition, while his cousin, Bustamante, sat at the head of government. As soon as my grandfather died, my father entered politics and the same thing happened in the next generation. He'd be prime minister or he wouldn't, and his cousin Shearer would be, or he wouldn't.

We were brought up to know our public duty: how to behave, how to be appropriate out in the world, how to be graceful and gracious as people who, if even only by reflected light in my third generation, were likely to be recognized. We were taught to control our nerves, to steel ourselves for public viewing, even for public speaking. But what we were never taught was how to be unknown, how to cope with being unrecognized, with having no official role, with being insignificant— how to be anonymous in a crowd. In my case, this caused my peculiar shyness, one I had not, like my famous father, actually earned.

Although my paroxysms of shyness kept Berne safely confined to my fifth-floor windows during the week, while my husband was at his office, the weekends were glorious. We would spread out the map and my husband would stick a pencil in some new direction and off we'd go to discover cheese from Emmenthal, or that Italian food wasn't all pizza, or a vividly painted wooden banana tree from Annecy (carved in the Philippines) that I took across the French border to assemble leaf by numbered leaf and set on the pristine carpet to remind me of sunlight and Jamaica.

I'd marvel at the white peacocks strutting over the brilliant green lawns at the Borromeo Palace on a tiny lake island across from Stresa, or the shortness of Josephine's bed, while my husband studied the military campaigns of Napoleon.

"I have never seen white peacocks. What's the point of peacocks without colours in their feathers?"

"They are albinos," my husband said, reading his guidebook. "It says here the guy who built this gave them to his wife as a present, along with this whole place. And Josephine's bed, she brought it with her when she and Napoleon stayed here."

The ghostly peacocks just kept strutting up and down the lawns around the palace, completely self-absorbed, extending their exquisite white feathers and crying out drunkenly, oblivious of their admiring audience.

And then my father arrived.

He came for a week, driving over from somewhere in Germany where he had addressed a conference. It is impossible to describe my excitement and frenzy, without also explaining that my father was all things in my world—my hero, nemesis, Achilles heel, idol and obsession, object of love, fury and ultimate fascination, my emptiness and too fullness, my ache of joy and pain of heartbreak. He had been like a fleeting miasma on my horizon all my life, someone as dear to me as an oasis in a desert for a nomad, and someone as rare. The times when I had him to myself were memorable, drafts from a lithium spring, the effects intoxicating—his intellect, his curiosity, the extraordinary connections he was able to make among all things and all ages—his unintentionally beguiling charm. When he was around, everything seemed brighter, richer, deeper, more agile or flexible, more dangerous, and any conquest more extraordinary.

When my father arrived, he was emerging from his "forty days." His 1970s decade of democratic socialism had stretched our economy beyond its endurance, but it was one of those eras that clanged like a bell embedded deep within a mountain—the depth of its reverberations came later.

My father now earned his living travelling through Europe and the States lecturing to political science students about his mistakes. Often on the road, he hadn't been able to keep up the diet and exercise regimen that had kept his six-foot three-and-a-half-inch frame at a lean hundred and eighty pounds, so he had gained a lot of weight. He huffed up my stairs like a tired old mule, stalling on each landing for breath and holding his waist in a typical Manley hiatus, and gathering his strength, as though ready to lift himself onto the next phase. With my father, in addition to politics, there were other seasons I had to contend with—his marriages. There would be five in all. He was emerging from his fourth marriage and, unknown to me, longing wistfully for his fifth.

My excitement, according to my husband, was oppressive. We watched my large father crouching and ducking to avoid the low-lying beams, the dangling lamps, the ceiling where it sloped. The spare room was neatly tucked into the edge of the roof, so he was permanently crouched in his bedroom. My husband and I had acquired two strays—my Fred in Barbados, his Freda in Montreal—and they had joined us on our travels. I had forgotten how much my father hated cats, thinking his irritation at my childhood Persian was simply due to his habitual squeamishness, as the animal had tizzic, a perpetual cough caused by eating ground lizards. My father hid his dismay, on discovering our cats, as best he could. Like all animals, however, they were fascinated by the stranger on their turf and, like most cats, were attracted to anyone who ignored them.

The visit was off to a hell of a start.

The following day we began my program. We took him to the bear pits to see the bears of Berne, and walked through the small town whose busy sidewalks ran like rivers of intent. My father strolled along looking somehow formal, even though casually dressed in a long-sleeved shirt and simple dark slacks—it may have been the outline of the vest beneath, or the calm elegance of his thin leather belt. His hands were reversed, hitched up on his hips, his elbows akimbo as though he made his way along a natural wake that others had opened up before him. But he didn't look comfortable, just looked down at his long shoes landing like planes, back wheels first, then toes coming down, left, right into the endless glibness of Switzerland's little capital city, past its bloodless-minded banks, past its quaint jewellers with their endless versions of precision, their ultimate claim on the human race—the cuckoo clock.

"My friend Jarmila, the seismologist, told me that in the drift of centuries, Africa is slowly pushing up the Alps," I said.

He liked that. It was the only time he really smiled that day, and gave his little "ha-ha" chuckle, which he repeated as though the story on its echo elicited a similar response. I hovered attentively, and tried to interest him. Occasionally, he'd look up and follow the eyes of people approaching him, watching them for too long, his expression fading into some unspoken disappointment as they hurried by. Sometimes he caught himself in a mirror and seemed drawn for a moment to its intent reflection as if unsure as to who it really was; as if unsure *he* really was. It made me think about the fact that in his home I never saw him hover at a mirror. He was a handsome man, but not a man of vapid vanities, his pride a thing trained to his serious social values.

He seemed preoccupied that day, and then after his long walk up the stairs, halting blowingly and painfully on each landing, he came home and captured the phone and went into his room, the plastic cord snaking under his door—a familiar habit that I had known all my life. It meant he was talking to his latest, fervent secret love.

But my youth was long behind me, and hopefully my jealousies—of him, his time, his interests, my siblings, Jamaica, and most of all his women, my stepmothers. So I invited him to share the secret, which I had already intuited. And he did. And this was such a happiness for me, sharing his new hopes, his fears and worries, his eternal capacity for romantic renewal—which one could never call romantic, like one could never call his charisma *charisma,* for I think these words somehow demeaned him, demeaned his intent by painting him a charlatan, a thing he never was. I felt the comfort once again of a familiar bond that seemed to be forged whenever I became his emotional confidante.

We set off for the little town of Gruyère to sample the cheese. We parked at the bottom of a steep climb, the mountain path winding like a grey thread up the manicured hillside.

"Good Lord, even the cows are tidy," noted my father as he walked a few steps and paused, and the wind gently fanned towards us the sound of the pretty brass bells around their glossy bovine necks.

We sat on the patio of a restaurant famous for its raclette. Even though the Swiss say only tourists eat fondue in summer, my father ordered it anyway, and ate heartily, rubbing his stomach occasionally, indulgently, the way he often rubbed our heads when we had been naughty as children, having committed misdeeds that he found funny because displays of unconventionality or rebelliousness secretly delighted him. And then the strawberries came with cream, Swiss cream, cream from Gruyère, cream as he had never seen or tasted it, he said—not even in Geneva.

His eyes really lit up, and his cheeks, the typical mulatto beige of the Shearer family, became flushed in the cool autumn air, and I realized he was for that moment really happy, thinking how the cream could last in memory long enough to be described to his new love when he got back to the phone. And I also saw in that moment that he was unhealthy, although at the time I had no idea what years of struggle this would foreshadow.

Between the surrounding hills, a lake sparkled, spotless and blue. Small islands rose obediently on the Lilliputian map. I suddenly thought of the time he visited us in Montreal, a city he thought of fondly for his brief time there as a student at McGill during the war.

"Remember when we wanted to pool our money and buy that island in the Laurentians north of Montreal?"

"Ha," he laughed and chucked up his chin. "Now that you say it, I do. Who was I there with?"

"Jean," I said. "It was only a hundred and fifty thousand dollars for a whole island, including a house and a pier and a snow-mobile. We should have tried to raise the money."

"It would have been too cold half the year," he said.

"But you could have had that remoteness you long for … your own little world … even a moat—the lake surrounding you!"

"Ah," he said. "But why need seclusion when one is anonymous?"

We took him up to the gates of the castle, but he was tired and so he sat on a bench with me while we waited for my husband to explore it yet again. My husband loves castles; he loves history in the way it takes shape as cities and landmarks, as statues and dedications. He is always a worthwhile tourist, lingering in war museums for hours over some era with his guidebook and notes.

My father and I sat there discussing how we both rush through passing towns head down, tire quickly of fossil rooms and bones in museums, and stroll through art galleries with no need for guides. Yet, years later we can remember an old man feeding a bird on Lake Como at Bellagio, or visualize the golden room of Gauguin at the Louvre and see the calm brown skin of the paintings' Polynesian women, and the light so different from that of the Caribbean sun. We can remember afterwards, outside, a thin white woman with a mass of black curly hair suddenly spitting at her black companion.

My father grimaced and pulled in his shoulders as he remembered. I walked him across the road to the souvenir shop, where he bought gifts for his two youngest children, younger than my sons—a music box for Natasha, a cuckoo clock for David.

But these idyllic times with my father are usually cut short by some urgent phone call; and by the following day one came. It was Hurricane Gilbert bearing down on Jamaica. For a while, we waited and tried as best we could to chart its course by the drips of information from the Swiss radio, TV and newspapers. But for all his frantic worry, my father was now powerless, useless—without influence. And the hurricane hit Jamaica dead-on in the way that hurricanes, so human in their individuality, can decide to do. Six storms can travel south along our shores waiting till they pass us to turn north to Cuba or Miami, and then the seventh will get curious, like a tongue that senses some small cavity in a tooth, and swerve towards our heartland of mountains.

Coastlines disappeared, houses were flattened, crops destroyed, people drowned or washed away, planes upended, boats dumped on land. My father paced up and down our living room, the only place where he could walk upright, muttering instructions and frustrations, stopping to try telephone numbers that had ceased to work, as Gilbert trashed us like a mad dog with a rag in its jaws, as my father's mountain house, and my late grandmother's, lost their shingles like thousands of tiny hats flying off the roofs of our world, the tall pine trees breaking their backs and tumbling down to be found weeks later by my father, where they lay on beds of their own strewn needles like fallen gods.

But there was no civil service, no fire brigade or police force to summon and instruct, no agency or department to address, no doors or windows to order boarded up, no rising water to assess, not even the howl of the wind to carry his words: He had to sit this one out. Nevertheless, my father decided to leave two days early, to return the car to Germany and get a convenient flight to London or New York and hope that by then the airport would be open in Kingston.

Early in the morning, we escorted him to the French border, where we decided to have brunch together before saying goodbye. This was the first time he had used the car since he had driven it to Switzerland. We led the way, and just before the border we stopped at a small cluster of buildings—a restaurant and a service station. My father stopped to fill the tank, waiting in the car for assistance.

"Go and help him," I said, realizing that it was self-service.

"Why?" My husband sat there waiting.

"Well, he can't do it himself," I said indignantly.

"Why not?" he asked.

"Well, he never *has*. He won't even know if it's self-service."

By now, my father had rolled down his window and was looking back at us. He stuck his hand out the window with a "what's happening?" gesture.

"Self-service," my husband called out.

"Look, he can't!" I shouted, exasperated. I didn't even know if we *had* self-service stations in Jamaica, and even if we did, I was pretty sure my father had never filled a tank with gas.

"And he used to run a country?"

My husband was being droll, but his comment infuriated me. I knew that my father, all his life, had been like a marked man in our society. If he were to fill a tank or post a letter, buy groceries or ride on a bus, everywhere he went he would be recognized, gawked at or applauded, waved to or pointedly ignored.

My uncle, a great rum-bar campaigner who courted his rural votes one by one, once said that my father was no good with less than twenty thousand people. My grandmother shrewdly added, "Only if the twenty thousand are there to see him!"

I knew how hard it would be for him to do anything informal or normal, and yet if you asked him to *open* a gas station or post office, or to *announce* a new bus service, he'd stand there in the spotlight and make a fine speech, bring the crowd to its feet, light up minds with excitement and wonder, negotiate for the rights and better wages of the gas station attendants, fight against the existence of self-service stations that deny attendants jobs. But to fill a gas tank himself—that I knew he could never do. I knew, because, somehow, neither could I.

"Neither of you has a sense of humour," muttered my husband, as he went to rescue my father at the pump. With the gas tank full, we headed for what was the only restaurant in the border village. Chez Nana's turned out to be a small seafood restaurant run by a large, melodic-voiced woman from Martinique who spoke a lilting broken English.

She welcomed us warmly, sat us down at a small table under a blaring television set, and left us with menus as she went to get the drinks.

While we studied the fare, my husband translating the French for my father, an unusually catchy, cheerful tune attracted my attention and I looked up at the television overhead. There were Robin Williams and Bobby McFerrin facing the camera doing a little jig side by side, hands on knees, legs bent, knees knocking, then ankles, hands criss-crossing, and singing the happiest little song I think I have ever heard.

"Don't worry, *da da,* be happy, *da da* …"

It was gentle and unassuming, so reassuring at a moment when once again I had to face being left with only a slip of memory, as my father momentarily sailed through my hand, a rich and silken, exquisitely brilliant magical scarf, to continue on his life's journey enchanting many more lives.

Our hostess escorted the waiter with steaming dishes of Creole chowder, which they placed before us, and she clasped her hands like a profound contralto about to sing. "*Bon appétit, mes amis* from the Caribbean," she said in a medley of all our island Creole accents.

My father, who had already raised his spoon to begin, stopped with his hand midair and looked up at her with a margin of hope in his eyes.

"How do you know we are Caribbean?" I asked her.

My father replaced his spoon and started to prepare himself to extend his shy, charming greeting on being recognized.

But the lady turned to my Canadian husband, with his deep tan and frizz of curly hair, the lone non-Caribbean person at the table, and rubbed the top of his head and said with delight.

"I see de colour right here in de curly hair."

I was sad when my father left, but I knew he would deliver the car and catch his plane to his stormy pond, and that along the way, once he hit Heathrow or Kennedy, people would know him and he could feel himself alive again, like a plant being watered and slowly emerging from drought, somehow back in the world, a small conflagration of light in a lens of recognition he had selflessly earned.

We drove back to Berne without him, the little song I had heard still in my head: "Don't worry, *da da,* be happy."

Visitation Rights

by Sandra Martin

When did people start including photo collages in their funeral rituals? Certainly, when my mother died it never occurred to us to set to work with scissors, glue and bristol board to make a display for mourners to view at the back of the church, as though they were judges in a school project. But then we knew who my mother was, her place in our lives, and ours in hers. By the time my father died of a stroke nearly twenty-five years later, the times and our circumstances had both changed so irrevocably that it seemed important, as one of my three sisters explained to me, to document the events and stages of his life—as though the exercise would help us hold onto the good parts of him. Even so, we didn't include pictures of our mother, out of deference to his second wife, our stepmother.

That is how I first came to see a photograph of my father that triggered an overwhelming desire to make one last attempt to figure him out. And that meant telling the truth, at least as I perceived it, about my father and his women—his beloved mother, his four revered older

119

sisters, his two wives and his four daughters, especially me, the difficult one—if only to quell my conflicting emotions. This is the story
that nobody in my family wants to hear publicly. It is the hardest piece
that I, "a seasoned journalist," have ever tried to write. And if it is still
opaque to you at the end, well, you aren't alone, because it will never
be entirely clear to me either.

The strangest thing about the picture is that there are no women
in it. My father is standing alone with my son outside a restaurant in
Montreal on a wintry day. It's an ordinary enough picture of two men,
one young, the other old, each with an arm around the other's shoulder. Their height, obvious affection and matching smiles connect
them genetically, but my eighty-five-year-old father, in his cap and
duffle coat, seems frail and tired, especially in comparison with his
vibrant, bare-headed grandson.

Was this gentle-looking man, with the beseeching gaze, the father
who beat me when I was a child? Everything that I know and yet still
don't completely understand about him—his rages, his tenderness, his
scorn, his vulnerability—are caught up in this casually snapped
photograph. He seems to be looking directly at me, which is absurd
since I wasn't holding the camera, but that's what happens with
photographs—the subject is frozen in a particular expression and the
beholder is free to ascribe motives and interpret expressions. That's
the way memory works, too; the past is buried under mounds of
experience. We are the ones who disinter it in order to explain or
assuage the present.

Sixty years separate my father and my son, a reality I had never
considered until I saw the photograph. That same age gap—the equivalent of two generations—divided my father from his father, a teeto-
talling Presbyterian born before Confederation in remote Prince
Edward Island. My father grew up on a small farm in an era of
kerosene lamps, outhouses and horse-drawn hay rigs—long before

"electrification" powered the world, as he loved to remind us. The youngest by a decade in a family of six children, he never knew his father as anything but an old man, a bearded biblical figure like Abraham. When my father was twenty-five, the age my son is in the photograph, his father was long dead and he was overseas, serving as a high-tech radar officer on secondment to the Royal Navy during the Second World War. While part of me rejoices that my son was born in luckier circumstances, another part reaches out to my father in empathy for the losses that shaped his early life and which compromised him as a parent.

My father escaped from the farm and from P.E.I. by winning a scholarship to Queen's University. His family was delighted, for they all had expectations of him and his intellectual prowess. But, while he could wipe the red soil from his boots, he found it much harder to shake off his need to please and defer to strong-willed women.

In 1937, he took the ferry to the mainland for the first time in his life, travelled by train to Kingston, Ontario, and enrolled in engineering, a program that he, a survivor of The Depression, hoped would give him "a slightly greater than zero chance" of finding a job. He flourished at Queen's, earning top marks and making lifelong male friends.

My mother was an unusual choice for a shy, socially awkward beanpole with little conversational skill and no aptitude for dancing or partying. More than two years older, she was vivacious, beautiful and self-supporting from her job as manager of the drugstore on the edge of the campus, where many students hung out at the lunch counter. (When people asked if she had gone to Queen's, she always replied: "Queen's came to me.") Her warmth and spontaneity, combined with her skill at making sandwiches and pouring coffee, must have disarmed him.

I'm guessing that he was intimidated by female undergraduates—not that there were any in his classes. As for my mother, the eldest daughter in a large farming family from nearby Wolfe Island, she probably thought of him as a brainy younger brother—until the surprising evening when he blurted out an invitation to walk her home after work. They corresponded on blue aerograms for the four years he served overseas in the Royal Navy, in capital ships such as *Rodney* and *Valiant*. After he returned, deaf in one ear from the blasting of the guns, he proposed marriage. What really attracted him to her, despite her lack of formal education, was her vitality and her spontaneity. She must have seemed the perfect antidote to the fear and death that had stalked him during the war.

Being in love was the easy part. The hard part was going home to P.E.I. to tell his family that he was engaged to a Roman Catholic, a liaison that to them was worse than marrying across racial or colour divides. His two eldest sisters were horrified by this dashing of their expectations, but he resisted their entreaties. His brother-in-law drove him to the train station, all the while exhorting him to change his mind if only to avoid "the blow to the family pride." My father once told me that his emotional turmoil on the ferry ride back across the Northumberland Strait to the mainland was worse than the fear he felt on even the most dangerous convoy.

Nevertheless, in what I have always believed was the first defiant act of my father's life, he married my mother in the Catholic Church—although he never converted, which was a disappointment to my mother. "Never marry a man of a different religion," she ritually intoned to us when we were teenagers. Religion wasn't the only difference in my parents' upbringing. My father, the cherished final child of aged parents, was bathed in love, even though the world into which he was born was chaotic. I never heard of anybody having raised a hand to him. Nevertheless, he was certainly in awe of his older sisters, after whom he named each of his four daughters. They were gentle and loving, especially to us, their nieces, but they could skewer you with an aptly turned "My dear."

My mother came from a different tradition. As a wedding gift, her father gave her his leather razor strop, with instructions to use it liberally on her children. She took the advice to heart and so did my father, who became an avid proponent of corporal punishment. Was he just following orders? Who can say for certain?

What fuelled his rage is still a mystery to me. It wasn't drink, for that made him mellow and expansive. Given his childhood, I suspect he had very little resilience for coping with the chaos and trade-offs of family life. Maybe if he had been less obedient as a child; or had had siblings closer to his own age; or had had younger parents and more financial security; or had enlisted in the army instead of the Navy, he would have learned a leadership style based on collaboration and teamwork. After the war, he became a nuclear physicist in the male-dominated department that Ernest Rutherford had made famous at McGill University, where the academic hierarchy, especially in those days, was built on deference to seniority and belief in a universe in which every problem had a solution, if only it could be computed.

As a husband and father, he wanted order, control and respect—all of which were in short supply, considering that two babies arrived in quick succession and my mother had to have a spinal fusion operation when I was two and my older sister almost four. She was in a body cast for months. Meanwhile, he was researching and writing a Ph.D. dissertation and supporting all of us on a veteran's allowance, without benefit of universal health care. That he graduated magna cum laude still astonishes me.

Did he beat us because he was frustrated, or were we particularly devilish children? Probably a bit of both. Certainly, spanking was in vogue. "Crying? I'll give you something to cry about" was a common expression at that time. "Pull down your underpants," he would order, when my older sister and I were very small, so that he could beat us on our bare bottoms.

When I was nearly four, we moved to Kingston because he had a teaching appointment at Queen's, his alma mater. He was also in the Navy Reserves. One evening, he was heading off to the "ship" when my sister and I, then probably five and six and dressed in our nightgowns, went out on the front porch and started chanting, "Na-nana-na-na, you have to go to work." He stopped halfway down the street, turned around and ordered us to stop. We did, until he turned and began walking away again. The third time we began chanting, he made good on his threat and stomped back towards the house. We ran inside and tried to hide. I got to our bedroom closet first and pulled the door shut behind me. My sister was hammering on the door, but it stuck and I couldn't get it open. She had to hide under the bed. He found her, of course. I can still hear her cries while I cowered safe and guilt-ridden in the closet.

Our lives weren't all punishment. I can remember him reading to us and car trips to my mother's home on Wolfe Island, especially after he accepted a teaching appointment at McGill and we moved back to Montreal. But fear of his censure was a constant. As girls, my older sister and I would be sent to his study to wait until he deigned to appear to mete out his harsh discipline. When the razor strop wore out, he found a two-by-two, which seemed to suit his grip even better—especially since he now used the basement, where it was harder for the neighbours to hear our screams.

As for my mother, she seemed eager to snitch on us to our father, despite knowing how he would respond to tales of disobedience or squabbling. Frustrated by housework and the tedium of raising four daughters in a suburban bungalow—there was a six-year gap before my two younger sisters were born two years apart—my mother needed a job to get her out of the house and give her something on which to expend her energy. Eventually, she found an outlet in volunteer work and local politics, activities that sustained her and brought her deserved recognition.

Being a professor at a university set my father off from the other men in our suburban community. So did his lack of interest in sports. My mother was the football and hockey fan. My father preferred to read the newspaper, to volunteer in the United Church, which he alone attended because the rest of us followed the dictates of the marriage contract and went to the Catholic Church, and most of all to closet himself in his study to write lectures or mark papers.

As a family, we were like a failed physics experiment. There were plenty of sparks flying from negative and positive poles, but they never connected in a meaningful way. As a teenager, I was embarrassed by my mother's very presence in that judgmental hauteur adopted by many adolescents, but that disdain was mostly a condition of my age. My father's revulsion was visceral. I knew deep in my bruised flesh that he was mortified by my curiosity about unconventional ideas, my frivolity, my attempts at humour, my appearance.

My older sister, the naughtier one when we were children, was much less rebellious as a teenager. As for my little sisters, they witnessed but didn't directly experience my father's wrath. It was as though they were raised by different parents, or so it seemed to me. How much easier it would have been for all of us if I had given in and conformed to my parents' expectations. Even I knew that. And yet, I couldn't resist ramming against my father's wishes with a naïve desire to explain myself and win his approval.

For most of my first two decades, I was furious with both of my parents: him for beating me, and her for serving me up. My fury fuelled my rebellion—for me, doing well in school was the equivalent of sleeping with the enemy—and my lack of achievement enraged my father all the more. He would insist, "In the Royal Navy we learned discipline" as he raised his stick. In *The View from Castle Rock,* Alice Munro writes about her father removing his belt from his trousers to beat her after having heard about a "falling-out"—such a delicately loaded phrase—between Munro and her mother. Of the moments before the raised belt descended on her flesh, Munro writes, "I would plead my case incoherently, in a way that seemed to make him despise me." That's not the way I remember the horribly attenuated minute between the time my father grabbed me by the hair or whatever appendage he could reach and began landing blows with his stick. I fought like an alley cat, kicking and punching and screaming abuse and hatred until his fury (or his strength) was spent or my mother appeared at the top of the stairs to shout: "That's enough!" Even though I made it worse for myself, I couldn't beg for mercy or forgiveness. All I had was defiance, and I flashed it like a shield, despising myself for the tears that invariably flowed down my contorted face.

When I was sixteen, he threw me down the basement stairs—or did he shove me and I fell? Whatever the case, I ended up in a heap on the cement floor. "Hit me again, you bastard, and I'll call the police!" I screamed at him. I don't know which frightened him more—what he was capable of doing in a rage or that I might carry out my threat—but he never beat me again, although he continued to issue ultimatums, curfews and demands for written declarations of subservience. When he ordered me to stop seeing the man who eventually became my husband, I ran away from university and from home, finding a room and a job as a clerk to support myself in the city where my boyfriend lived.

Ultimately, rage consumes too much energy, so you've got to let it go if you want to be an adult. As for my parents, I loved them the instinctive way children do, and I suppose they loved me the way parents do, and so the estrangement eventually collapsed in a kind of wary détente. We never discussed my grievances or theirs, although they still tried to control me and my ideas when I was in their house. Besides, I got married (although my husband refused to be wed within a thousand miles of my parents) and my mother became ill with breast cancer when I was in my early twenties, and so everything changed, including the familial power structure. For the first time, they needed me, or so I told myself.

During the eleven years of my mother's heroic but terrified struggle, my father turned into a loving, gentle nurse. The cancer controlled both of them. Her strength, her very being, was spent fighting her disease, and that meant keeping it a secret from "outsiders." All aspects of their lives were subsumed in a futile battle with death, a struggle that conjoined them and made them closer than I had ever remembered. He knew his role and his duty and he performed admirably. We all marvelled at his patience and kindness, for my mother often camouflaged her fear and her pain with bitterness and rage. What surprised me, on our frequent trips to Montreal with our baby son, was how much my father turned to us for conversation and companionship. It was as though he was siding with the living in order to cope with the dying.

He ordered a bouquet of red roses with baby's breath for her coffin because those were the flowers she had carried at their wedding, a romantic gesture that still touches me. Resolve got us all through the funeral, which was held in the United Church, as my mother had taken a shine to the minister and his wife some years earlier and had— surprisingly, to me—abandoned the Catholic Church. Afterwards, my father was bereft, his purpose spent. Where he once had four older sisters to care for him, he now turned to his four daughters, who were eager to lavish affection and attention on him—especially my youngest sister, the one who was still living at home.

Neediness changed him from a stern and judgmental disciplinarian into an expansive and generous father and grandfather. "Oh let the boy be," he would say if I tried to subdue my rambunctious son from turning somersaults on the living room furniture. As a toddler, my son had looked up the length of my father's tall frame and pronounced "Big Man." I latched onto the name as a way of christening this new and kinder iteration of our relationship. Big Man liked nothing better than to talk with my husband about military and political alliances during the Second World War and stay up late with me or my sisters to retell family stories about his childhood on the Island. I loved these sessions because they showed the gentle side of my father and they connected me to him and to his past.

His father's family had come from the Isle of Skye in the 1840s. Two generations later, my grandfather was the one who stayed on the family farm while most of his siblings, including his twin brother, went to the mainland, especially to New England (or the "Boston States," as they were called) to practise medicine. He was highly literate, as Scots Presbyterians who followed the teachings of John Knox were wont to be, and he married well, but he was a frustrated and indifferent farmer.

My grandmother's family had come from Inverness, in the Scottish Highlands, at about the same time, but they had prospered both economically and intellectually. One of her brothers was a decorated First World War veteran, and another was knighted. The latter, having married well, returned to the Island every summer, where he lived in a lavish house, entertained expansively and, along with his brother, often helped discreetly with his sister's precarious finances.

By the time my father was born, in 1919, his only brother had left home, and his four older sisters were teaching in the Prairies or away at Island schools. His siblings were ghostly figures, flitting in and out of his life, setting him sums to do on his slate when they were home and cosseting him like a favourite plaything. Essentially an only child, he was six when he watched his father almost perish from pneumo-nia—a deadly infection in the days before antibiotics.

His father's illness brought one of his sisters and his older brother home. Full of grandiose and doomed schemes to revolutionize the farm, my uncle was also stubborn and argumentative. Besides, he smoked, drank and swore when he was angry—all of which deeply offended my grandfather. The stock market crash in 1929 drastically slashed the price of potatoes, and the deeply mortgaged farm fell into disrepair. My father told me only once about his "thudding despair" as he watched his older brother, his back rigid with bitterness, stomp down the road, leaving the dilapidated farm forever. It was 1932, my father was thirteen, his mother was fifty-nine and his father was seventy-three. He must have felt both trapped and terrified about what was to become of him.

His brains were his salvation. The next year, my father won a full scholarship to Prince of Wales College in Charlottetown. After hearing the news, his maternal uncles, both of them university professors, climbed into their green Overland motor car on a Sunday afternoon and roared over from the big house at Orwell, demanding to see "the boy."

They felt his head for bumps of knowledge, and then quizzed him on his examination papers, jocularly despairing of his answers until they came across a question about the evils of alcohol and tobacco. This they fell upon "like a brace of mongoose," as my father described it. "The boy" began his righteous spiel, describing how alcohol weakened one's character and destroyed moral fibre while his uncles, reeking of cigars and whisky, fell about themselves, pledging reform and eternal abstinence. Then they climbed back into the Overland so they could make it back to the big house in time for drinks before dinner.

I used to love hearing this story, which my father would tell late at night if he had a glass of Scotch in his hand. Now I wonder what it must have been like to be the ball, as my father once described his role, in a tennis match played by his mother's brothers, and to be forced, by youth and deference to his affluent relatives, to participate in a "home" game in which his father's values and authority were ridiculed while the old man watched helplessly from the sidelines.

My infant daughter, who was born nine months after my mother died, also sparked a story about the uncles. We took her to Montreal to be christened in the church where my mother's funeral had been held, on the first anniversary of her death. Afterwards, my father rocked my daughter in his arms, chortling and beaming, and exclaimed: "The first redhead to be born into the family in four hundred years!" Substitute "Roman Catholic" for "redhead" and the remark was a direct reference to the delighted comment that his uncle, the one who taught at Queen's, had made after meeting my mother nearly forty years earlier.

His grief was powerful and so was his loneliness. On the second anniversary of my mother's death, he sent me a diptych that opened to display a photograph of my mother standing on the shore on the Island with her birth and death dates. The opposite picture was a similarly posed shot of me in the same spot, with my birth date and an expectant dash. I can still feel the dread that plummeted from my chest to my feet as I remembered that photo session and its now bewildering implications. Was he expecting me, a married woman with two small children and a job, to act as a substitute for my mother? Or was he recognizing something in her that had been passed on to me? Flustered, I crammed the diptych in a drawer until I could figure out how to respond. It rests there still.

Odd to think now how surprised but happy we were when my father suddenly announced, about three years after my mother's death, that he was engaged to be married. He was sixty-seven and she was sixty.

He and his fiancée had much in common: grown children, Scottish ancestry, a love of order, shared faith in the United Church—indeed they had met because their congregations were amalgamating. Bizarrely, their first spouses were buried in adjacent plots in the same cemetery. Metaphorically, my father was slated to be trapped underground for all eternity between the outrageous demands of his first and second wives.

For all their similarities, my father and his bride had at least one serious difference: She did not share his love of family—at least not *his* family. Before they were married, we organized a dinner party at my father's house, at which she announced, "I always said I wanted grandchildren, but I never expected to marry a man with five of them." I tossed off the remark at the time as a joke, but its significance grew when, with my father a silent presence on the telephone extension, she asked me not to bring my children, then three and seven, to the wedding. As the years passed, access to my father became increasingly restricted. And yet he never defied his wife, almost as though he had become emotionally as well as physically deaf—at least to the needs of his children and grandchildren.

Although we lived five hundred kilometres away, in Toronto, they were often "too busy" to see us when we were in Montreal because she had organized an event with her adult children and there wasn't room for us at the table, or in the backyard or in their five-bedroom house. My husband and I used to joke about suing for visitation rights. My father still phoned us, but he was no longer a spontaneous or enthusiastic part of our lives and he didn't seem aware of how much his wife dominated every conversation, every friendship, every decision—even about food and drink. For years, neither coffee nor beer was allowed in the house.

My father would sit quietly, with a slight apologetic smile on his face and that beseeching look in his eyes, unless she had gone to bed. Then he would haul out his secret cache of Scotch for a night-cap in his study (now a refuge rather than a star chamber) and a conversation that wasn't dominated by "we think" or "we don't like." People said he was happy, but to me his new life was a toss-up in which he balanced his terror of being alone against his fear of displeasing his second wife. I never got the chance (or the nerve) to ask how he felt about the inversion of his old authoritarian role in our family or how he could condone his children being treated as interlopers in his home.

Now I realize that my stepmother saw all the women in my father's life as rivals, and that included not only the ghost of his first wife but his four daughters as well—especially me, the "troublesome one." We had so much more shared experience with him, we could catch his eye at a gathering and exchange a knowing look based on a common view of the world; we could tease him about being Cordelia to his Lear—although Shakespeare was gaining a deeper and more sinister resonance as my stepmother tightened her hold on my father. In her insecurity, my stepmother was afraid of us. That's why she turned into the gatekeeper who lowered and raised the portcullis, denying or granting access to her husband. My three sisters were much more tolerant of her behaviour, but my reaction to our upbringing had made me abhor tyranny and reject appeasement. I kept wanting to rescue my father, to see him resist her bullying, but he seemed worn out and unwilling to risk defiance.

And then my father, by now in his eighties, became sick. A cardiologist diagnosed congestive heart failure and put him on a powerful blood thinner which caused such prolific nosebleeds that a visit to the hospital emergency ward was often required to staunch the flow. At my stepmother's insistence, the cardiologist referred my father to a cardiac surgeon, who performed open-heart surgery in 2003 without telling my father to stop taking his prescribed blood thinner. He was rushed back to the operating room at least twice that first day in desperate attempts to keep him from bleeding to death.

By the time he finally emerged from hospital three months later, he had undergone seven operations, including plastic surgery to repair the damage to his sternum from a hospital-based infection, and lost so much weight and muscle tone that he had to learn how to walk again. Physically weaker, but spiritually stronger, my father had survived more confrontations with death that dreadful summer than in all of his wartime service.

Afterwards, he loved to tell about his drug-induced hallucinations—one of them was about my stepmother poisoning him and his frenzied attempts to save her from being arrested on a murder charge. I always marvelled that he had the nerve to relate this story while she sat stony-faced by his side. Once, I caught his eye during the telling but he quickly looked away. He had another memory, of me sitting beside his bed while he lay seemingly unconscious and attached to myriad tubes and machines. "I sensed you there and I could see your face in profile, like a cameo," my father told me. And then, his eyes welling, he said, "I could feel your hand stroking my arm and you were saying 'we all love you.'"

I was stunned by this fortuitous recollection, as I had only been sitting by his bedside after appealing to the nurses to override my stepmother's stipulations about who could visit and for how long. And now he was telling me that he had actually heard and remembered my whispered declarations. After a horrible adolescence, my father and I had reconnected when my mother was dying; now that he had survived a grossly negligent medical mishap, I was determined not to lose him again.

So, when we made the thousand-kilometre round trip to celebrate his eighty-fifth birthday and saw him for only three hours over the entire weekend—and never alone—I held my tongue until I got home. Then I phoned and invited him to come to visit us—on his own. Much to my surprise, he agreed, and we had a splendid weekend eating and talking, sitting by the fire, and driving into the countryside. As my husband reminded me, and not for the first time, "Your father is always capable of doing the right thing, once it is pointed out to him."

Spending Christmas together was out of the question, but he did invite my son and his girlfriend to have lunch at a local restaurant before the holidays. That's when the photograph was taken, the only one we have of grandson and grandfather alone together as adults. Eighteen months had passed since his medical catastrophe, but looking at that picture now, I can see that my father's post-hospital pinkness is turning grey. The hand that is reaching into the pocket of his duffle coat is bruised from blood work, and fatigue is etched around his eyes. All that remains of his former vigour is the happiness in his smile.

Early in the new year, I phoned to say that we were going to be in Montreal at the end of February to take our daughter to an open house at the university she was planning to attend. The dates were fixed. After checking with my stepmother, he called back to tell us they would be "busy" that weekend. Enough, I said to myself, realizing that if I accepted "busy," I might never see my father again. I pushed the point. And finally, over the course of a desperately stressful week for all of us, he defied my stepmother and assured me that he would spend time with my family when we were in town. The cost was what my father described as "a fatal breakdown" in my relationship with my stepmother.

The evening of the "fatal breakdown" remark, I called my father. My stepmother answered the phone in an agitated voice and said she had no time to talk because my father was having muscle pains and she had to change the sheets so that he could get into bed. Muscle pains? Change the sheets? Why aren't you going to the hospital? I wondered as she put down the phone. An hour later, she called back to say that my father had asked her to phone to tell me that he was feeling better and that he would call me the next day. In the middle of the night, the phone rang. Another medical procedure had gone wrong and my father was clinging to life in a local hospital. We rushed to the airport to fly to his bedside, but it was too late. My son met us in Montreal with the news that my father was dead.

This was the end of sitting in his study, exchanging family anecdotes, sipping Scotch as the ice cubes clinked in our glasses, sharing a companionship painfully nurtured out of brutal conflict—and the end, too, of any hope of understanding why my father was so compliant to female authority. At the time, I thought perhaps he had seen death as the easiest resolution to the conflict with my stepmother over "visitation rights." And then, when I finally got back to Toronto, I found a note in his handwriting in the pile of mail, telling me how much he was looking forward to our planned visit later that month.

On bad days, I still beat myself up for killing my father. Was my insistence on making plans to see him the added stress that precipitated the final assault on his heart? On good days, I believe he died committing the second great act of defiance in his life, affirming his love for his daughter against his second wife's opposition. Although I can't know for certain, at those moments I like to think he was remembering the way he had defied his family's wishes to make that lonely trip across the Northumberland Strait in 1945.

What I do know is what I learned from living with my father: a hatred of bullying, a career-limiting defiance of any form of authority, a super-nuanced wariness and an unspoken fear that I would turn into a child beater myself. The fact that I didn't has a lot to do, I think, with my husband's tolerance, the encompassing love of my children and my own ability to intellectualize my situation. From an early age, I learned how to step outside myself and observe what was happening with a clinical eye. As a parent, I put this childhood training to advantage. If my kids infuriated me, I picked them up and walked until my rage subsided, even if it meant circling the room with one of them in my arms.

Since I hated authority, I fully assumed that my children had the right to hit me back if I ever raised my fist to them. Because I didn't, neither did they. And yet, when I look at my now grown red-haired daughter, the one who was never beaten, but who combines super-charged charm and defiance, I wonder, Where did that feistiness come from? And that makes me think of my mother and her ineluctable female legacy—a force that my father craved and feared all of his life, and I take an odd solace from that unsettling power.

My Father's Afterlife

by Lisa Moore

When I was twelve, I wanted to paint a midnight sky on my ceiling with yellow stars. The walls would be pale blue sky with spray-painted clouds. The midnight sky would drip down the walls. I told my parents about my idea over supper.

My father did almost all the cooking and he barbecued in all seasons. He liked to serve my mother. He liked to get her drinks and cook for us and he did the dishes. We ate a lot of steaks and hamburgers and tossed salad with Kraft dressing and baked potatoes. In the mornings, he peeled us grapefruit and put the separate sections around our plates so they formed flowers with a maraschino cherry in each centre. These grapefruit were waiting for us when we came to the table. He liked to let my mother sleep in.

Big drips running down the walls, I said. My father took me out the next Saturday and bought me rollers and spray paint and we looked over the paint samples for a shade that might pass for a midnight sky.

My childhood was full of permission; it was a sort of ambush. My parents trusted me and there was nothing I could keep from them. They let me do whatever I wanted. I wanted to never let them down.

My bedroom was in a house in the country on Hogan's Pond. The pond was big and had an island at one end; our house was in front of that island, sheltered from the wind. We skated fast in the winter on the pond, if the wind was behind us and the ice was smooth. We skated until it was almost dark and I'd hold my arms out and let the wind push me. And when we came off the ice my ankles hurt and my laces were frozen and it felt strange to walk in my boots on solid ground.

My father bought the land while it was cheap and he and my mother built the house together on the weekends and during the summer holidays. We had a pale green Chevy, and my sister and I slept curled up on the back seat on the way home from a weekend of swimming and canoeing, pouring concrete and hammering. The road was narrow and unpaved, and the car rocked slowly through the potholes and the alders, full of dust. We had to be home in time for *The Wonderful World of Disney*.

There is a photograph of me at the age of four standing in the long, swaying grass at the water's edge, beside a baby bassinet. The photograph is overexposed, sunlight fills the floating clouds of fluff lifting from the fireweed and the water is blazing with sparkles. My father is in this picture, shirtless, his back to the camera. He is looking out over the water, figuring out how to build the wharf.

My father had an idea that whatever we wanted, we would have it. I can almost feel him thinking it while I look at this photograph. If we wanted it, he would get it.

They wanted this house, he and my mother. It had shag carpet throughout, gold and khaki upstairs and on each step of the wrought iron spiral staircase. There was a two-tone blue in my parents' room to match the velvet wallpaper. A fireplace encased in mirror, stucco ceilings, exposed beams, plaid furniture in orange and black. It was the mid-seventies. The upstairs of this house was all one room—living room, kitchen, dining room—with two giant patio windows facing the water.

The front door was between the windows, and I remember a thunder-and-lightning storm, rain drumming the picnic table, gushing from the eavestrough, zigzagging in fast-moving runnels on the glass. I heard my father's car door and heard him pounding up the stairs to the verandah. When he reached the first patio window there was a shockingly bright smack of lightning. It was a pure white light that drained everything of colour; my father's red jacket, the trees, and the water beyond all became a dull metallic grey. My father was suspended in the window frame for a beat, like a single frame of a film snagged in a projector. Suspended, still, saturated with unnatural light. Then he disappeared.

The door crashed open, hitting the wall. I was screaming when he burst through the door. He was soaking wet, laughing, dropping groceries, and he hugged me. He pressed my face into his chest, his big hand on the back of my head. And the thunder rumbled like orchestral drums before a curtain goes up.

We were the thing with my father—my mother and sister and me. We were what mattered. That's what it felt like. A big life was being built for us and my father had what it took. What I felt for him was adoration. He was probably flawed—of course he was; I know he was, but he died before I could ever come to believe it.

I think of him clearing the land and building the house, he and my mother, together. I can see her on a rickety scaffold painting the side of the house in her bra and jeans and—hearing a car coming down the driveway—starting to crawl, gripping the wobbly plank with both hands, trying to get to her shirt before the car turned the corner.

I can see my father's back turning pink in the sun, working the shovel through wet cement in a wooden trough. He knew how to build a house. Newfoundland men of his generation seemed to be born knowing how to do it. He cooked rabbit and seal flippers and partridge and he knew how to make a very good pastry. I'd watch him rip the fur off the rabbits and he showed me the gullets of the partridges, cutting them open so the berries and leaves came out whole.

Before he married, my father lived with his mother and baked bread every morning and handed over his paycheque at the end of the week. He had a brother who went to the mainland at sixteen, and another brother whom we didn't see often because, as my father put it, he was a man who valued his privacy.

Dad worked as an accountant at Furnace Withy on Water Street in downtown St. John's until he started his own construction company and, for a short while, we lived large. We travelled to Barbados and Jamaica and stayed for a month or two in each place, and there is a photograph of me, at age ten, waltzing with my father on an outdoor dance floor with the night sky over our heads and a steel drum band playing. I'm wearing glasses and a peasant dress and I'm slightly chubby. I'm looking at my feet in this picture, and we are both grinning and caught in the splashy wash of the flashbulb, darkness obscuring the other dancers, except the shoulder of a lady in a bikini top and the rim of one of the drums at the edge of the frame.

My husband took our daughter, Eva, to India this year. They brought home thirty hours of video. There is a shot of my daughter leaning out of the open door of a train and there are streaking flashes of water on the rice fields under her outstretched arms. She turns back to look at my husband and she smiles and you can see in this few seconds of video the love between them. It is a through-and-through love. They are two of a kind, my daughter and her father.

Eva is just turning sixteen, the age I was when my father died of a cerebral aneurysm. He and my mother were buying lobsters at the side of the road that afternoon and he complained of nausea and handed Mom the car keys. I was in a play that night—at the high school drama festival—and they were coming to see me. I expected them to be waiting in the wings but I found instead a neighbour and friend of the family, a man who was also a police officer. He was dressed in his uniform and had a kind of stiff formality that I recognized as alien to him.

A few years later, I remember asking this neighbour if he believed in life after death. He wasn't a man naturally given to philosophical chit-chat. He was driving me into town because he was going there himself and my mother was busy. I was in the back seat of his car and I leaned over the front and just asked him. I watched the colour come up in his neck to his hairline. I realize now that my question was flippant, a violation of his privacy, but he knew I was ignorant of all that, and responded with a sensitive caution. He switched the radio off and a palpable discomfort filled the car and he turned the radio back on.

I had been raised a Roman Catholic, but my parents had given up going to church. I had insisted on going myself and I'd prayed every day. But when my father died, I felt about God the way you feel when an absorbing movie ends and I stopped believing altogether.

Our neighbour finally said he thought my question was pretty heavy talk for a girl my age. He flicked the rearview my way and inadvertently caught my eyes, and he flicked the mirror back. The rest of the drive was in silence. I had forgotten all about the question by the time we got to town. We were at the lights before the Avalon Mall when he said: Maybe you should think about something else.

It was the suddenness of my father's death that was most staggering—the unrelenting finality. Gradually, very gradually, I came to realize that everything to come would not have him in it. Grief becomes more acute as time passes, undiluted, and vivid. How thoroughly present my father had been; how thoroughly absent he became. It was impossible to believe, but it was irrefutable. And when my daughter was born, eleven years later, there were my father's ears. This infant, a month and a half premature, so tiny in my husband's large hands—how could such a creature, small and brand new, have the exact same ears my father had, and the curve of his temple? I saw them as soon as the doctor laid her on my chest and I began to sob. There was my father, just when I needed him.

I ask my friend Holly what she remembers about my dad.

I remember him being patient, she says. He drove us everywhere and bought us a lot of pizza. I remember you losing your contact lens and him looking for it and he found it in a spider's web on the leg of a picnic table. Do you remember that?

And from this delicate, peculiar memory, a whole summer comes back, when we were fourteen. Painter pants and checked Levi's shirts and curling irons and *Grease* in the movie theatres. We suntanned with cucumbers on our eyes and made squashed banana face masks and washed our hair in lemon juice.

My father's construction company had failed and he'd bought a convenience store. My parents worked back-to-back shifts, taking off only Sunday afternoons together. For a long time there was very little money. I can hear the relentless adding machine on the dining room table. My father punching the keys, the machine grinding and spewing tape that showed how much things cost. It didn't seem to make a difference. It was a huge difference, but one that didn't matter.

Dad encouraged me to start a sandwich-making business. Egg sandwiches, ham, pressed turkey, tomato and roast beef. We went to a wholesale store together so I could buy oversized jars of mustard and mayonnaise and an industrial roll of plastic wrap. He had me keep a notebook listing expenses and profits. My father said I couldn't take a weekday off because working people were counting on me. They had built my sandwich into their day and they came to the store early in the morning, and the sandwiches had better be there. These were some things I would have to understand: I had to be dependable and hard-working. I should never give up.

He paid me out of the till at the end of each week and I made a lot of money. I kept him company in the store for hours at a time. He had nightmares, he once told me, that there would be cars at the pumps, waiting for gas, but he'd be serving customers at the counter inside. The cars would try to tear away, burning rubber, and he would run outside and grab their fenders and hang onto them, digging his heels in.

Sometimes the store would be empty and I'd read a book and put my feet up. If it was raining, we'd listen to the rain. My father stacked the shelves. There was an eighteen-year-old boy named Rick who worked for my father pumping gas. I was afflicted with a paralyzing crush. If Rick was working, halfway through the shift he would come over to the counter and buy a bag of chips and a Coke. He always bought the same thing, and he always gave me a five-dollar bill. It didn't matter. I could never count back his change. He would hold out his hand and I would get it wrong and get it wrong again. There was nothing any of us could do about the situation. There was no way to pretend I was not blushing, no way for Rick to withdraw his outstretched hand. This rigid moment, while I stared down at the coins in the cash register drawer, would take a very long time to pass. My father would continue to slide the cans of dog food over the shelves. Rick was kind and waited, and he and my father never shared a complicit glance. We were united in the act of pretending there was nothing out of the ordinary. We all got through this moment, every Saturday, as best we could.

My sister says my mother cooked.

Of course she cooked, my sister says. She did Sunday dinner and macaroni and cheese and that rib dish. You just want to believe Dad did all the cooking.

What would Mom say? I ask.

Mom would say Dad did all the cooking, she says.

And the barn, Holly says. Your father built you that barn.

I wanted a horse and I got one. Every morning, I dragged buckets of water from the laundry room sink over the yard and up the hill in the snow. I'd wear my winter boots and flannel night-gown, and the barn smelled of grain and molasses and manure and frost. The horse was too much for me. She needed exercise, and I hung on while she galloped away with me down the centre of the icy winter road, bucking and rearing, pawing the clouds. She finally knocked me off, on one occasion, by trotting under a low-hanging branch, which caught me across the throat. I was lying flat on the road, the wind knocked out of me, listening to the horse's hoofs clattering on the pavement. It took the rest of the afternoon to find her.

How heartbroken my father was when we had to have our talk. The horse would have to be sold, he said. We couldn't afford her. There was nothing he could do. He was shocked to see my relief.

He made us a puppet theatre out of the box the dryer came in, and sewed puppets out of old socks with buttons for eyes and had me write the script. He made us a giant Easter bonnet out of cardboard, covered in Christmas wrapping paper and bows and pictures cut from magazines—a place for the Bunny to leave our chocolate eggs. When I wanted to audition for the drama club at high school, he went to the library and brought home a record of *Macbeth*. He watched my sister dive every morning at six from the balcony of the Aquarena. She always checked to make sure he was watching before she threw herself off the board to execute three hard, fast somersaults.

When we were very little, he put us to bed, lying between my sister and me, telling us stories about princesses and dragons and poor young men who fought evil and won and fell in love, a love that lasted forever and ever. He made up these stories as he went along, and they were full of drama and bravery and suspense.

Last night, when I was putting my six-year-old son, Theo, to bed he asked me if you still have dreams when you're dead. I laid his storybook down on my chest and closed my eyes.

I'd been canoeing with my husband that evening. He'd bought a second-hand canoe and had repaired it and wanted to try it out right away. We drove out to Hogan's Pond with the canoe on the hood of the car, resting on Styrofoam blocks. It was an evening without wind, and the sun was big and a deep, dark orange and the light was fiercely pink on the water and fading fast. Small trout broke the surface. We paddled past what had been my parents' land. Our house had been torn down several years before and there was a new house that spread itself over as much of the waterfront as it could.

We floated there for a moment, the paddles resting over our knees, not talking, and I remembered, as if out of nowhere, a hot summer evening long, long ago when my father came home with Jesus boots. They were big Styrofoam pontoons, one for each foot, and you could walk on the water. Someone had brought them into the store and offered to sell them to my father.

Theo and I were lying on his narrow bed and it was as though I were still at the pond, floating in the canoe. The bed seemed to be floating beneath me. I was tired from the heat and exercise, and the great, prodigious, mounting feeling of summer coming on, all at once.

When you're dead there's absolutely nothing, I said.

I'd forgotten who I was speaking to; didn't realize I had spoken out loud; but it was too late.

Nothing, Theo said. He was astonished. His astonishment filled up the bedroom. It was as though the red sun and the midnight sky and the glare off the pond and all the fireweed had come through the room on a blasting wind. Theo sat up on one elbow and stared forward, into the dark.

I didn't mean it, I said.

And I am suddenly sitting on the wharf, digging my feet into the squeaky Styrofoam footholds of the pontoons. I am twelve and I'm in the blaze of red sunset on a summer evening, just before dark. I push off the wharf and I'm trying hard to dig my heels in but there's no friction. I'm shrieking with laughter and my arms are swinging around like windmills and the pontoons slip and slide. I'm trying to walk on the water and my father is calling from the wharf: You can do it.

Loving Felicite

by Sarah Murdoch

One evening, a few years before his death, my father recalled one of our more horrifying family dramas. "I'll never forget," he said, "the time you phoned me at work to tell me to get home fast because you were afraid Felicite was going to murder Grandma."

I'll never forget it either—my drunk mother weaving dangerously around the house; her mother, my grandmother, then well into her eighties, barricaded in her room. I was around fifteen, and felt overwhelmed by those three intruders—disgust, shame and fury—who always showed up when my mum was on a bender. On this occasion, there was panic, too, which is why I'd called my dad at work. He came home immediately, and gently, lovingly, put my mother to bed.

That he harked back to that day surprised me, because we rarely talked about those occasions when my mother fell off the wagon. We both preferred to remember the woman we knew when she was sober: a magnificent eccentric, given to 3 A.M. jaunts to the laundromat, where she knew interesting people were to be found, or out having mad adventures with Dino, the cross-dressing burlesque queen who lodged with us for a while. When she wasn't drinking, my mother was a real character, full of enthusiasm and energy.

The big difference between my dad and me, when it came to my mother, was that he unfailingly regarded her with tenderness and affection whether she was drunk or sober. To me, she was an unpredictable, scary character, given to abrupt transformations and crazy behaviour—like the time she opened the car door, presumably to throw herself into the road, while my father was driving down the New York State Thruway (I lunged forward from the back seat and flung one arm around her and grabbed the door with the other hand). I couldn't count on her for even the most ordinary parental task. After she showed up sodden at my bridal shower at the suburban home of my future mother-in-law, I screamed at my father for letting her out of the house and exposing me to such monumental humiliation. I was mystified by his forbearance—and I suppose I still am, thirty years after her death.

No matter how badly my mother behaved, my father remained enchanted with her. There was no marital breakdown, no bickering, no ultimatums, no gradual alienation of affection—quite the opposite. For the entire thirty-seven years of their marriage, my father was passionately involved with my mother, to the exclusion of almost everything, and everyone, else.

My father liked to say he was one of the last of the Edwardians, born in December 1909, a few months before the king's death. I'm one of the first of the baby boomers, but my upbringing was more akin to my father's era than the postwar years. For most of my childhood, I was brought up by my grandmother, who was more like a governess than a relative—teaching me, disciplining me and making certain I was presentable for my brief daily interactions with my mother and father. Grandma fed me, clothed me, sat next to me when I practised the piano and conducted weekly tests in spelling and arithmetic. I lived with her in a flat in London, England, a few blocks from my parents' home. There was a housing shortage after the war. Their place wasn't big enough. My mother worked. Those were the stated reasons. The truth was that my parents liked their life as it was—just the two of them.

They had been married for seven years when I was born: He was thirty-seven, she was thirty-three, older than most first-time parents of the day. They'd pretty much decided not to have kids. Then one night they returned home after an evening of pubbing and changed their minds. They made love without precautions, just that one time. Next morning, they agreed that perhaps they'd been a trifle hasty— alas, too late. My mother told me this story when I was around twelve (she greatly enjoyed inappropriate disclosure), but I wasn't at all distressed to learn I was the result of such a whimsical desire to procreate. She assured me that though she didn't like children, she and my father were delighted to have me after I arrived. One's own children are different, she explained, and I believed her (though not to the point of ever undertaking any childbearing of my own, I must add).

But though I had no doubt that my parents loved me, I also knew—a belief underscored repeatedly by my grandmother, whose continued role in the household depended on my needing her—that their primary relationship was with each other. I still have the letter my father wrote to my mother on the day I was born. It is a sentimental note, filled with his declarations of love for her, his determination to make us both happy, his delight at the arrival of this flesh-and-blood manifestation of his love for her. I weep every time I read it.

My father, who dreamed of being a novelist, was an executive in the electronics industry in London. My mother, who wanted to be an

actress, taught dancing, took on modelling jobs, worked in a department store and, for a time during the war, drove an ambulance. God
knows why they thought moving to Canada to create a new division
of a British manufacturing company would satisfy their ambitions.
But running his own show was a step up for my father. In Canada, he
would be the managing director of the company, the boss. My mother,
who found multiplying by ten a challenge, was the treasurer.

We arrived just before my fifth birthday, and after moving a few
times we settled in Willowdale, north of Toronto. My grandmother and
I shared a room on the top floor of the house, my Snow White poster
on the wall on my side of the room, her autographed photo of Liberace
on the other. My exposure to my parents was mostly limited to short,
formal encounters in the evenings, when they returned home exhausted
from work—after which I was dispatched to my grandmother.

Actually, there was a third pillar to my upbringing: summer camp.
I spent two months at Little Buckaroo Ranch every year from the age
of five, our first summer in Canada, until I was old enough to be a
junior counsellor, at the age of seventeen. That first year, I was by far
the youngest camper. My counsellor taught me how to tie my
shoelaces. The second year, I learned to stand on my head. By my fifth
year, I could stand on a horse and twirl a lasso. Most of the important
life skills I've acquired were learned at Little Buckaroo, away from my
parents and my beloved grandmother who, unwisely, but understand-
ably, wanted me to remain her helpless darling girl forever.

My father and my grandmother lived under the same roof—
though a storey apart—for the better part of twenty years, and he
always addressed her politely as "Mrs. Kirby." He didn't like her. He
blamed my mother's incapacitating insecurities and mounting anxi-
eties on her. I can't remember him ever coming upstairs. Not once.

My parents, meanwhile, were as closely involved with each other as
they had been in England. More so now, since they worked together,

had lunch together and came home late together. On weekends, they stayed in bed until late in the morning, reading, dozing, chatting. I would perch on their bed, delighted to be part of this contented circle.

How different the narrow-minded Toronto suburb where we lived must have seemed compared to the congenial life they'd left in Chelsea. Instead of writing and acting, Derrick and Felicite endured the long drive down Yonge Street every morning to the old brownstone that was the first home of the Juno Floor Polisher Company of Canada. The window display consisted of a huge flight cage filled with tropical birds, a floor polisher standing sentry on either side. Exotic birds were one of my mother's enthusiasms, and I suppose my parents hoped this fine display of finches and budgerigars would bring customers through the door. In the basement at home, there was a similar arrangement: a huge flight cage, the home of dozens of tropical birds, connected by the basement window to another flight cage in the backyard. Smaller breeding cages lined the basement walls, where mating couples, say a pair of Javanese temple birds, awaited their broods.

I adored my father, probably even more so than most little girls. Because my grandmother was the disciplinarian, the educator, the chore assigner, the finger waggler, my dealings with my father were entirely pleasurable for both of us. And where other kids' fathers were staid and boring, mine was smart and funny. He was always an excellent companion—interested and interesting—and he never talked down to me. In short, he gave me a sense of specialness, a gift I treasure. I was shy with grownups and other children, but never with my dad. With him, I felt like myself.

Three stories come to mind, significant because in each one the adult isn't responding to the child the way fathers and daughters usually do. Each is typical of the honesty and spontaneity with which my father always engaged with me. He didn't treat me like a little kid.

And when he was with me, he didn't behave like a conventional, stuffy adult. Maybe we met each other halfway.

- I am about seven, and one evening I try out a gag on my dad that's been going the rounds in the schoolyard.

  "What do bees make?"

  "Honey," he says.

  "Fresh! How dare you call me honey," I say, and slap him across the face.

  He slaps me right back—not as hard as I hit him, but enough to get my attention. I am too shocked to cry. I am shattered. This is a father who has never struck me. I think he was shocked by my striking him, and reacted instinctively. I now know, first-hand, how hurtful even a playful slap can be.

- I am eight or nine, and Dad and I are exploring a second-hand bookstore not far from the office. He hands me a Victorian book of fairy tales, open to a grotesque drawing of a child splayed in a giant web, with spiders, snakes and various oversized insects advancing. I am fascinated but not horrified; this sort of outrage is common in children's literature and I'd seen worse. Many years later, my father tells me he felt ashamed of himself after he showed me that picture. He had had that very book when he was a child, and the drawing had given him the horrors for weeks. He wanted to see if it had the same effect on me.

- I am ten or eleven, and one day I rifle through a drawer of old photographs. I come upon a picture of a little girl. She is about my age, has blond hair and is wearing a white dress. I am on high alert, immediately suspicious. I somehow know she has nothing to do with my dark-haired, olive-skinned mother. But who could she be?

When he comes home that evening, I confront him, photo in hand. He explains that this is his daughter, Carole, from his first marriage, and that she is ten years older than I. He hopes one day I will meet her. I had known about his first marriage (a wicked, selfish woman, to hear my mother tell it, whom my father had to marry because she was pregnant). But until then I had not known it had produced a daughter, my half-sister.

In all three stories, you might question my father's behaviour, if you happen to be one of those conventional adults who feel it's poor form to slap your child, give her nightmares or conceal from her the existence of an older half-sibling. I have turned out to be the least stuffy of adults imaginable, and it is largely because of my father. I never got the sense he was humouring me, as adults so often do with children. He treated me as though I were his younger self and showed me that a grownup never has to forget what it is to be very young.

In my teens, my family—not a cohesive unit at the best of times—seemed to come completely unstitched. The floor polisher business failed, despite the tropical birds and an aggressive telemarketing effort. Later, a powdered-milk business flopped, as did a plan to sell a university savings scheme to parents. My father got his real estate licence and tried selling houses for a while. The situation was dire, but I only realized this later. My father became increasingly remote, irritable, stressed. He started seeing a psychiatrist. "Unresolved conflicts" was all I was told.

My mother acquired a shrink, too, for more obvious reasons. Her alcoholism became evident to me when I was twelve and a family vacation to Montreal had to be curtailed. That was a preview of coming attractions. After that, there were four or five, sometimes six or seven, such episodes a year, often on the eve of a holiday or an event that for some reason was stressful for her. I learned to identify some of the warning signs and would beg her not to give in, but she always did. My father would put her to bed, where she would stay for days, drugged on Promazine, to help her through the withdrawal.

She went to all the big treatment centres—Homewood Sanitarium, the Donwood—and small private hospitals in Toronto (she dried out with Brendan Behan in one of them shortly before his death). She was the unhappiest drunk ever, filled with remorse during and after each binge. Her problem was a central fact of our lives. Indeed, she would take me to Alcoholics Anonymous meetings with her—we shopped around, going to meetings both in affluent neighbourhoods and grubby church basements.

For my part, I was no longer a shy little girl. Over the course of the six months leading up to my fourteenth birthday, I started playing hooky, took up smoking, got caught shoplifting at the local Zellers, siphoned gas from trucks in the municipal parking lot, discovered sex and failed grade nine. Now I was assigned a psychiatrist too. My grandmother soon declared me incorrigible and moved down the street to live with my Uncle Joe, Felicite's brother.

Maybe there were other girls my age having sex in Willowdale, but I didn't know them. My boyfriend was eighteen, and when my parents found out, very soon after the fact, that I'd lost my virginity, my father demanded that he be charged with statutory rape. At his trial, the boyfriend received a suspended sentence (not surprising, given that it was consensual and I wouldn't dispute the claim that he thought I was sixteen). My poor father, the very embodiment of a cultivated Englishman, stood up in court and declared, furiously: "He should be castrated." I was mortified. It was my fault that this private man had been pushed to such an excessive pronouncement.

That was the beginning of my difficult teens, and suffice to say I wasn't a model daughter in the years that followed either. We moved downtown (my mother in particular had always hated suburbia), to a house, then an apartment, a stone's throw from then-swinging Yorkville—which of course I embraced. At seventeen, I was charged with possession with intent to traffic after my best friend returned from Morocco with what the police said at a press conference was the largest hashish haul in Toronto history (a mere two kilos—a bagatelle by today's standards). The day before my arrest, I'd smoked marijuana for the first time. It was the same old story. No matter what aspect of youthful criminality I turned my hand to, my parents always seemed to find out right away—or, as it happened in this instance, my parents, the police and the national media (I'm only a little bit ashamed to admit that I was proud that we made page one of both *The Globe and Mail* and the *Toronto Star*).

Maybe getting caught was the whole point of my outlaw years. Certainly, my father had always demonstrated a high tolerance level for egregious behaviour (both mine and my mother's), so was I simply competing with her, substituting sex and drugs for booze? Was I out to get my father's attention, to punish them both, or seek notoriety elsewhere because they just weren't available? Why teenagers do what they do is never simple. And remember, I was a girl who had been brought up in a household where unconventional behaviour, being different from the pack, was prized. Yet despite all my escapades, despite several tangles with the law, despite a distinctly lacklustre high school career, I always knew I would turn out just fine. And I was right.

All parents blame themselves more than they should. Mine certainly did. They blamed their absence from my life, my mother blamed her drinking, my father blamed my grandmother. My father even blamed himself for my pot bust. A month or two before my arrest, he had published an article in *The Globe and Mail* arguing for the legalization of marijuana on grounds that it is safer than tobacco and, really, not all that damaging. ("Smoking? Go to pot," said the headline).

So, when I was busted, my father hired Arthur Martin, one of Canada's best criminal lawyers, who used that article as a central thread of my defence: The poor child ran afoul of the law because of her father's seditious writings. The other thread was that we were innocent kids who'd got in over our heads, which was mostly correct. My co-conspirator and I were sentenced to two years' probation.

The prospect of twenty years in the slammer does much to concentrate the imagination of even the most determined juvenile miscreant. There were no more scrapes with the law. I worked in an office for several years, got married, returned to school, got a degree in journalism, then a job at the *Ottawa Citizen,* got divorced, returned to Toronto and got married again. My father was enormously proud of me. Or perhaps just relieved I wasn't in jail.

My mother died at sixty-two, her body spent by drink and late-onset diabetes. My father was inconsolable. We spent Christmas and New Year's in Aruba that year, because he couldn't tolerate the idea of spending the holiday alone in Toronto. On Christmas Day he told me he could no longer see the point of living. I was shocked by the depths of his grief. But in time it became easier, and indeed in some ways he came into his own after her death.

He continued to write a weekly crime fiction column for *The Globe and Mail,* twenty-two years all told, right up to the week of his death. He was regarded as the elder statesman of Canada's crime fiction community and was a founder of the Bootmakers of Toronto (the local chapter of Canada's Sherlock Holmes society) and, with my second husband and several others, the Crime Writers of Canada. Its President's Award, given occasionally for extraordinary performance in the service of crime fiction, is named after him. (You will have observed that my family has an affinity for courtrooms, in fact and fiction.)

For the first time, he was earning a reliable stream of income, mostly from the Ontario government, where he put words into the mouths of several cabinet ministers. He wrote two books: one about Agatha Christie, and then, at the age of seventy, a second on noteworthy Canadian disappearances. There were several much younger women whom he would squire to cultural events. I know for a certainty that when he had a bit too much to drink he was capable of making passes at them, unsuccessfully as far as I know. A girlfriend of mine—one of his favourite dates—once remarked that he was the only man she'd ever met who shot his cuffs, that charming gesture by which gentlemen of the old school abruptly and stiffly thrust their arms out of their jacket sleeves in order to reveal a small amount of shirt cuff and a flash of cuff link. It was the Edwardian in him.

It was in this final phase of his life that I really got to know my father. Not the idealized hero of my childhood, and not the often petulant man I knew in my teens. At least twice a week, I would stop by his ground-floor apartment at the corner of Lowther and Huron. The separate suite attached to the apartment, which had once housed the flamboyant Dino (who drifted off after a year with us) and later my terrified grandmother (who died in a nursing home at ninety-four, and thank God my mother had nothing to do with it), was empty. My old bedroom served as his office.

Sometimes I'd drop by for a quick visit after work. But more often we would loosen our tongues with copious quantities of red wine, smoke far too many cigarettes and talk for hours. We had variously intense, hilarious, difficult, painful conversations about everything that had touched our lives. Our worlds converged. We developed friends in common. And ideas. It evolved, seamlessly, into an extraordinary relationship. He delighted me as much as he had when I was little. And I him.

And, still, I didn't have him all to myself. After my mother's death, my half-sister, Carole (my rival, that little blond-haired girl) came to Canada after a career in the Italian film industry. She, too, wanted to know her father before he died. Their relationship was entirely different. Every morning, one would phone the other to deconstruct that day's *Globe* cryptic crossword and discuss events of the previous twenty-four hours. Douglas, my husband, said the minutiae with which they occupied themselves reminded him of a Jane Austen novel. Often, my father and Carole and Douglas and I would convene at a restaurant or one of our homes. Her arrival in Canada had a wonderfully restorative effect on my father in the last years of his life. And me? Slowly, I lost a rival and gained a sister.

My father died of cancer (all those cigarettes we smoked) at the age of seventy-six, ten years after my mother. He left me a file containing his will, his funeral instructions and a list of who should be notified on his death. There was also a letter for me, in its way just as sentimental as the one he wrote to my mother on the day I was born: "I know we love each other," he wrote. "If it was only a matter of the time, consideration, gentleness, uncritical support and companionship you've given me over the past few years, you'd just be a model of daughterly dutifulness. But, of course, it went much further. You always sparkled with brightness, wit, wisdom and charm when we were together. I could almost believe you enjoyed my company as much as I did yours. Partly because it often took me back to happy days with Felicite, partly because there's the constant wonder of the separate, individual person you have grown to become."

He couldn't have said goodbye in a better way. My mother, as she was in life, remained front and centre, the great love of his life. But, finally, I had a place with him too.

Dancing with My Father

by Marina Nemat

"Look what you've done now! You've killed your mother!" my father said to me in Persian as the paramedics carried my mother on a stretcher down the narrow flight of stairs of my suburban Toronto house. Standing in the tiny foyer with the front door wide open, I shivered in the cold October wind that carried the scent of winter, relieved that the paramedics didn't speak our language. But one of them looked at me with questioning eyes and I guessed that he had heard the rage in my father's voice, which was as sharp as broken glass, bleeding with raw, confused anger. As always, my father was trying to place blame, to find somebody responsible for my mother's sudden illness, as if that would fix things and make her well.

The paramedics rushed my mother past me, and I had a moment to study her face; it was a little paler than usual and the lines around her brown eyes seemed deeper. But there was more: Her eyes were different; they were not as stern and condemning as they had always been. She looked like a defiant child who had been caught red-handed but didn't regret what she had done, not even for a moment. I followed the paramedics and my parents through the door, and tears rolled down my face. I wiped them with the back of my hand. I was stronger than this. But here I was, a thirty-three-year-old woman, feeling like I was eight years old again and back in Tehran.

I watched the lights of the ambulance disappear around the corner. Then I went back into the house, which my husband and I had bought two years after our arrival in Canada as landed immigrants in 1991. My parents had followed us two years later to be close to their only two children: my brother, who had come to Canada in 1979, and me. The top half of the wall of the stairway was painted yellow, the bottom half a bright pistachio green and a wide border of blue and white flowers separated the two. I had always wanted to paint the walls of the stairway, but working a part-time job at McDonald's and being the mother of two young boys, I had never gotten around to it.

I locked the door behind me and, unable to carry my weight any longer, sat on the floor in front of it. I was grateful that no one was home; my children were at school and my husband was at work. I knew I had to call and ask him to pick up the kids and come home so we could go to the hospital and find out what had happened to my mother. But I couldn't move.

"Look what you've done now! You've killed your mother!"

Was my father finally dealing with what had happened in Tehran more than sixteen years earlier when I had been arrested and imprisoned in the notorious Evin prison? I knew that my incarceration had taken its toll on my parents. But it had taken its toll on me, too. I hadn't thought about Evin in years. I had never talked to my parents about what had happened to me there, because they never asked me about it. Now my mother was dying, and they still didn't know.

In a strange way, we were like complete strangers. No one at home knew the real me. But how could I tell them? Where would I start?

How could I tell them that I had been tortured, had come very close to execution and had been forced to marry one of my interrogators and to spend many nights with him in a solitary cell? And there was more, much more. The only way for me to tell them was to start at the very beginning and to speak of every moment, every single thing that had happened behind the walls of Evin.

The phone began to ring, but I didn't dare answer it. What if my mother had died? What if my father was right and I had killed her?

My parents and I had never gotten along. As a punishment, when I was a child, my mother used to lock me out on the balcony of our apartment in downtown Tehran. We rented two connected apartments on top of a small restaurant and a furniture store at the northwest corner of the intersection of Shah and Rahzi avenues, where my mother ran her beauty salon and my father his dance studio. This was before the 1979 Islamic revolution in Iran, back when dancing was not considered evil.

Our three bedrooms, small kitchen and bathroom were in-between the salon and the studio on either side of a dark, narrow hallway. I cannot remember the details of why my mother locked me out on the balcony, but I was a curious, opinionated and articulate child who wanted to know everything and never took "no" for an answer. "No" always set an intriguing challenge for me, and I always responded to it with "why?" And my mother, who was beautiful, busy and short-tempered, simply didn't have the time or patience to get into never-ending discussions with me, so she came up with the perfect punishment that kept me out of her way.

I hated the balcony. It was either too hot or too cold, and worst of all, it was lonely. However, this was where I learned the art of patience, a virtue that didn't come naturally to me. One thing I hated even more than being locked out on the balcony was being humiliated, and this was why I never made a scene; I never screamed, banged on the balcony door or stomped my feet. I cried silently and watched the street from the top of the bamboo shades encircling my one-by-three-metre roofless cell.

The paved four-lane street seethed with traffic during rush hours and the air smelled of exhaust fumes. On the other side of the road, Hassan Agha, the vendor who had only one arm, sold sour green plums in spring, peaches and apricots in summer, cooked red beets in autumn and various kinds of cookies in winter. At the other corner of the intersection, an old blind man held his bony hands to the passers-by and cried "Help me for the love of God!" from morning till night. In front of our apartment, the large, mirrored windows of a fifteen-storey office building sparkled in the sun and reflected the movement of the clouds. At night, the neon lights above the stores came on and coloured the darkness.

My sentence on the balcony would last from half an hour to three hours, and for most of this time, I could hear a waltz or a tango seeping through the windows of my father's dance studio, and I sometimes heard his voice saying, "one, two, three … one, two, three …" In my mind, I could see my father's students, elegantly dressed couples, spin and dance to the music, and I wished I could be a part of the forbidden world of the dance studio. But my father never let me in there when he was working. Sometimes when I awoke very early in the morning and everyone was still asleep, I would go into the studio and swirl around to an imaginary waltz until I became dizzy and collapsed on the cool, brown linoleum floor that smelled of wax.

As a child, I was afraid of my father. What I remember most about him from those days is watching him sit on his favourite black leather chair in the waiting area of his studio every evening, reading the paper. His posture was always perfect and as straight as a ruler. If I disturbed him by saying something or making a sound, he would look at me with his serious amber eyes, his mouth an unbending line that seemed incapable of ever breaking into a smile. He didn't have any patience for young children. I knew quite well that if I misbehaved, he would slap me on the face, which was the most humiliating thing I had ever experienced.

This was how I grew up, an outsider, watching my family from a distance, as if a glass wall, which became thicker with each passing day, stood between us. I found refuge in books, school and friends, and I spent most of my time reading and studying. Having always been one of the top students in my class, I decided to become a medical doctor when I was twelve, and all my teachers encouraged me, telling me that with my perseverance, I could become whatever I set my mind on.

The Islamic Revolution happened when I was thirteen and turned our world upside down. From my window, I watched the revolution unfold, slowly at first, but then it turned into a flash flood, engulfing the streets, washing away the normalcy of our lives. Our street, which had always been congested with cars and filled with pedestrians, who strolled or rushed along or haggled with vendors, was empty and silent. Even the beggars were gone. Soon, military trucks appeared at every corner. Once every few days, hundreds of angry demonstrators filled the street, bearded men leading the way and women wearing chadors following them; with their fists raised in the air, they screamed, "Down with the Shah!" and "Independence, Freedom, Islamic Republic!" For the first time in my life, I heard shots fired; the military had opened fire on the demonstrating crowds. My mother ordered me to stay away from windows, and, this time, I obeyed her without an argument.

Even though the revolution was gathering momentum, my parents believed that a bunch of mullahs and unarmed civilians would never defeat the Shah's military. But they were wrong. The Shah went into exile; Ayatollah Khomeini, who had been in exile for years, returned to

Iran; the Islamic Republic of Iran was born; and with it, our world and all the rules that had held it together collapsed. Dancing was declared satanic, and my father began working as an office clerk at his friend's stainless steel factory. He hated his job but was hopeful that the new Islamic government would not last very long. Looking back now, I realize how devastating it must have been for him not to be able to dance, but I was only thirteen, going through adolescence as well as a violent revolution, and I was too busy trying to understand the merciless new world that was taking form in front of my eyes.

Wearing makeup and beautiful clothes and reading Western books became illegal. And before I knew it, my dream of becoming a doctor slipped away because young fanatical women of the Revolutionary Guard, most of whom didn't even have a high school diploma, gradually replaced our teachers. These unqualified new teachers spent most of the class time with political rhetoric, and when I protested, I was told that I could leave the classroom if I didn't like the new order of things—and I did, and by doing so, I unintentionally began a school-wide strike that went on for three days. During the next few months, I started a school newspaper and wrote articles against the government. My parents were aware of most of my activities, but they never tried to stop me; after all, by normal standards, I wasn't doing anything wrong.

I was arrested at ten o'clock at night on January 15, 1982. I was only sixteen years old. During the next two years, my mother and father suffered a great deal. They knew that political prisoners were tortured in Evin. They had heard about the rape of young girls and knew about daily mass executions. Every day they waited for the phone call that would tell them to go to the prison gates to collect my belongings because I had been executed.

Most prisoners were allowed regular visits with close family members, so I saw my parents once a month. A thick glass barrier divided the large visitation room in half. For the first few months of my time in Evin, there were no phones in the visitation room, so we couldn't talk and used a sign language instead. Armed revolutionary guards stood in every corner and carefully watched everyone. My parents cried constantly, and I tried to smile and told them I was all right. At one of the visitations, about five months after my arrest, I told them I had converted to Islam from Christianity, but they didn't ask why. They knew I had been forced to do it. No one dared question what went on in Evin.

When I was released, my parents pretended that nothing out of the ordinary had happened, as if I had been away on an extended holiday. The first night that I was home, we all sat around the dinner table, and I watched in astonishment as my parents talked about the weather. It took me days to understand their behaviour. I finally decided that their silence was their way of protecting themselves as well as me; they didn't want to know about the pain and horror of my time in prison, so they pretended it had never happened, hoping we would all forget it. But I didn't forget. I pushed my memories into a dark corner of my mind, where they remained dormant for close to twenty years. After my release from Evin, I became a prisoner of silence.

As it turned out, I had not caused my mother to have a heart attack on that day in October 1998. She had gallbladder cancer and had to undergo surgery. My mother had known about her cancer for a couple of weeks but had not said a word to any of us. We asked her why she hadn't told us, and she said she didn't want us to worry.

My father had blamed me for my mother's illness because he was angry, he was hurt and he felt helpless. But I had gone down the path of anger and blame, and I had learned that placing blame only brought temporary relief. The pain always returned, even stronger than before. Only forgiveness could truly heal. But how could my parents forgive me if they didn't know the truth, if they didn't know what had happened to me and why I was the way I was?

My mother had told me that I was "harsh" and "difficult." She and my father didn't understand why I couldn't be like "normal" people and care about normal things like shopping, vacations and luxuries. When their complaints about little things upset me and I told them that they were being unreasonable, they always stopped talking to me for days. After Evin, I had expected my homecoming to make things simple again, but it hadn't. I hated the silence surrounding me, but I didn't dare break it.

Both my parents were of Russian descent and, although not religious at all, were Christian. My Russian grandmothers had married Iranian men who had gone to Russia for work before the Communist revolution of 1917, after which both families were forced to leave that country because the husbands were not Russian citizens, and foreigners were not allowed to remain there any longer.

My father's parents, Esah and Xena, left Russia to go to Iran when Xena was pregnant with my father. They arrived in Tehran after my father's birth. One morning, shortly after their arrival in the capital, Esah, who was a jeweller, went out to sell the jewellery he had brought with him from Russia to buy a house for his family—but he was murdered, and everything he had with him was stolen. Xena, who didn't speak Persian and was a stranger in Iran, managed to survive after this. She eventually opened a boarding house, never married again, and provided a decent living for my father and his sister, Tamara. When my father was in elementary school, many of his schoolmates and teachers mocked, teased and bullied him because he was a Christian. He never talked to me about his childhood; I learned a little about it from eavesdropping on my mother's conversations with her friends.

My mother passed away from cancer in March 2000 before I told her the secrets of my past. After we buried her, my prison memories came back to life and haunted me until I finally began to put them on paper. Writing was much easier than talking. I didn't have to face anyone. I didn't have to worry about the judgments people would place on me. My first readers were my husband and my closest friends, and their understanding and encouragement helped me to take the next step and to begin sharing my story with the world by telling it to a reporter.

I knew I had to speak to my father about the newspaper article before he saw it in the paper. He was in relatively good health and living by himself in a seniors' building. The first year after my mother's death had been very hard on him—they had been married for more than fifty years—but he had slowly recovered. Now he had a new social life and had made friends with a few of his neighbours. He exercised for more than an hour every morning, went for walks and to his favourite café with a friend, and, as always, he enjoyed watching soccer on television. Still, my body began to shake the moment I picked up the receiver to dial his number.

"Hello?"

"Hello, Papa, it's me, Marina," I said.

"Hello my dear. How are you?"

"Not bad. How are you?"

"Not bad, I guess, for an eighty-four-year-old old man."

"Papa, I have something important to tell you …" A sharp pain spread into my chest.

"What? Are you ill? Are the children ill?"

"No. There's going to be an article about me in the newspaper and I want you to know about it before you read it somewhere. When I was arrested …"

"Marina, please don't …"

"But why not? You need to know."

"I'll read the article."

The thick, invisible wall that had always separated us remained as impenetrable as ever before. Why didn't he want to hear me out? Was his fear of my past, of the terrible things he knew I had experienced, so strong that he would still push me away after all these years?

I had no choice but to accept his decision, and we said goodbye.

He called me after the article was published and told me he had read it.

"I'm proud of you," he said.

I was shocked. This was the first time in my life that my father had told me he was proud of me. But he ended our conversation as quickly as possible; he was still running away from me.

After all this, I still felt a desperate need to sit down with my father and talk to him about the past. I needed answers, and I wanted to hear them from him, but I didn't have the courage to face him. The opportunity came up when my proposal to produce a radio documentary about my experiences as a political prisoner was accepted. The producer told me that documentaries always had a connection to the present; only telling the story of my past was not going to be enough. I had told her about the complications of my relationship with my father, and she was astonished about the silence I had faced after my release. She suggested I should interview him and explore how my experiences as a political prisoner had affected our relationship. Then she supplied me with a microphone and a voice recorder.

A couple of days later, I went to my father's apartment. I had not said anything about the documentary to him. He made some tea, we sat at his kitchen table and I put the microphone and the voice recorder on the table. He wanted to know what was going on. I suddenly felt a strong sense of authority. I wasn't only Marina any more. I had a microphone. I was a reporter.

"I want to interview you," I said and told him about the documentary. To my surprise, he agreed to do it. I began by asking him how he had felt when the revolutionary guards arrested me and took me away. He said he had felt absolutely helpless, that there was nothing he could do to save me. I knew how he must have felt. He was supposed to protect me, but he couldn't. On the night of my arrest, I saw him cry for the first time since his mother's death. Now that I was a mother, I knew how painful my arrest had been for him. I asked him if he had done anything to try to save me from the prison while I was there. He said he had tried but that all his efforts had been useless. In a way, my parents had been even more helpless than I had been.

"What do you remember about the night I was released and came home?" I asked.

"We were very happy to see you," he said.

"I remember we talked about the weather and normal things. I was shocked that nobody asked me about the prison."

Back then, their silence had frustrated me and had left me confused, but now I knew that most political prisoners' families usually chose silence over dialogue, believing it was the best thing to do.

"I thought it wasn't suitable to talk about it. Everything was behind us," my father said.

"As time went by, I was hurt that no one ever asked anything."

"Well jail is jail, and we knew that it was not correct to remind you. I didn't want to hurt you by making you think about the past. We knew that terrible things had happened to you, but we didn't know what they were and we were glad we didn't know because if we did, it would hurt us, and why would we want to do that? So we decided to stay away from it."

I wanted to tell him that all I needed back then was a shoulder to cry on. I needed someone to know and to understand. But my parents stepped away from me, protecting themselves and believing that they were protecting me as well. This was about survival instincts, and I understood them very well. Silence was an indestructible member of my family; I was convinced that even a nuclear explosion would leave that familiar wall standing in the midst of our ashes. It had become my father's way of life, his companion.

I had decided to break my silence because, as a former political prisoner, I had come face to face with torture, rape, loneliness, loss and death, and I had come to learn that I could be truly free only if I faced the past and tried to make sense of my survival by speaking out about all I had witnessed. But my father had lived with silence for far too long and trusted the false comfort it provided. It was too painful for him to look into my eyes, knowing what they had seen. And while I no longer blamed him, I knew we could never have a deeper, more meaningful relationship.

My father and I see each other every once in a while, and we some-times talk on the phone. But he has shown me that he wants to keep a safe distance from me. "The past is the past," he always says, so we only talk about the present. I had hoped that the hardship my parents and I went through would bring us closer, but it pushed us further apart. For years, I tried to begin a dialogue with my father; I even resorted to an interview, but all my efforts have failed. My father has never danced with me and he never will. This is the simple truth, a truth I have accepted, even though the pain it has caused me may never diminish.

The Change

by P.K. Page

It was only when my father was dying that my vision of him changed utterly. He who had always seemed larger than life—not out of reach, but heroic—shrank to the size of an ordinary human being. It was instantaneous, shocking and inspiring.

I must have had a sense of scale when I was quite young, for despite the fact that we lived in a small house, with clearly less money than our friends (his pay as a major in the Royal Strathcona's Horse in Calgary in the twenties was three dollars a day!), I was sure that "*my* father" was "better than *your* father," in the words of our terrible taunt and brag. Better, he may not have been, but he was clearly different. To begin with, his groom, with a saddled horse on a lead rein, arrived at our front gate every morning so he could ride to work—brass buttons glinting, riding boots and Sam Browne polished to a high shine. What other father did that?

Although it was never talked about, I knew he was brave. He had won three DSOs in World War I and been mentioned in dispatches six times. These phrases meant nothing to me in themselves, but they had authority. And from the time I was a very small girl and had seen him jump onto a bull and hang on by its horns, I knew he was a daredevil, seemingly fearless. Too, I had watched him play that hair-raising cavalry game in which a tent peg is driven into the ground and a mounted player at full gallop, sword drawn, leans dangerously out of his saddle to lift it into the air at sword point. It is vivid to me still—the sound of hooves thundering, dust rising, the heat of a prairie summer hammering us, and the triumphant moment when he, my father, held the tent peg aloft on his sword. Also, although not witness to the event, I remember the tale of how he jumped into the Bow River, polished boots and all, when an elderly Sarcee driving a horse and cart down the Corkscrew Hill had somehow missed the final turn and ended up in the water. I presume the horse saved itself, but it was my father who saved the old lady.

There was something romantic about my father. People said he looked French. I could not judge that, but he was attractive—dark with grey eyes and high cheekbones. More interesting to me were his crooked little finger and his right forearm with the tattoo of a frog snapping at a fly. Now, I can't imagine when, why or where he got the tattoo, an act seemingly so out of character with everything else about him; but then, it was further proof that he was different.

In addition, he bought horses from Chief Starlight. Who else had a friend with a name that opened up the night skies as it was spoken? Family lore has it that when my father's cousin in London sent him the first Dunhill lighter ever seen in the Canadian West, he gave it to Chief Starlight because of the look of wonder on his face when my father lit his cigarette for him.

But what went with the daredevil and the generosity was an independence of spirit, a disregard for public opinion—the spinoffs from which, for me in my teens, were cause for embarrassment, if not outrage.

I wanted to conform. I wanted my parents to conform. *Oh please, God, let them go to church or at least not drink shandies on the verandah on Sunday mornings as the worthy, upstanding churchgoers walk by.* Why did they have to speak with English accents? Dress differently? Laugh so much? Even our furnishings were different. No respectable navy blue carpet or Axminster—but a burnt-orange carpet, for heaven's sake! The fact that it was Chinese and very beautiful didn't count. And the dark oak furniture, carved by my parents, was totally unlike the mahogany in the houses of my friends. Why was I unable to make my family see as desirable the flat, grey norm I so longed for us all to be part of?

It became clear to me in my early teens that I was a changeling or adopted—an idea that had, at an earlier age, filled me with terror. Now I embraced it. It explained everything. Surely my real parents wouldn't embarrass me at every turn. How many times did I have to explain that "all the other kids" could do this or that, forbidden to me? And how many times did my father patiently point out that one didn't have to be a sheep? He tried hard to teach me difficult lessons—about love, about possessing one's own soul, about selfishness. I remember them still. They began when I was eight or nine, after I had walked through a puddle in my new shoes. The talk that followed was not a lecture; he didn't chastise me, but it was then we discussed selfishness in some depth. And I was awed.

What adolescent doesn't want to be a clone of their friends—dress the same way, do the same things? Why couldn't I be confirmed without having to undergo a soul-searching conversation that was totally beside the point, as I saw it? Did I want to be confirmed because of my friends, he asked, or did I have a sense of what confirmation meant? Did I really want to join the church? If I knew what I was doing, he would be supportive. I didn't know what I was doing, of course, so I suffered twice—once for my superficiality, and once because I felt I was letting him down.

He had ingenious methods of teaching. It was as if he already knew about aversion therapy. When my brother and I started that interminable, "I did! You didn't!" routine, he made the two of us sit on facing chairs and continue until he told us to stop. This probably wouldn't work with the modern child. But it did with us. In no time, we were laughing. And when I was a little older, my transgressions were dealt with by his arguing the case from my point of view while I argued it from his. A mind-expanding exercise.

He taught me any number of practical things. Sometimes he actually showed me how; sometimes I just hung around while he was doing them, learning by a kind of osmosis, as apprentices did in artists' studios in the Middle Ages. At quite a young age, I was able to change fuses, light a gas furnace with a long spill made from newspaper, roll an eyelid inside out to remove a foreign object, roll a cigarette, sit a horse. And his advice, if advice it was: that I was no daughter of his if I wouldn't try anything once.

He expected a lot of me and my brother—too much, I sometimes felt at the time. We learned to accept blame, to apologize when in the wrong. No lying, no pouting, no sulking, no self-pity, no squeamishness. I feel now that it was as if he wanted us to aspire to some higher order, some level of consciousness that perhaps he himself had attained. A level at which humour and team spirit were "givens." I don't remember him or my mother ever gossiping or bad-mouthing their friends and acquaintances. In fact, when much later, I discovered the world, I was appalled by the sniping and backbiting that went on among adults. I wasn't prepared for it.

My father's love of horses and the curious circumstances of his young life led him into the army, but I think his soul was that of an artist. He had a "feel" for things. He read, acted in amateur theatre, and drew with great accuracy. His high-relief carving of quarter-cut oak, for which he kept his tools as sharp as razors, was controlled and sensitive. This sensitivity was also extended to my own early attempts at poetry. He was interested. Genuinely interested.

From this distance, I may be putting too romantic a gloss on things. If there is a bigger truth, or a smaller, than the picture I conjure up, it escapes me now. I see my father as measured, patient, fun-loving and larger than life. His sun sign was Sagittarius, the archer, and his ruling planet, Jupiter or Jove. He was a straight shooter, loyal and jovial. That there could be so perfect a match between him and his stars almost makes me believe in astrology.

He was fifty-nine when he died. At the height of his career. It was 1944, and he was Commander-in-Chief of Atlantic Command, with headquarters in Halifax. I was twenty-seven, holidaying by the sea in New Brunswick, when my mother phoned, telling me to come quickly. My father had had a serious heart attack. Dying? How was it possible?

I arrived after an all-night drive and went straight to the hospital. In a bare, aseptic room in a white bed lay a small, crumpled figure. It was hard to believe it was my larger-than-life father. For the first time, I saw him as a human being. Mortal. And also, for the first time, I saw the burdens he had carried all his life. Illnesses, accidents, pre-medicare doctors' bills, clothes for growing children, tickets for pantomimes, roller skates, bikes, tennis rackets, with never enough money. And he—this small man on the bed—had borne them all, with vitality and good humour. He was not superman; he was life-sized, an amateur, like me. And I realized, at what was a heartbreaking time in my own life, that if he could do it, I could do it. That was his last gift.

Man Down!

by Emma Richler

For my mother

When I am very young, my mother purchases two old portraits, for my father's delectation, of the famous bare-knuckle boxers Daniel Mendoza and Tom Molineaux, posed in attitude, at the scratch. The portraits move along with us from house to house and country to country, and Dad, not much prone to gazing fondly at art upon walls, gazes fondly upon these portraits, the subjects always facing away from each other, and the frames misaligned for good measure, a pleasing and sensitive picture-hanging wrought by my mother who faces the facts about boxing and Dad's romance with boxing, and how men and animals must fight, etc., yet chooses not to be reminded of such things on her daily perambulations through the home, breezing by these two portraits she bought for my father, of two men poised like tigers, in eighteenth-century attitude, in the stance classical— Molineaux, to complicate matters, being a freed American slave, illiterate, a bruiser and never champion, Mendoza, educated, unusually articulate and, in the ring, famously artful, "scientific," as the saying goes. He was a great champion, and a Jew. I know where Mum's empathy lies. She does not need to parade it.

I gaze fondly upon the portraits also, from year to year, gaining height by increments as I stand alongside my dad, yet no greater grasp, I think, of the appeal of Messrs. Mendoza and Molineaux. My dad feels the glamour of boxing and passes it on to me in some mute manner. I do not question it.

"Daniel Mendoza," he says.

I do not recall his mentioning the freed slave by name, and I happen to know now that the two boxers never met in the ring. I like to think that in a battle between Daniel's science and Tom's power, science would win out before brutality maimed him. I like to think so, though I am in the myth-dispelling vein.

I may be guilty of mythology by supposing my father identified with Mendoza, but I am sure I love Mendoza, flaws to boot, because of my father. I note that of all the favoured epithets used, mistakenly, to describe my dad—"shy," "curmudgeonly"—curmudgeon irks me particularly. Dad was private, absorbed and economical with words, especially ones spoken aloud. To simplify: Those who do not wish to be hurt by his manner call him shy, those who choose to be affronted call him curmudgeonly. My dad was too grand a man to be curmudgeonly. Not pugnacious, not curmudgeonly. Dad's fights were never petty things. He was a fighting man, yes, but his battles were epic, championship bouts only.

I am in the myth-dispelling vein.

Here comes autumn and days of clearer thinking. I hope so. I walk with Captain, my dashing sixteen-month-old black Labrador retriever. I walk on Primrose Hill, and the park is sparkling green and blue and sharp with no shadows, yet I will entertain fancies regarding my fine dog and his Field Trial Champion gundogs, his champion pedigree of generations. I walk tall with my gundog, my gun crooked open over my forearm in the correct fashion, my gun invisible to all but me. I am a good shot. Here comes autumn and days of clear thinking!

Yesterday, the rain raced down at an angle, still summer-soft, and in between sessions of slanting rain, the wind buffeted my ears, noisy, and I thought how when a man dies, this is how the myths and fables race in, at speed, filling the head with racket, and so, being fanciful by nature, I must be careful, because Sandra Martin has asked would I write about a time, a place, an event, so far as I understand it, that elucidated my dad for me in some way, providing some new perspective, and I said, yes, I will, in the steamy summer and now it is autumn and I know that family, too, can suffer from myths and fables concerning the loved and departed, and furthermore, I worry that my father never did anything to surprise me, to cause a shift in perspective, not really, not ever.

Let me see. One evening in a restaurant in Covent Garden, following a marvellous reading my father gives at the National Theatre, I note his upper lip turn pale, a telltale sign in our family of an imminent throw-up situation, and as my dad excuses himself from the table, I announce quietly how Dad is about to be sick—a case, surely, of post-performance nerves and too much Scotch on an empty bread-box, whereupon a member of extended family reacts in disbelief and horror, this nervous throw-up state not in keeping with a certain version of Mordecai. I say nothing. When Dad returns to the table, he orders a large cognac and large espresso, instantly reassuring the disbelieving relation, who reckons the order of large espresso and large cognac suitably brawny, and quite seemly. The moment of vulnerability disappears in the fog of myth-making. Myth is so quick.

I try not to colour the memory of my grown-up, clear-sighted anticipation of Dad's nerves and Scotch-fuelled barf with the terrible recent memory of food catching in my father's esophagus in a London restaurant, the nausea heralding his awful, precipitous death too few weeks thereafter. His demise, as my mother would have it. My mother faces the facts regarding death and tragedy, but chooses not to use the word *death* in reference to my father. His demise, she says, with an arrested look of startling poignancy.

Strangely stifling today after that promise of autumn, the air still and sticky, inducing an edgy feeling in me, and recalling a summer morning at our lake house in the Eastern Townships when I wake early, very early, jetlagged and restive, to sit in the glass-walled sunroom overlooking the bay, a favourite place of my dad's on summer evenings, where he delighted especially in watching storms rush in to convulse the waters and flex the trees, calling me in to watch with him—Em! Em! Quickly!—as I also have a thing for storms. We sit in the dark, the better to see, drinks in hand, and chortle with affectionate derision at Mum, who fears a storm, worrying about trees and wildlife and water levels, and omens in the brutishness of the elements, and the passage of space shuttles, pollutants and other effects of manmade incursions into the atmospheres and stratospheres. She is not beguiled by weather. She has respect.

I sit in the sunroom this early morning on a visit from London, with only my parents in the house, and I hear their bedroom door blasting open suddenly; it can only be Dad, opening up as quietly as he knows how, and he is impervious to me in the next room espying him through a glass wall, quite naked, slipping his dressing gown on as he marches to the kitchen, taking the opportunity to scratch his own back as he goes, gripping the cuffs and swiping the material across his shoulders like a bather with a towel after a cold immersion. I see my dad through glass and am glad he does not see me, because he would be embarrassed where I am not, being altogether grown up and clear-sighted, and untroubled by the inherent vulnerability in a naked parent. I see through glass clearly. I am very grown up.

Now, what? I walk with Captain and strip off my jacket to tie it by the sleeves around my waist, amazed at Indian-summer warmth, as if the seasons were working backwards. My mind is set for autumn. Today's brazen warmth takes me by surprise. Did Dad ever surprise me?

I remember one spring in London, when Mum flies to Toronto for my nephew's third birthday, leaving my dad alone in their Chelsea flat for a few days during which period he rings me in my North London flat with surprising regularity for a man not at ease with telephones. He even braves the voicemail system when necessary, just to keep me apprised of his movements and activities in this calamitous while without her.

"Em. This is Daddy. I'm finished work and I'm going for a walk."

"Em. This is Daddy. I'm home. I'm not resting. I'm reading."

We are in the full throes of BSE, a.k.a. the "mad cow" crisis, and he rings in the evening, before the Channel 4 news, quite excited about BSE.

"Em! I'm going to watch the news, see how many cows died today. Ha ha ha ha!"

He calls after the news.

"Em! Guess what I had tonight."

"What, Dad?"

"A hot-dog omelette!"

"You had that last night, Dad!"

"I know! That's what I want to tell you. Listen. If you eat the same meal every night, YOU DO NOT HAVE TO WASH THE PAN. AND, YOU CAN USE THE SAME PLATE!"

"That's great, Dad."

"Yeah. And here: WHAT is the point of making the bed in the morning? YOU ONLY MESS IT UP AGAIN AT NIGHT!"

"That's true, Daddy."

"THERE IS TOO MUCH WORK DONE AROUND HERE! I am going to tell Florence that!"

"Okay, Dad."

On the day of her return, I receive regular bulletins from him, important information to do with cleaning and shopping.

"THIS PLACE IS A PIGSTY! Em, I wiped the counters! I fluffed up the cushions! I put away ALL the dishes! I'm knocked out! I'm exhausted! Now I'm going shopping."

"Again?"

"Yes! I've got tons to do."

He makes several trips and tells me everything he buys and what a tough job it is hauling it all home, the bouquets of white flowers, the quails' eggs, the salad leaves, the smoked salmon, the bread from Poilâne, the champagne, the Evian water, all of it. Around 8 P.M., he rings to say he needs a nap, and please, Em, wake me up in an hour, which I do, and he does not sound sleepy, his voice instead full of industry and endeavour.

"Daddy, did you rest?"

"No. I'm peeling quails' eggs."

"Dad! You need a nap!"

"Ah, I can't," he says, "I'm too excited."

This surprises me, I think, a little. Not the craving, the excitement, the still-blazing love, but the admission, the involvement of me. For a man who only ever really needed Mum to know him, he tells me much that night. He dreams of her much.

The rain is so tremendous on the way home from Primrose Hill, Captain begins to pull like a sledge dog. He is in a hurry to get us home and out of the weather, but I need to make a pit stop beneath a café awning, being blinded by rain, my spectacles as sheeted with water as a Formula One driver's in a squall. I stop hunching my shoulders and give in to the storm, drenched to the marrow of me. There is thunder and lightning, and I imagine in sudden violent changes of weather not the effects of space shuttles or even mere chaos theory, but the motions of spirits, of maybe a great ghost personage waking and wandering suddenly, like Neptune in the waters, causing shudders in the elements. What weather is this? Who goes there?

I am in a huddle of people under the café awning and I am mindful, again, of pugilism, of fighting men battling some two hundred years ago in diverse bucolic locations in and outside London, battling on occasions, for hours in bright, blinding sunshine or into fading light and shadows, in all weathers, slipping in mud or on ice, blinking in the rain, the blood, the claret, as it is known, coursing down their swollen faces straight into the ground beneath, the boxers milling and bruising on until one goes down, my father, his lifeblood coursing down into the floor beneath, his body erupting finally, protesting—no more! No more!—and my hopeless hope is that his agonies of mind, his great teeming mind, were brief, oh please.

I peruse Jack Broughton's famous rules of 1743.

Rules to be Observed in All Battles on the Stage

VII. That no person is to hit his Adversary when he is down, or seize him by the ham, the breeches or any part below the waist: a man on his knees to be reckoned down.

Man down! Man down!

II. That, in order to prevent any disputes, the time a man lies after a fall, if the second does not bring his man to the side of the square, within the space of half a minute, he shall be deemed a beaten man.

Daddy surprised me, yes, he did, because though I am ever so grown up and clear-sighted, I supposed him invincible, poised forever, as I suppose, like Mendoza toeing the line, at the scratch, poised in perpetuity, in attitude, in the stance classical.

They say it may turn unseasonably warm this afternoon, that it may rain tonight; anything can happen, that's the truth of it, but there is a distinct chill this morning as I step out with Captain and a half-moon is high and bright in a crystalline sky. Here is autumn and days of clearer thinking.

Ah, Daddy, come to the scratch. Rise! Rise.

Drive

by Eden Robinson

We drive a 1996 silver Ford Taurus, a common car in Kitamaat Village. I have waved warmly at one of them on my morning walk, thinking Dad was out for a drive, and the driver has turned out to be someone else. You can't undo a friendly wave, can't explain non-verbally, *uh, oops, thought you were my dad* and so you are stuck being eagerly approachable and having the people in the *other* silver Taurus give you half-hearted *who-the-hell-are-you?* waves back.

Our previous vehicle was a true rez car: a muffler-rattling 1988 white Pontiac Grand Am with silver polka dots (where Dad had spray-painted the rust spots), a cracked windshield and a driver's side window that was stuck three-quarters of the way up and duct-taped shut against the rain. We were stopped at a roadside check, and when I opened the driver's side door, the police officer gave my smokehouse clothes and samurai topknot a suspicious once-over. I put no effort into my appearance on Sundays when Dad and I go to the Mount Layton hot springs. We soak in the mineral hot tub and float in the big pool and have a coffee before we go home.

"What's your postal code?" the officer asked, examining my licence.

"Uh. Oops. Kept meaning to get that updated."

"How out of date is this?"

"I haven't lived in Vancouver in …" (mentally trying to remember when I moved home—was that 2003? 2004? It's 2005, so that's, uh, let's see—) "a couple of months, at least."

"Does that really matter?" Dad chimed in. "Her licence is valid, isn't it?"

A pause, while the officer gave Dad a once-over. "You are legally responsible for changing your address within ten days of moving."

Lord, I wished I was wearing something low-cut and had at least put lipstick on. I once watched my sister talk her way out of a ticket for doing a U-turn in front of a police car just outside the Pacific National Exhibition in Vancouver, but she was wearing bicycle shorts and a tank top. She didn't even have her driver's licence with her.

Dad and the police officer debate the law a little longer before we are let off with a warning. A line of cars is waiting behind us. I shut the car door and we drive off in silence. A part of my brain is turning the incident into a short story. I'm always half-present (or half-absent if you are a pessimist) from the current timeline. That's why I can't drive in cities. I flew out to Toronto to help my sister after her laser eye surgery and I drove her kids to daycare and they moaned in their safety seats, "Aunty, why is this taking so loooong?"

Afterwards, I drove my sister to Home Depot and had to enter the QEW, a four-lane highway connecting Toronto and Niagara Falls.

"Merge! Merge! You have to speed up to merge!" she shouted, chest heaving, clutching her protective sunglasses. She learned to city drive when she was a cub reporter at BCTV, and every day she fought Vancouver traffic to get to her stories and meet her deadlines. "It's called the acceleration lane because you have to *accelerate!*"

"We're okay," I said. "Someone will let us in."

"Speed up! Oh, God!"

Me, to myself: This conversation reminds me of my favourite show, *Mayday*, on the Discovery Channel. They always play recordings of the pilot and co-pilot's terse conversations just before the plane goes down in flames.

"See?" I said cheerfully. "We made it."

The speed limit was one hundred kilometres per hour, but everyone else seemed to believe that the speed limit was actually one hundred and twenty kilometres per hour.

"You have to keep up with traffic! Get in the slow lane!"

"But this is the speed limit," I said.

I learned to city drive in a sleepy two-stoplight town which, confusingly, has been named Kitimat but spelled differently from Kitamaat Village, where we live. The village is the main Haisla reserve, eleven kilometres from town. Dad took me out to the logging roads and we trundled along in our station wagon. On my maiden voyage on the Terrace highway, I hit a family of grouse. The feathers splattered up from the grill.

I pulled over and shut the engine off. My eyes grew hot and my throat caught. I hadn't even seen them until I was on top of them, a mama grouse leading a line of chicks across the road.

"Want me to drive?" Dad said.

I nodded. We exchanged seats. I went around the back so I wouldn't have the image of the body parts stuck in my head. I tried not to cry.

"They were just birds," Dad said.

Roadkill aside, the Terrace highway is my kind of driving—a long, winding road with mountains on one side, the sparkling river on the other and only our car and a speck so far ahead it could be a bus or a semi. I watch for black bears. They feed on the new grass on the side of the highway.

"You have to learn to be a Sunday driver," Dad said. "Gas hit one-nineteen a litre today. They say it's going to be one-fifty this summer."

I tried hard not to roll my eyes. Dad pumps the imaginary brake on the passenger's side if he thinks I'm going too fast. "I'm not speeding, Dad."

"I know, I know," Dad said. "But if you go five clicks slower, you'll save gas."

"Do you want to drive?"

"That's not what I'm saying. If you go ninety, even ninety-five, it adds up."

The road to town is narrow and filled with hairpin turns and steep hills. People who drive the road every day go about seventy kilometres per hour. The speed limit is fifty. When Dad drives to town, he has an entourage of cars behind him. Sometimes they'll get too impatient to wait for one of the three passing areas and try to overtake him on a corner, blindly trusting their luck. When I'm driving, I pull over once there are three cars behind me. This annoys Dad.

"I'd never let them pass me," he says. Or, "You're going the speed limit. You don't have to worry about them."

Dad was a driving machine in his younger days. He commuted from Kitamaat to Greenville when we were children, a three-and-a-quarter-hour drive. His idea of vacations was to see how far we could get before we had to turn back. Mom's idea of a vacation was to see how much we could shop. When Dad and I went on our jaunts, Mom would wave us goodbye, saying her back had had enough of Dad's jalopy.

We drove to Dawson in 1998 for the one hundredth anniversary of the Gold Rush. I took a panoramic disposable camera and my pictures of him have majestic backgrounds. (Dad sits in the cab of his prized but worn-out denim-blue Ford F-150, and it's hard to get him to smile. He's tired, he says. I have trouble adjusting to this. My father is the Energizer Bunny: He go-go-goes. He has a tremor in his right hand. His older brother has Parkinson's disease, and he hasn't told me yet but he suspects he himself does, too. "This may be my last trip," he kept saying. People try to clue you in about themselves.)

I hate driving stick, and rode the clutch. By the time we reached Pelly Crossing, we were both exhausted. We had a late lunch at the greasy spoon beside the Indian gas station. I noticed a man in blue jeans and a jean jacket because he reminded me of a younger version of Dad right down to the slicked-back pompadour. The man talked to one of the attendants, asking if he knew anyone who was heading north, and the attendant shook his head and the man struck out towards the highway.

Dad and I lingered over our fries. I was in the early stages of coffee psychosis and I was crashing and distracted. I'd slept badly in our motel room by the junction near Watson Lake. The mattress had sagged like a hammock. The *Discover the Yukon* brochure said Pelly Crossing is halfway between Whitehorse and Dawson. I wanted to cry. My arms had no functioning muscles left and (I know I said it before, but it bears repeating) I hate stick.

"Can you drive?" I said.

"For a little," he said. "But we should find a motel soon."

"Okay."

We passed the hitchhiker before the bridge and I looked at Dad and said, "I wonder if he can drive stick."

Dad examined the man in the rearview mirror. "Ask him."

He did a U-turn on the empty highway and I rolled down the passenger side window. "Can you drive stick?"

The man looked hopeful. "Yes."

"We're trying to get to Dawson," Dad said.

"Me, too," he said.

"And we're tired," I added.

"I got a truck just like this," the man said. "I'd have no problem driving."

Dad took the middle seat so he could sit between us. I'm sure he was being chivalrous, but I think it was unnecessary given that I'd been driving for two days in my grubbies and I outweighed both Dad and the hitchhiker put together. I didn't say anything, and the hitchhiker climbed in and geared up faster than Dad or I could have and we rocketed down the road. Our speed reminded me of a seventies TV show called *The Streets of San Francisco,* which opened with cars going airborne after taking hills too fast. Dad's face contorted with alarm.

"I hope you don't mind," the hitchhiker said. "But I'm late for my girl's birthday and if I don't get home soon, my ex is going to kill me."

"If we get pulled over, you're paying the speeding ticket," Dad said.

He laughed. "No speed traps up here."

The hitchhiker (I've forgotten his name. It was something simple—Evan, Ed, Eric) told us he'd driven down to Ross River to help his father fix his roof and his ex had been furious because he'd promised his daughter he'd be at her fifth birthday party and he'd said he could do both, but then his truck broke down. Dad and Hitch then lapsed into mechanese: The wacka wacka broke and the mechanic said wacka wacka wacka and he couldn't get a wacka wacka for three weeks. Dad nodded his head. Once your wacka wacka goes, good luck getting your heap to start. Cue the rueful laughter.

Hitch had worked in a mine near Dawson when he was younger; that was how he'd met his ex. She was Han, pronounced like *Han* Solo, not like *Ham,* which they found insulting. Dad said we were going to Dawson to play tourist. His interest in the Gold Rush began because he heard stories about local men who had gone north to try their luck.

Hitch told him about his mining days, and then they talked fishing, and drowsily I watched the trees blur by.

We tore into Dawson barely an hour later and arrived at his ex's house just as the party was breaking up. We knew his ex without Hitch having to point her out; her back stiffened when she spotted him exiting our truck and her glare could freeze hellfire.

"I'd give you a tour, John," Hitch said. "But, uh …"

"Good luck," Dad said.

Dad hates "wasting" money on hotels and I hate camping, so we compromised on a motel owned and operated by a woman whose eyes constantly wandered around the room even when she was talking to you. We gambled at Diamond Tooth Gertie's with the American tourists from the Skagway cruise ships and I won seventy-five dollars and lost it all and went home late that night with the sun still shining and people playing a soccer game in a field near our motel. Dad said he'd be home when he lost his twenty dollars and didn't come home until early that morning. He has a weakness for the nickel slots.

We spent the day in Dawson (panning in Bonanza Creek, touring, shopping) and had enough time left over to stay another night, but getting to our destination never holds Dad's attention and so we were off at 4 A.M. Outside of Dawson, we stopped for a car that had broken down. Three Han women stood around the rear left tire. The driver was in her mid-forties and she said she was travelling with her daughter and her grandmother. They'd gone to Skagway to pick up her daughter (puffy-eyed and forlorn and kicking the ground), who was getting out of a bad relationship. By luck, they'd met a man selling king salmon and they were loaded down and the driver said she'd considered ditching the spare tire so she could squeeze in some more fish, but decided not to be greedy and now she was glad she hadn't.

The grandmother, hunched and frail, smoked by the side of the road and I invited her into the cab to warm up because the morning air frosted our breaths. We listened to the radio and watched Dad and the driver change the tire, and when he was done, he opened the door for the grandmother and tried to help her out, but she grasped his hand and told him she had prayed for someone like him—a strong, generous man who would save them; she had prayed hard and here he was. Dad's face reddened and he ducked his head, pleased and embarrassed to be the answer to someone's prayers.

Close to home, we bumped off the highway onto the gravel road that leads to the Mount Layton hot springs. We used to be clockwork regulars, but now we come once a month or so. The every-Sunday regulars recognized Dad and they exchanged pleasantries. Dad used to drive us crazy when we were kids. Leaving the village to run errands in town, he would roll down his window and stop to chat with anyone who waved him down. Sometimes it would take us an hour to get from one end of the village to the other. You can stroll the same distance in ten minutes.

I went to the ladies' change room, dumped my stuff in a locker and waited for Dad in the hot tub, which has a roof. The big pool and the baby slides were under the open sky. You can float on your back watching the clouds roll by, but it was too cold that day to do that without heating up first. I closed my eyes and relaxed. Dad has his own speed. He'd be there when he was there.

He can drive to the hot springs himself. He's renewed his licence. The process was harder for me than for Dad. Neither of us had expected the letter from the Superintendent of Motor Vehicles. Dad's seventy-four and we thought retesting didn't start until you were eighty. But because of his Parkinson's, his file had been given a medical flag. Dad was pragmatic, wanting to know what hoops he needed to jump. He dutifully studied the books and passed his medical and visual and written, but then flunked his first driver's test for going forty kilometres per hour in a thirty-kilometre-per-hour school zone.

"We have zero tolerance for speeding in school zones," the tester said. "It's an automatic fail."

"You have two more chances at the driving exam," one of the women in the motor vehicle office said.

"And if I flunk those ones?" Dad said.

"You get to be chauffeured around."

Dad signed up for a retest, but it was in early January when I'd be visiting my sister in Toronto. We argued about this over dinner. I said he should reschedule so I could be there, and he rolled his eyes.

"I *can* take the test myself," he said.

"But you'll need a licensed driver to help you practise and stuff," I said.

"We'll figure it out," my mother said. "We're not invalids yet, Eden."

And so I flew out to Toronto, and cried on the plane and cried in my sister's guest room at night when everyone was asleep, and couldn't understand why I was crying until I realized I could not imagine my father not driving. His vehicles in various stages of repair cluttered our lawn and our basement. He loved his cars and his trucks and taking off on a whim, and I wasn't ready for it to end.

The day of his test, I couldn't bring myself to call home. When the phone rang and my sister answered, I listened for clues and she sounded pleasantly surprised, so I wasn't caught off guard when he told me he'd passed. I whooped and he laughed and the world was right again.

"But I have to retest in two years," he said grumpily.

"How's your picture look?" I said.

We talked, and then he said he had to go get some groceries before the stores closed and I said, "I love you, Dad."

There was the usual pause, but instead of hanging up without saying anything like he usually does, Dad said, "Your car misses you."

The Archaeology of My Dad

by Rebecca Snow

Subtlety is not my father's forte. Why else would he choose a night in Monte Carlo to throw a monumental twist into our lives? It was the latest port of call on our annual summer sailing holiday, and the first time two of my siblings and I had properly been together for months. Mythical Monte Carlo—a city that until that point existed for us only in the movies—now the indelible, visceral backdrop for a dramatic declaration.

The way he told us will haunt me forever. "Now kids, I have something very serious to tell you. You might find it shocking, or sad, and it might change your lives." My worst nightmare began to unfold in front of me. He was dying. I couldn't believe it. I was sitting between my elder brother and my younger sister. My heart stopped. I wanted to slap my hand over Dad's mouth. I could see that Mom knew what was coming, and I wanted her to stop vacillating between the comforting, brave smile and the gravely serious face. I wanted the ridge the restaurant sat on to give way so I could slip down the precipice into the harbour and float off in a sea of bobbing Monaco poker chips. Anything to stop Dad saying what I thought he was going to say next.

"You may be angry," he said. *Damn right I will be; I've been praying daily since Mom taught me The Lord's Prayer—I even blow God a kiss every night.* And now my painfully adored father was about to stage some sort of exit from our lives?

As a kid, my worst recurring nightmare was Dad being stabbed in a supermarket in front of me, his wobbly whistle fading away as he bled to death in front of me. Dad is a well-known television host in Britain, and somehow his public exposure disturbed my young active mind. When the IRA started blowing up journalists in London, I'd check under his car for bombs on a regular basis, much to his amusement. I was petrified of a life without Dad. Once I tried to tell him how much I loved him, but couldn't quantify it properly in words, so ended up blurting out, "Dad, I'd take a bullet for you." It was an absurd thing to say, but his strip of a mouth stretched into a smile, his faraway eyes wrinkled up, and he put his huge, great hand on mine.

Are we naturally more devoted to the parent that we resemble the most? It is biological fact that I am my mother's daughter because I dramatically screamed out of her womb, demanding that the umbilical cord be sliced from around my neck. But it is even clearer to me that I am my father's daughter. I have his pencil-thin lips, long nose with a bump at the bridge, and inelegant, big-knuckled hands. My maternal grandmother occasionally flinches when I inadvertently pull a face and I know she's just seen Dad in my features.

Dad and I both point at people when we talk to them. We find it hard to control the volume of our voices, we hate small talk and love crosswords and maps; we both wake up in the middle of the night panicking over something that pales into insignificance in the light of day. Dad knows that it disturbs me to be so like him. He sighs and puts his arm around me and says, "You are a bit of a social misfit like your father"—

as if that is some consolation. I even have his whistle. My friends always laugh at me because I whistle with a trill, a wobble, like a man.

He continued: "About thirty-three years ago, I was on holiday in the Middle East …"

Hang on, this doesn't sound like a terminal illness! The thought of him leaving my mom shot into my head.

Dad tends to airbrush his past with a sheen of gentle forgetfulness. He never talks about leaving his first wife and two kids, for example, but one memory broke through recently when Dad recalled, with some surprise, how his two small kids used to hide under the table when he picked them up from their mother's house at weekends. Now adults, my half-brother and half-sister are still trying to work out their relationship with Dad, and he can't figure out why.

For most of his life, Dad didn't really "get" the family thing. His childhood was worlds apart from mine. In a very English way, he was sent to boarding school at seven, and the only story he tells about the experience was that he was bullied into sending his teddy bear home after one week of being there. His mother received a pathetic little package in the mail, with no explanation, just the bear inside. He doesn't remember his dad ever hugging him. His parents both died well before I was born. Perhaps that is why I find him so much more vulnerable than my mom.

When I was a kid, I fantasized melodramatically about my parents divorcing, guiltily realizing that if they were to separate, it would be an easy decision to stick with Dad. I knew that I would choose him because I'd feel sorry for him. He doesn't realize it, but he'd collapse without his family. The image of him packing a little suitcase with hankies and socks, going into the conservatory to pick up his beloved African statues that Mom has always hated, and exiting our front door forever with his precious ancient history books tucked under his arm was too much for me.

These thoughts were whizzing through my mind in Monte Carlo when Dad finally reached the point: "I met a rather wonderful French woman, and well, one thing led to another. We were quite careless ..."

My elder brother's eyes widened; "Oh my God, Dad ..." And like a domino effect, the realization hit me, and then, after a delay, my little sister gasped.

Dad was telling us that he had just discovered he had a thirty-three-year-old son. I had a new brother, who in turn had a son himself who was about half my age. I was sixteen and suddenly I had five siblings instead of four.

Matthieu, a young man from Paris, had phoned my dad at the office a month earlier. He had introduced himself warily, mentioning his mother's name and his date of birth, and asking my dad if he could possibly be his father. Without missing a beat, Dad replied, "Well, are you tall and handsome?" I think Dad had been trying to make himself laugh. Would he have panicked otherwise? He was trying to make us laugh, too, there in the restaurant in Monte Carlo over our half-eaten dinner.

We weren't quite ready to laugh. But we weren't crying either. My first reaction was utter relief. So he wasn't dying, and he wasn't leaving Mom. I could put my nightmares back in their box. Then I felt resentment: typical Dad, saying it all the wrong way, jolting me into a panic.

I find it slightly puzzling to understand where my devotion and attachment to Dad came from. Dad has always referred to children as "luggage," and he carried us, as babies, under his arm like inconvenient bundles. When we were kids, he worked hard all week, missing our bedtime because he was anchoring the evening news. He believed that fathering involved dragging his small, complaining children out to a historic battlefield in the rain on a Sunday. He would spend the day telling us about the Battle of Hastings. Then we'd go home to read about the discovery of the tomb of Tutankhamen from his favourite book, *Gods, Graves & Scholars*. I used to sit there listening to the stories, eating my yogourt with a blob on my nose, just to see if he noticed, which he never did.

We weren't neglected by our father; we knew he loved us very much. But to him, we were not kids—we were curious little people who could be entertained or ignored at his convenience. He would talk to us as though we were adults and never over-indulge us like many of our friends' fathers.

Dad nicknamed me Hatchibombotar when I was five. It is the name of the street cleaner elephant in the Babar books. I used to wonder why he didn't name me after the cute princess elephant, Flora, or the ballerina elephant? Even Coco, the clown elephant, would have been easier for a child to relate to. But a street cleaner …?

He has a strange mind, and is half deaf, which appears to make him forget our names for some reason. A friend once called my house asking for me, and Dad said, "Rebecca who?" He is an emotional enigma. One minute, he is completely detached and forgets you exist, and the next, he's so overbearing that you feel suffocated. He was never the kind of dad who noticed whether his kid was walking beside him or two blocks behind him, but he used to run beside my train waving, and breaking my heart, as I went back to university every semester.

After my father's bombshell disclosure, my little sister and I walked in silence back to Monte Carlo harbour ahead of the rest of the family. We got into our pyjamas and squeezed into the tiny bathroom to brush our teeth, staring at each other's shocked faces in the mirror. We climbed into our cabin and turned off the light. Then, through the dark, came a little, excited voice: "Bec, this kind of thing only happens in *Neighbours*." The melodrama of our favourite soap opera was the only point of reference that we had to cling onto as our heads spun with the idea of a new sibling.

I went over the math again to make sure that I shouldn't hate Dad for the revelation. When Matthieu was conceived, Mom had no idea Dad even existed and we kids "weren't even thinked of," as she used to say about life before we were born.

And that is when I realized how little I knew about Dad's past. I didn't know what his nickname was as a child, whether he did crosswords with his dad, how much he loved his parents, how many girlfriends he had or their names. I was brought up on stories of my mom squabbling with her siblings, cheerleading with a huge beehive hairdo, flirting with Boy Scouts on canoe trips, and touring Tuscany with an Italian hunk called Rocco.

We used to laugh because all the photos of Dad in his youth are fairly straight, all static, black and white, while Mom has colourful pictures of "Pussy Galore" parties, a boyfriend writing her name in the sand on a beach, and endless happy friends. It was as though they came from different eras. Dad's past was not in Technicolor like Mom's was. Mom always joked as we looked through our family scrapbooks, "Your Dad is the only person I know who missed the sixties completely!"

And suddenly Dad had a "Rocco," too—or at least a Roccette. Until this point, I'd never really imagined him as a young man. Now, with this new aperture into Dad's past, I looked at the once-distant photos of Dad at twenty-six, standing in a Greek amphitheatre or sitting at a newsdesk, and my imagination ran away with me. Who was standing just out of frame? Some beautiful Greek woman? His dad proudly taking the photo of him at his first job? I had always thought it strange that someone so captivated by history and archaeology found it so unimportant to think or talk about his own past. Now, suddenly his past was being disinterred and exhibited for us all to wonder over, especially the lost sixties.

The British tabloids loved the story of Dad's newfound son. *"My love child and my new family," "Don't tell me you're my son!" "I have a secret son!"* the headlines screamed. Unlike us, Dad was relieved when the news went public. He no longer had to worry about who the press would find out from, and what distorted story they would produce. I was never one of those kids with famous-parent-resentment syndrome, but this episode made all of us frustrated with Dad because it should have been a private matter. Dad almost took for granted that we'd welcome a new brother into the family, but to have to grin and deal with it publicly? Overnight, the issue was suddenly between Dad, us and *The Daily Mail.* We had photographers outside the house and Dad had to hide out at friends' houses until the press withdrew for the night.

Digging deep inside myself, I failed to find any feeling of resentment towards my new brother. I was fascinated to meet him, and I went with my dad to the airport to pick him up the first time he came to visit. He had agreed to fly over with his wife and meet the family for a weekend. I was excited, quizzing my dad about what he was like— asking, "Does he look like me? Will I recognize him even though I've never met him?" I scrutinized every man who came out of the arrivals gate until my eyes hurt. I didn't know him at first, but when he was standing in front of me, I saw my dad in him. I wanted to shout, "You have our nose! You have our chin!"

But I also didn't want to scare him off right away. I was suddenly petrified that he'd be disappointed in us, his new family. What was this thirty-three-year-old stranger thinking when he stared at his teenaged sister? A sister was a new phenomenon to Matthieu. This self-induced revelation had landed him a second father, two half-brothers and three half-sisters.

There could never be any doubt that they are father and son. The doctor who did their DNA test must have had to suppress a smile when they came in saying they wanted to make sure they were related. How hard was it for him not to blurt out, "Guys, save the thousands of pounds; do me a favour, take a look in the mirror"? It is blindingly obvious; they are identical.

After the initial shock and excitement, I did feel a little suspicious. Can you really spend thirty years not knowing that there is a version of you living and breathing and having your grandchildren somewhere else in the world? I had to believe Dad when he said that he knew nothing about his eldest son for half of his life; otherwise I'd hate him. I took my lead from Mom, who was unconditionally supportive about it. Some members of the family kicked up a fuss, and Dad did not try to stop them. Instead, he held up those large, frank hands of his in confused surrender.

If Matthieu had been born after the siblings I grew up with, then it would have been a different story. That phone call Matthieu made to my Dad would have rumbled the earth that my family is solidly rooted in. A fault line would have ripped through our happiness, thrown us all off our feet and eventually left each one of us on little dry, sad islands very far away from the dad who had betrayed us by having an affair. And seeing him standing there with his little suitcase and *Gods, Graves & Scholars* under his arm would have broken my heart.

Perhaps Matthieu considered all this before he boldly picked up that phone. What had brought him to contact Dad after all those years? He had wanted to find his real father because he had children of his own. He had started to wonder about the missing half of his family. He wasn't holding out for new relationships; he had a very happy family and a non-biological father whom he loved. Still, meeting Dad and the rest of us explained so much to him.

As a kid, Matthieu had always surprised his family with inexplicable character traits. He loved orienteering and displayed an interest in all things military. He made a cadet force out of his cousins and brothers, and marched about ordering them around. They called him "Little Hitler." No doubt he was play-fighting the *maudit anglais* as any proud, history-loving French boy would do. His laidback French family wondered where on earth this eccentric, verging on fanatical, tendency came from.

Cut back to my dad, aged twelve, arranging his Irish cousins into battalions and acting out famous battles. Fast-forward forty years to Dad marching his own children in a military formation around Buckingham Palace, teaching us to "present arms" with our umbrellas.

I can't help but think that Matthieu would have appreciated those family marches around the palace more than we did, but I wonder how horrified he would have been as a child fighting his Anglo-French wars, to learn that he was biologically as English as he was French.

As well as the genetic parallels, some uncanny coincidences link Dad and Matthieu. Estranged father and son in London and Paris, both married blonde Canadian girls from the same neighbourhood in Toronto. Mom and my sister-in-law went to the same high school. My mom's sister went to university with Matthieu's mother-in-law. The world can be terrifyingly small.

I still don't really know if my dad was hugely strong or far too emotionally detached about discovering he had another son. He has never talked about how he dealt with the revelation that he had missed half of the life of his eldest child. But he is from the generation of British males for whom being emotionally clued in is alien. Dad probably had to wave goodbye to his emotions when he packaged up that teddy bear at boarding school and sent it home to his mother. I have been told that Dad did not cry at his own mother's funeral. But, in the end, I think that the entire Matthieu incident jerked Dad into an emotional awakening.

Several years after the Matthieu revelation, I was spending some time exploring the archaeological ruins of Latin America (*Gods, Graves & Scholars* had the intended effect on me). I fell in love with an

Ecuadorian, and after six months I had to leave him to go back to England and university. I was devastated. I was by myself in transit in Guatemala for a week and my heart was in pieces. Naturally, I expected my mom to be the most sympathetic and comforting to me. But, to my horror, on the phone she told me to get over it and try to enjoy my last week of travelling. I was weeping pathetically when Dad came on the line, and he started to try to comfort me. I was ready to say something along the lines of, "You, of all people, won't understand, you emotional clutz ..." when he softly told me about a girl he had once met in New York when he was in his teens. He said that she was the first person he fell in love with, and it was the most painful thing to leave her; he understood why I was so unhappy. That was exactly what I wanted to hear. He knew how I felt. To me, this was the most sensitive piece of fathering he had accomplished. He was digging hard into his past to try to identify with his nineteen-year-old lovesick daughter, drawing from his own experiences way back in the depths of his mind.

Coming face to face with that part of his past ten years ago was good for Dad. He's turned into a late-blooming family man. It took him more than thirty years to ease into fatherhood and break through the emotional barrier so carefully built by his quasi-Victorian upbringing and confused sense of family.

It is wonderful to watch Matthieu and Dad discover each other. They laugh like boys when they exchange stories about strange character similarities. We meet up in London, Paris and Toronto, and it feels very natural when we are all together. Dad was greatly amused to take Matthieu's eldest son to a museum in London recently and send his Anglo-French grandson back home with a photograph of himself posing next to a waxwork model of the Duke of Wellington, that great English general who finally defeated Napoleon and the French at the Battle of Waterloo.

Dad (the unlikely family man) now has a total of five young grandchildren from his first two sons, who are all very attached to him. They spend hours with him, playing chess or working on his model railways (something that we as kids showed little interest in). Dad still talks to them like they are adults. He visibly adores them, and he only occasionally forgets that they are beside him, holding onto his hand. No doubt he will soon begin to read *Gods, Graves & Scholars* to them, but this time around he seems a little more clued in about it all. Is he making up for lost time, conscious of filling the absence that he left in their fathers' lives?

When I see Dad with his grandchildren, I wonder what his father would have been like as a grandfather. I never knew him, and Dad hardly talked about him, but not having a paternal grandfather is disturbing. I sometimes squint at a bent-over white-haired old man, trying to imagine he is Dad in ten years' time. But it is no good. I simply cannot imagine him as an elderly man.

I am terrified when I think of my kids missing their grandfather. In an echo of my recurring nightmare when I was a kid, my worst fear now is that Dad won't be around to be an absent-minded, unconventional but overwhelmingly doting grandfather for my little bits of "luggage" whenever they come along.

Becoming Canadian

by Tina Srebotnjak

If you travel along Dupont Avenue in Toronto's west end, you come across a place called New Canadians Lumber. I have never driven by that spot without being strangely and deeply moved. I know nothing about the company—other than that it's a lumberyard—and maybe the name doesn't mean anything. But to me, it's shorthand for the Canadian immigrant dream. We leave our homelands, we come here, we build new lives.

That is my family's story, and it all starts with my father. As I write this, it has been six months since his death, and as happens after such a great and irreplaceable loss, he has been very much in my thoughts. Especially since he left us a memoir—we found it only after he died— and so in these bittersweet days, it has been my journey to follow his.

The memoir was written in a notebook, in his beautiful hand. It was entirely in Slovenian, the language of his birth, except for the last four words, which were in English, the language of his adopted home-land. The memoir broke my heart all over again, because it spoke volumes about the kind of man my father had been—a man who gave up everything to grasp a new life, and whose gratitude for that life was unbounded. This is how it starts:

> I am aware that the evening of my life is getting near to its inevitable ending. Many times, I've thought I should describe to my family the life I had in the time of the Second World War. I want my children and my children's children to know my past. For this reason, I've decided to start writing today, so they can feel really happy they are in Canada.

My father then tells us his war story, which was one of constant upheaval and escape. He was only nineteen when Germany invaded Yugoslavia in 1941, and was soon conscripted to work in a munitions factory in Austria. As the war continued, the factory's quota was upped, and my dad worked twelve-hour shifts, seven days a week. Eventually, he decided he'd had enough, and lit out for the nearby Swiss border. He picked a rainy night for his escape, hoping the weather would mean fewer border guards, but he was caught. It was his bad luck that that same day five French prisoners of war had escaped from a nearby camp, and the German guards were convinced my dad had had something to do with that. He was turned over to the Gestapo, and sent to a concentration camp just outside Vienna. It didn't take him long to realize that the camp was a holding tank— when a sufficient number of prisoners was collected, they were shipped out to Auschwitz or Dachau. Again, he plotted an escape, and this time he was successful. He headed for Vienna and wandered aimlessly around the city, trying to figure out what to do.

Finally, he decided to take a huge risk—he would throw himself on the mercy of the Vienna police. A sympathetic captain listened to his story, and advised him that the only out he could see was for Dad to join the German army. It wasn't ideal, but it would get him out of the crosshairs of the Gestapo. So, that's what he did. He was sent to the eastern front, was wounded twice, and finally, in 1944, on his twenty-second birthday, he managed to hook up with the Czech resistance, where he spent the rest of the war. After the war ended, he was conscripted yet again—this time by the Russians, as a Russian–German translator. Finally, in August 1945, he was free to return to Slovenia, and what he hoped would be a normal life.

For a time, it was. He met my mother. The way she tells it, she was walking up a hill and he was walking down. The view must have been pretty good from both sides, because love bloomed. He wrote her a wildly romantic letter asking for permission to court her. If she refused, he told her, the ship he was preparing for his life's journey would surely founder. This is a story I heard for the first time only after his death, and I cherish this glimpse of him as a young man in love.

My parents married and started a family. By 1952, they had two little girls, but again the wide world intervened in their lives. Yugoslavia was by then a communist country, and Dad had to do his time in the Yugoslav army, where they had a daily "political hour." Dad quickly discovered that if you were not a member of the Communist Party—and he had no desire to be—and especially if you had served in the German army, even as an unwilling conscript, your future in Slovenia was pretty bleak. In fact, he soon learned there were plans afoot to send him off—yet again—to a forced labour camp in the southern part of the country.

That was when he decided to leave. On a lovely June day, he told two lies. He told my mother he was being sent on a work-related course, leaving her a letter that she would receive that evening as she waited to meet him at the bus stop. His rationale was that when my mother was questioned about his whereabouts—as she surely would be—she would honestly be able to tell them nothing. He told his employer he was at home sick. This ruse bought him some time, enough to leave Yugoslavia on foot and cross over into Italy. In the following months, he made his way to Austria. From there, he emigrated to Canada, signing on as a farm labourer to pay back the cost of his passage. He scrimped and saved, and finally, in 1955, he was able to bring his family to Canada. We were by now three little girls, as my mother had been pregnant with me when he left.

Those three years were very hard for my mother. Initially, she was ashamed and heartbroken that her husband had left her and her little girls behind. Then, as Dad started writing to her about his plans, and sending her parcels filled with little trinkets from Canada, she knew that soon she too would have to leave her world behind. When the time came, she said a wrenching goodbye to her own parents, with whom we'd been living, and the four of us boarded the *Arosa Star* in Bremerhaven, bound for Quebec City. What was Mom thinking on that ten-day journey, as the only home she'd ever known receded in the distance and she headed for a new start with a husband she hadn't seen in three years? When I ask her that question, she tells me she was mostly giddy with anticipation. Soon, she would see the man she loved, and her family would be reunited. She told me she used to think of it as "wanting her own bread," meaning, I think, that she would once again be mistress of her own house. The future was unknowable, but she was anxious to take up the challenge.

Meanwhile, my father was driving from Highland Creek, Ontario, to Quebec to pick us up. He had a beat-up old car, and inevitably, somewhere en route it broke down. He managed to get it to a mechanic, a man who spoke almost no English. But they communicated well enough for my dad to explain that he was on his way to pick up his family. The mechanic spent two hours fixing the car, and when it was time to settle the bill, he refused to take any money. It was, he said in his rudimentary English, his gift to our family. My father's first encounter with the Two Solitudes was an extremely gratifying one.

Dad continued on his journey and was waiting at the dock when we landed. My mother spotted him right away. "There—the man in the furry collar!" she excitedly told us. (My father had described what he would be wearing in a letter, and although she identified him right away, he couldn't see us.) It would be another three hours of waiting—while we went through the immigration process—before we finally ran into his arms. And so it was that at three years of age, I saw my father for the first time. I have a hazy memory of this, but realize it may be wishful thinking. What I do have is a recently found treasure, a picture of the two of us that must have been taken in our first few months together.

I knew the bare outlines of this story, but very few details. When I was young, I asked my father questions about his past, but he never answered in any detail. And of course, my own life seemed far more fascinating to me than the distant past, and to my great regret, I just stopped asking. That all changed in October 2005, when my father rose to speak at a family gathering. The occasion was the fiftieth anniversary of our arrival in Canada. We had dinner at a lovely restaurant, and all five children (two boys had been born in Canada) and their children were there. Mom and Dad, so unassuming in everyday life, looked like European royalty that day. Mom spoke first—about the great joy her children had brought her. Then Dad stood and told us how hard the decision to leave had been, and how proud he was that he had made it. He wanted a future of endless possibilities for his children, and that was what he had delivered. At the close of his speech, he said, "And to end, I'd just like to say that whenever my time comes, do not be sad for too long. For you will see a smile and happy expression on my face, with the knowledge that I did achieve what I set out to do."

What he also achieved that night, I came to see, was his farewell to us. He hadn't yet received a formal diagnosis of the lung cancer that would take him just two short months later, but he knew in his heart that time was short. Not a guy normally given to big splashy events, he had agitated for this party for weeks. When I watch him making that speech on tape now (thank God, we recorded it) it couldn't be clearer to me what his intentions were. This is what he wanted us to remember.

The Canada we came to in 1955 was nothing like the Canada of today. Multicultural Toronto was still in the future. In the early days, we lived on a farm that no longer exists, having long ago been swallowed by the suburban sprawl of Mississauga. My sisters and I were the only ethnic kids in our school. In a class filled with Linda Smiths and Jane Clarks, my name stood out like a beacon of otherness. I can still remember how I would squirm on the first day of school every year. The teacher would have a class list, and would proceed to read everyone's name. Eventually, she would pause, look confused and vaguely alarmed, and I knew she'd come to my name. Not only was my last name a killer, but my first name was also unheard of. Martina is a name you hear quite often these days—thank you Ms. Navratilova— but in my day, it was thought to be bizarre, and distinctly uncool. (I finally switched over to Tina in high school.) Years later, my poor brother would be saddled with Aloyz as a first name, which pretty soon bit the dust in favour of Tony.

As I got older and developed the confidence not to want to be like everyone else, I came to love my name. It *was* unique, and although it remained difficult to pronounce, it became increasingly common to meet people who also had exotic names from elsewhere. When I married, and had the option of changing my name to the much easier "Stewart," I didn't consider it for a moment. Tina Srebotnjak was quite simply who I was, and suddenly to become someone else was just not on.

But when you're young, mortification lurks around every corner. School lunches were a good example. In the days before the perfume of garlic was appreciated, our "smelly sandwiches" were another embarrassment. We would often bring salami to school, and I can recall asking my mom to make me "Canadian" sandwiches, which, from what I could tell, were composed uniquely of peanut butter and jam. And we girls were certainly not fashion plates. Thank goodness for those Catholic school uniforms! I still cringe when I look at my First Communion picture—I am the only girl out of fifteen wearing heavy black shoes.

My parents also didn't do what most immigrants today do—they didn't find a community of their own and settle there. We were assimilationists. There was a big push to learn English and fit in with the people around us. We girls, aged six, five and three upon arrival, learned the language in a heartbeat, the way kids do, but for my parents, it was much more difficult. My dad spoke English pretty well, having been here for two years already, but my mother was completely at sea. I so clearly remember the little book she used—little stick figures, with phrases underneath. The one that always did her in was "I put my hat on my head." "Hat" and "head" sounded exactly the same to her, and we girls would dissolve in laughter as she announced that she was putting her head on her hat. But mostly, she relied on us to learn the language. It became the rule that we would speak English at home. The good news was that my mother picked up the language in no time, the bad news was that we kids lost the Slovenian of our birth.

My early childhood was idyllic. My dad was the foreman on a farm, and a house was provided to him as part of his salary. We girls just loved it—fifty-five acres of strawberries, beans and apple orchards. Irrigation sprinklers to run through in the summer (although we learned quickly that it wasn't done to run through them nude.) My dad worked hard, and my mother cleaned the farm-owner's house. We had very little money, but didn't know it and so lived in oblivious contentment. One of my fondest memories is of my dad coming home from the fields at dinnertime. I would run to greet him, and he would hoist me up on his shoulders. I would cover his eyes with my hands, and he would make a great show of losing his way. He'd be heading right for the apple tree in front of our house, and I'd be squealing with laughter, shouting, "Not that way, Daddy!"

There were no vacations, and not many treats, but boy did we appreciate the special things when we got them. Every once in a while my mother would take us shopping with her, and we would sit at the lunch counter at Woolworths and order hamburgers and cokes. I have eaten in Canada's finest restaurants, have had spectacular meals in France and Italy, but none of them can match my memory of those burgers.

Most of the time, though, we ate at home. My father worked two jobs his entire life, one full-time and one part-time. I know that means he must not have been home a lot, but my recollection is that he was around all the time. I think that's because when he was home, he was really present. He and my mother simply did not go out, and if they did go to visit a friend, we went with them. We didn't know what a babysitter was. Partly it was a money issue—every spare cent went towards a down payment on a much-longed-for house.

As an adult, I realize what a sacrifice that was. Not the missed dinners out, but the isolation of living without a social or family network. Unlike many immigrants, we came on our own. There was no extended family here to greet us, and none ever came. We didn't move into a Slovenian community, and although my parents had a few Slovenian friends, we lived our lives in English. How hard that must have been for them, to always live outside their comfort zone, to speak so rarely in the language of their dreams.

We were renters, of course, and we moved several times in the hope of trading up. (I went to four different elementary schools, and each time my name had to be introduced all over again.) There was an ill-fated venture on a chicken farm, where we lived for two years. But finally, in 1964, my parents bought a house, a brand new three-bedroom bungalow where my mother still lives today. Next to their children, that house was everything to them. They took such joy in every small improvement they could make. They didn't believe in buying on time, so we accumulated pieces of furniture at a slow but steady pace. It was years before my mother allowed us to take the plastic covering off the living room couch and chair. My dad would paint the house from top to bottom every few years, the windows were blindingly clean, the driveway was swept—*swept*—continually, and the gardens were impeccable. That house had curb appeal to burn.

Unfortunately for us girls, though, my mother demanded perfection inside the house as well, and we had a full roster of duties. There were stacks of ironing to do, not to mention dishes, vacuuming, dusting and making beds, all of which were carried out with military precision. And every Saturday, it was down on our hands and knees to wash the kitchen floor. Our friends would be at the mall, and we'd be home cleaning. We hated that, but we never thought of rebelling. I have a crystal-clear memory of doing the floor (wash, wax and polish) with my hair in giant brush rollers—my idea of getting dolled up for a date. My parents were both surprisingly relaxed about boys, although I think that's because my sister Rose, the oldest, had already fought many battles on that front.

My father was a self-taught handyman, and he had a great work-shop in the basement. He was a man who felt that everything should have its place. Each of his dozens of screwdrivers stood in its own little slot, and each Christmas decoration of my mother's had its own little hook in the cupboard he built for her. Opening that cupboard was like stacking nesting dolls. There was not one inch of unused space. In fact, the entire basement was his handiwork. He finished the rec room, built a little cold cellar, and when I was in university, carved out a separate bedroom for me. (Up till that time, the three of us girls—young women by then—all shared one small bedroom.) That new room of my own was my sanctuary for the remaining years I lived at home.

Dad's great gift as builder and fixer was something we as adult children all benefited from. He built fences, finished bathrooms, installed plumbing, hung wallpaper and painted walls for each one of us in turn. But as generous as he was with his time and expertise, he could be a stingy man when it came to compliments. While my mother gushed at every achievement, no matter how loosely you applied that word, my dad was strangely unforthcoming. If I brought home a great report card or won an award, he acted as if it was nothing less than he expected. When I became a television and radio host, and people would sometimes recognize me, he went out of his way to be unimpressed. That's not to say that he wasn't proud of me—I knew he was—he just wasn't a man to whom praise came easily, something all five of us children had to learn to accept.

In 1971, my parents fulfilled another dream when we became Canadian citizens. My mother and father knew they would be quizzed about their knowledge of Canada, and they pored over their study guides, memorizing the capitals of all the provinces. It was a family joke that my mother was so flustered by the good looks of the Mounties in attendance—she says it was their shiny boots—that she couldn't remember the capital of Saskatchewan when asked. She passed anyway. If you ever want to appreciate Canada, go to a citizenship ceremony. They are festivals of hope and love—you can feel it coming in waves from the assembled families when they are called up to receive their certificates.

As each of his children went out into the world, I think my dad felt his own life had been validated. He became a grandfather, and in the last year of his life, a great-grandfather. This is the last paragraph of his memoir:

> Today I live alone with my wife—all three daughters and two sons, who were born in Canada, have grown and gone. My children all have good jobs. I think about that many times, and I figured out that my long journey was satisfying, because I finally got to Canada, and my family and I got Canadian citizenship. We live in prosperity; we don't miss anything.
>
> And then those four words in English: "O Canada, thank you."

O Dad, thank *you*.

My Father's Shoes

by Susan Swan

If I had sent my father a letter a few years ago, I would have written something like this: "Dear Dad. Thanks a lot, you narcissistic son of a bitch, for ignoring me most of my childhood and giving all your time to your patients instead of your family. And thanks another bunch for dying from overwork when I was seventeen. Why did you work so hard anyway? I'll show you by shutting you out of my heart and making a name for myself as a writer. Your resentful, mad-as-hell daughter, Susan."

If I sent the same letter now, I might say: "Dear Dad: Why has it taken me all these years to see you as a person? And to understand that your reasons for working so hard as a country doctor had nothing to do with me? Your early death was tragic, but your values of judiciousness, loyalty and compassion for others have been a moral compass all my life. By the way, I've never stopped writing about how much I love you. Susan."

How did my father go from being the object of my anger to

someone more human? To begin with, my father's shoes were bigger than the shoes of other fathers I knew. As a small girl, I used to put my favourite doll inside one of his size-twelve brogues from Dack's and push it around as if my doll were driving a motor launch like the one my father kept in a Penetanguishene boathouse. His huge shoes—brown brogues for his brown suits, black brogues for everyday wear and two-tone brogues for summer—were arranged on closet shelves below the drapery of his gigantic clothes. Nearby, a tall dresser sheltered a mountain of white handkerchiefs and the handmade white cotton shirts whose pockets had been especially enlarged so they were deep enough to hold his custom-made spectacles.

The bedroom he shared with my mother in our Midland, Ontario, home was like a stage set awaiting a giant in a fairy tale. Big-headed and dark-haired, my father stood over six foot four in his stocking feet and weighed close to three hundred pounds. He was too big for our household scales, so he went to the train station at night when nobody was around and weighed himself on the freight scales. As a girl, I was fascinated by the sight of him in a doorway, his body blocking out the light except for a few bright rays winking up and down the edges of his large frame.

When I was invited to my friends' houses, I always noticed that their mothers would clean up their living rooms and wax their kitchen floors because "the doctor's daughter" was coming. Next to the minister, my father was the most important person in our town and I coped with his larger than life persona by escaping into a world of stories and make-believe.

I had no idea then that these playful games would continue into my adult life. Instead of struggling to fill his oversized shoes, I (unknowingly) devoted my imagination to his memory and tried to re-create my lost parent from the shoes up. Building on fragments of experience, I wrote about imperfect yet vital father figures in my novels. Like my father, these literary characters were often flawed physical giants, lacking the time (and the foresight) to help their fictional daughters mature into adults.

Last year, I began working on a novel about a country doctor named Morley Bradford. (This character had appeared in a marginal way in an earlier novel of mine, *The Wives of Bath,* and closely resembled my father. In this new work, Morley is now the focal point of the story.) Not long after I started my book, I had a dream about meeting my father outside the old Carnegie Library in Midland. He was hurrying (no doubt off to see a patient), but I stepped in front of him and said, "Dad?" He stopped and exclaimed, "Suzabelle!" Holding each other lovingly, we stood looking into each other's eyes. He was still taller, but I was my full height and the age I am now and the two of us were smiling as if we were seeing each other as people for the first time.

Waking up from my dream, I realized that for years I had been dealing with my imagined father—not my real parent. He had acknowledged me in the dream and I had returned the favour, and my dream suggested it was time to exchange my child's understanding for an adult perspective. It struck me that my new book required me to look at my father differently, that I had to try to get inside him instead of peering at him from the character of his daughter, Mouse. To help me write from this perspective, I decided I needed to research my father's life and find out who he was.

My father was born in Cabbagetown in Toronto on September 11, 1901. His father, William, a postal worker, was a tall man too, and his mother, Gertrude Smith, was a public school teacher. The Swans were from County Cavan, Ireland, and had been recruited by the 66th Regiment in Ireland in 1823. They were shipped to Quebec and eventually applied for land grants near Penetanguishene in the 1830s.

Most of the Swans stayed on the family farm on the Vasey side road near Midland, Ontario, but my grandfather moved to Toronto and my father grew up in the family home at 36 Metcalfe Street. My father's parents lived as a low-income family. However, my grandfather's government position made him more financially secure than many of their neighbours living in what was then an Anglo-Irish slum.

My grandmother's family came from Whitby and was well-to-do. Her father, my great-grandfather, was a button manufacturer from England who built an English farm on the grounds of what is now the Whitby Mental Health Centre. My grandmother was a member of St. Peter's Anglican parish in Cabbagetown. According to a family story, Winston Churchill, who was on a tour of Canada, dropped in to the church during my father's christening. That chance encounter led to my father's somewhat portentous full name: Dalton Churchill Swan. But to his friends, he was always "Tudder" or "The Great Tudder"—the nickname my grandfather gave him when he was a baby.

My grandmother had exacting standards. If my father scored ninety-eight percent on his math test, she would ask why his mark wasn't one hundred. His response was to study harder to achieve this goal. When my grandfather William died, my father was only twelve. My father took responsibility for the family even though he was the youngest boy. After all, my father was already several inches taller than his older brother, Minto. The day after my grandfather's death, a family friend invited my father into his parlour and gave him a cigar. "You're man of the house now, Tud," he said. "Your mother is depending on you."

Nobody explained to my father that he was too young for the role. Three years later, his high marks catapulted him into medical school; he graduated as a GP at the age of twenty in 1921 and he began supporting his mother financially, a task he performed for the rest of his life.

He took the offer of an assistant's position or "locum" with a doctor in Midland and fell in love with Georgian Bay. He married Jane Cowan, who grew up in Sarnia, Ontario. Tall, blonde and extraordinarily beautiful, she met my father through friends of her parents who lived in Midland, and she found my father more thoughtful and compelling than the young men her own age. They were married June 13, 1942. I was born three years later and my brother, John, two years after that. As small children, we were proud of our father and we thought the fathers of our friends were sissies because they cooked food on the barbecue and played with their children.

My father worked an eighty-hour week. On Monday, he started operating at the Midland Hospital at 8 A.M. At noon, he came home for lunch in our roomy brick house on Hugel Avenue, took a nap and was in his office on Midland's main street by 1 P.M. He stayed there until 6 P.M., when he came home again for dinner. By seven, he was back in his office, still seeing patients. At 9 P.M., he set out on his house calls. At 11 P.M., he came home for a cup of tea with my mother before bed. But nighttime didn't necessarily mean rest for my father because he was often roused from his sleep to deliver babies or rescue victims in a traffic accident. In those days there were no paramedics, and my father and the other doctors were expected to pull people from the burning wrecks and sometimes do surgery on the spot.

On Saturday, he went to the office and followed the same relentless schedule except that he didn't operate. In the early years of their marriage, my mother says my father also worked Saturday nights, when farmers around Midland came to town to do their shopping. On Sunday mornings, like many physicians in the mid-twentieth century, he went to the hospital dressed in his Sunday best, a striped black director's coat and black trousers, to see how his patients were recovering from their operations. Then, if we were lucky, if there were no boating or automobile disasters, my father would take us on his

Sunday-afternoon calls to Balm Beach or Lafontaine, small communities outside Midland. After his house calls were over, we would picnic with him at the beach, but the gaunt, exhausted man eating my mother's egg salad sandwiches seemed to look right through me as if I weren't there.

Occasionally, he would break into one of his favourite calypso tunes like a robot whose power button had been mistakenly pressed, springing him back to life. I loved those moments when my father sang because I felt he was inviting me to understand that he was not all work. But the tunes often died on his lips, and he would return to eating as if he'd never uttered a sound.

If I was in awe of his work habits, I was also impressed by the stories others told me about my father's legendary fortitude and courage. For instance, I knew how he had saved himself in the 1920s, when he was a young doctor visiting a logging camp on Hope Island in Georgian Bay. On my father's way home from Hope, a January storm came up and he lost his bearings. Somehow he had missed the path of Christmas trees marking the winter highway on the ice from Hope Island to Thunder Bay, and he was going round in circles far out on the frozen bay. To make matters worse, his horses had begun to rear and whinny because they were spooked by the clear black ice that resembles open water. So, he decided to let Tim, his fox terrier who always rode next to him on the sleigh, find the way home. The horses stopped panicking when they saw Tim adroitly picking his way across the ice and followed the dog through the blizzard to Cedar Point on the mainland.

In another story, my father helped a frightened lightkeeper on a remote Georgian Bay island when his son had an appendicitis attack in a November gale. The storm meant the lightkeeper couldn't leave his home on the Western Islands, so my father said he would walk him through the operation step by step over the ship-to-shore radio. My father was unflappable; he told the lightkeeper that taking out an appendix was an easy operation because the appendix lies close to the skin of the abdomen.

My father's calm bedside manner reassured the lightkeeper, and the man agreed to perform the operation with one of his wife's kitchen knives. Luckily for the lightkeeper, my father also had the presence of mind to call the coast guard, who arrived just as the man was about to cut his son open in a re-enactment of the Abraham and Isaac story. When the coast guard brought the boy to the mainland, my father was waiting on the dock to rush them to the hospital.

Even when my father was sick and dying, he made himself rise from his bed every night to give a morphine injection to a lake-boat captain ill with cancer. My father had given his word to the boat captain that he wouldn't let him suffer, and come hell or high water, my father intended to keep his promise. My father's will was formidable, and it was focused on helping others.

John Kenneth Galbraith once said that the superior confidence that people repose in the tall man is well merited. "Being tall, he is more visible than other men, and being more visible, he is more closely watched. In consequence, his behaviour is far better than that of smaller men."

My father was one of Galbraith's tall, good men, and even when I was angry with him for neglecting me, I never thought of criticizing his character. My father was open-hearted and non-judgmental. He never looked down on the people he helped, and his big, sad blue eyes signalled unguarded depths of compassion—an expression I didn't see in other men's faces.

He had been a top scholar at university and he still loved to learn. By his bed, next to the cabinet with the white hankies, he kept a pile of German grammar texts so he could speak to the German immigrants who had arrived in Midland after the war.

Because he was generous and a tad too trusting, people sometimes took advantage of his good nature. In 1929, my father's friend embezzled my father's savings, so he didn't have the money to go back to medical school and specialize in surgery, his first love. That's why he remained a general practitioner in Midland for the rest of his life.

Not that any betrayal could dampen my father's determined spirit for long. He believed in the myth of the invincible giant and failed to understand that giants aren't as strong as they look. They usually die young, worn down by gravity, and in my father's case, by overwork. However, my father's optimistic nature kept him from understanding the undertow that goes with the myth of Brobdingnagian proportions.

Was he cut out to be a father? Certainly, he excelled at caring for others and he was a kind man. But he was driven by archetypal healing energies, which he gave to others. A family friend used to warn me with a sigh, "Shoemakers' children don't have shoes." I was four when I was taken to the hospital for an operation on my tonsils. My father wasn't allowed to operate on his own child, but he towered over me in his surgical whites while another doctor applied a chloroform mask to my face. I struggled against it, screaming that the man was trying to kill me. As I lay shrieking on the hospital table, my father said, "Suzabelle, just relax. We're not going to hurt you."

Things were always going to be fine, according to my father. My mother said my father was the only person she knew who never had a crisis. When the public school across from our house burned down in the middle of the night, my father woke up to take a look and quickly went back to bed. My brother, mother and I stayed up to watch the shocking spectacle, terrified that the showers of sparks were going to catch fire on the cedars by our house. My father said there was no danger of that, and it turned out he was right. In the morning, our house stood safe and sound and he set off for his 8 A.M. operation.

But I was beginning to distrust my father's upbeat approach. A week before the tonsil operation, he had told me it wouldn't hurt when he pricked my finger to take a blood sample, and it felt like a bee sting. I cried that morning in his office because he hadn't told me the truth. So, when I awoke after my tonsil operation and felt pain, I wouldn't speak to my father. For a month afterwards, he couldn't bring his black doctor's bag into the house because I would start screaming.

As I grew older, I tried to emulate his stoicism. When I broke my left arm at the age of twelve, I pretended I was fine. I knew I'd hurt myself badly, but it was the first day of the summer holidays and I didn't want to wear a plaster cast. So, for days afterwards I lied to my father about my arm. Every evening, he would examine me and I would swing my broken arm up over my head and say, "See, Dad, no pain." My mother noticed I didn't move my left arm much when he wasn't around and pressured my father to look at me again. When he did, I admitted that my arm hurt like the dickens and he quickly took me to the hospital and slapped on the unwanted cast. Even so, within a week I was playing golf with one arm and swimming by holding my arm (tightly wrapped in a plastic bag) out of the water.

Neither the high marks on my report cards at the Midland Public School nor my budding stoicism made my father really notice me. I can't remember a single one-to-one conversation between us when I was growing up. Frustrated, I wrote a letter to Norman Vincent Peale, asking the famous advice columnist of the 1950s what to do about a father who worked too hard and didn't pay attention to his children. Unbeknownst to me, my mother never sent my letter; instead, she showed it to my father, who apparently found it endearing.

It made no difference. Nothing did. Not the appeals of his wife or his children or the warnings from his friends, who told my father that one of these days he was going to die of a heart attack. He would smile and promise to take us on a holiday, away from his ringing phone. Then he went back to work, driving himself through his exhausting days. He refused to accept that he no longer had the youthful stamina of the doctor who could stay up all night and play poker and then operate all morning, and as the years went by, he would arrive home for dinner worn out and discouraged.

Although he had no spare moments to play with me or with my brother, a fun-loving athlete, he made time to nag John about his performance at school. Once, I overheard my father angrily lecturing my brother about his marks. I was shocked when my father said, "Look, you are my only son. You have to do better than this." I remember thinking, "Say that to me, Dad, and leave my brother alone. I'm the one who likes to excel. I won't let you down."

I felt outraged. If my father was determined to overlook me, then I would match my will against his and make the world pay attention. I would show my father by making a name for myself as a writer, and I vowed that I would shut the door forever on the small town where my father's obsession with his work as a country doctor fell like a shadow across my childhood.

Of course, I didn't realize that instead of shutting the door on my early years with my father, I would spend a lifetime searching for a relationship with him in my books. Nor did I appreciate how the tragedy of his early death would affect me. The dream I had a few months ago, about my father and me standing outside the Midland library, suggests that I am not only beginning to acknowledge the impact of his death but that I can understand him for who he was.

In November 1963, the week that U.S. President John F. Kennedy was assassinated, my father came down with a mysterious flu. After a week in bed, he went to the hospital and I never saw him alive again. I was away at boarding school when I was told that he had died early one morning of an unknown cause. My mother said he'd been offered a chance to go to a specialist in Toronto, but my father had elected to stay with "the boys," as he called the other doctors. Midland Hospital had been good enough for him as a young doctor and it was good enough for him now.

My mother didn't have an autopsy performed. Later, it turned out that some of the men in my father's side of the family suffered from a rare form of heart disease, and this is probably what took my father's life too. His funeral was held in Midland's Anglican church in early December; most of the population in Midland and Penetanguishene showed up, including two farmers wearing high wading boots. They had walked through the snow all the way from Lafontaine, a small francophone community about fifteen miles outside Midland. One of them sobbed brokenly when he shook my mother's hand.

My brother and I were shocked by the outpouring of love for my father. He had brought many of the people in the church into the world and now they were watching him leave it. He had taken out the tonsils of the notorious murderer Mel Wilke in Penetang's Oak Ridge, and the gallbladder of the orchestra leader, Lawrence Welk. Criminal or celebrity, he had looked after them all. He just hadn't managed to look after himself.

I am sixty-one now. In a year, I will be sixty-two, the same age he was when he died, and it's taken me all this time to understand that I've spent much of my life searching for a way to keep my father close, and to recognize that I didn't want to share him with the community—I wanted him for myself. My mother says my father thought she would know best about child raising, and like many men of his generation he didn't understand that his nurturing was needed, too. Of course, he was dead wrong about that.

As a young woman, I didn't understand that writing novels would lead me back to my father and let me see how much I still miss him. But I believe the act of making things up has helped me to know him a little for who he was. Writing about loss doesn't heal the hurt. However, it does describe what the hurt is, and that is a step towards accepting it.

I chose a writing career to have a voice and a separate identity from my old childhood persona as "the doctor's daughter." I intended to be myself, but it turns out that being myself means accepting my father as part of me.

Portrait of the Artist as Father

by Emily Urquhart

JUNE 2006

The room is stuffed with earnest-faced art students wearing name tags, seeking their benefactors in order to thank them in person. It's the second time I've accompanied my father to this annual event, and each year I'm surprised by how many scholarship winners turn up at the Ontario College of Art and Design's awards ceremony, although I suspect attendance is mandatory.

Still, the fear that the student designated to receive the scholarship in my brother's name may not be in the room makes me stiff with anxiety. It's unlikely that my father will dwell on the absence for any length of time, as he's a fairly content fellow. But still, the *idea* of his disappointment is paralyzing.

The previous ceremony had a funereal feel and I swore I'd never return, but when my father asked me to join him again this year, I couldn't say no. The first recipient was a gracious young woman. This year's winner is also female—a relief. If it were a boy, comparisons would be inevitable.

My father (white-haired, wearing a white suit-coat) follows me through the crowd sipping Chardonnay while I scan name tags. He wants to meet the recipient of the Marsh Urquhart Memorial Scholarship, but she's difficult to find in the crush of students. I ask a boy in a rumpled sweater if he knows the person I'm looking for, and he does. He went to high school with her. She's just over there—the small one with the dark hair. I'm relieved, but still tense.

I introduce her to my father. He shakes her hand and inquires about her work. I interject with jokes and benign questions whenever I detect a hint of impending silence or discomfort from either party. When I think she's had enough, I make a move to end the conversation with an offhand comment about dinner reservations. After everyone has said goodbye, I usher my father through the crowd and out into the early evening light. We find a restaurant where we talk about art, my brother and how nice it was to meet the scholarship student. We've gotten through it again, and I'm off-duty for at least another twelve months.

FEBRUARY 2004

I imagine my parents in the kitchen of their Stratford home, quietly discussing my future. My mother has pulled one of the brightly coloured chairs away from the table and sits beside the telephone while my father lingers by the back door. They finish speaking and my father slips quietly out into the late afternoon. There is a light snow-fall, so he leaves tracks as he walks down towards the river with the intention of looping back once he reaches the frozen bank.

Inside the house, my mother is holding the receiver of the tele-phone and dialling the international code and seven numbers that follow. The first two calls don't go through. On the third try, she reaches me in my apartment in Kyiv, Ukraine, where I've lived for five months while working for an English-language newspaper. I pick up on the first ring because I'm expecting the call.

"Your father couldn't tell you this himself," she says. "But he feels that terrible things are happening to you in that country, and he wants you to know that if you need to come home, he will buy you a plane ticket right away."

The previous evening, after growing tired of a party at the U.S. Marine House—with its large relief sculpture of Lenin eyeing the American-style saloon bar opposite—I'd decided to go back to the apartment. My roommates stayed on, and so I did something very practical. I hailed a taxi. A real one, with official-looking lights and a running meter (normally I flagged down an unmarked car and bartered over an appropriate fare with the driver).

Shortly after the cab dropped me off, I was walking through the archway that leads into my giant, Soviet-style building complex when a man approached me and firmly grabbed my hand. I don't know what he said and I don't ever want to know. I struggled, and the white mitt I was wearing came off in his hand, freeing me. Just as I turned to run, I was knocked off my feet and dragged into the unlit archway by a previously unseen accomplice.

They kicked me in the ribs and the head, and were trying to reach the purse that was looped tightly across my chest. I made the task increasingly difficult by kicking back, screaming and biting, but eventually the more brutal of the two threw me onto my stomach and, quite swiftly and daintily, lifted the bag from around my shoulders. They ran off into the night, leaving me lying in a snowdrift with no house keys, no money and no identification.

I picked myself up and stumbled into a nearby café where the night cleaning staff let me use the telephone over and over again until my roommates returned from the party. By the following morning, I found that walking was made almost impossible by the spike of pain that shot up from my tailbone with each step.

The assault and ensuing injury, which had prompted the phone call, were the final pieces of bad luck that had been relayed to my father via my mother. Earlier that week, my ex-boyfriend had hacked into my email inbox and found a particularly humiliating passage from my private messages to cut-and-paste and send back to me with his own comments. He found a second outlet for his rage in creating a thinly veiled hate-site directed at me. And, finally, to go with what I believed was a broken tailbone, I'd also recently suffered a broken heart—the details of which were never passed on to my father—God willing—by my mother. But I think he had a pretty good idea.

My mother is the medium through which our family channels all unpleasant information, whether it originates with me, her stepchildren or my father. It is a gloomy but nevertheless crucial role.

Statements like, "No, we cannot pay for your (insert: divorce, wedding, mortgage, weird art project, trip to Tallinn)" and "Your child has decided not to pursue (insert: higher education, the birth control method, a career)" are part of her repertoire of communications.

And there are many of us to communicate with. Describing my blended family reminds me of those logic problems from math class involving two trains travelling at different speeds. When my mother met my father, he was already a successful painter, lumped in with a colourful group of artists from London, Ontario, who were being written about in art magazines and *The Globe and Mail*. She was twenty-four and he was forty, a divorcee with four children. My oldest (half-) sister was seventeen when I was born. My oldest (quarter-) nephew is twenty-five (he is four years my junior) and my youngest (quarter-) niece is one. I am the youngest sibling of five and also an only child. I exist because those two trains (my parents) passed each other on the tracks at a specific moment in time and collided.

I'm not exactly sure how my mother described the events of that week in early February 2004, but my father saw my surroundings as the source of my troubles.

Maybe he believed that this spate of bad luck could have been avoided if I'd stayed in Vancouver, or if I'd been offered a job in Paris instead of Kyiv. If I could have nursed a broken heart and dealt with cyber-terrorism while strolling in Les Jardins du Luxembourg, life would be bearable. If I'd been attacked in those gardens by, say, Pierre and François behind the Medici Fountain, as opposed to Igor and Yuri in a Stalinist archway, I might have put my years of French lessons to good use and reasoned with the two thugs. It was important to my father that I learn to speak the language of the country that has entranced him for nearly fifty years, so I slogged through French grammar from the age of five, but Russian, Ukrainian—those languages were entirely new to both of us.

On the telephone, I am still absorbing my father's indirect request that I should come home when my mother delivers his final message: "He also wants you to know that he loves you," she says, before the line fills with static and the connection is broken for a third time.

My father grew up in a funeral home on Main Street near the corner of Lundy's Lane in Niagara Falls. His mother, grandmother and maid overfed and overcared for him and his younger brother. His parents sold the family funeral business, as they did not want their two boys bearing the burden of the dead. Tony, my dad, drew at night while listening to radio soap operas, and in his teens earned himself a place at the Albright Art School in Buffalo. Although he chose art over the funeral business, death is a constant theme in his work—from his enormous gravesite paintings of the early eighties to his recent skull-and-bone sketches. (A month before the OCAD awards, I saw the skeletal drawings pinned to the corkboard that covers one kitchen wall and is always a staging ground for my father's next creative move. I was initially worried by the skulls, but then his work is always organic in theme.)

During his twenties and early thirties, my father lived in London, Ontario, with his schoolteacher wife and their four children. He had a job at the University of Western Ontario, and his career as an artist was going well. I think it was a happy time, and certainly in the artful black and white photos of my siblings as children, it looks light-filled, with few dark shadows.

It didn't last. I don't know at exactly what point their life together began to deteriorate or what role my father played in the destruction of his first marriage. I do know that his first wife was an alcoholic and that she started drinking at a late stage in their fourteen-year marriage.

Should I be smug-faced and thankful that my father's initial family fell apart? After all, it provided the basis for my existence. What I've learned, though, is to respect his past—linked with that of my siblings—and to accept the sorrows that followed in its wake.

In the early seventies, a judge decided that my two brothers would stay with their mother in London, so my two sisters moved with my father to Waterloo, where he had secured a teaching job at the university. My mother, a young widow, entered their life a few years later. I followed early one morning on a sunny day in February, just ten months after my parents were married.

Our first house was a cacophony of fighting teenaged girls (the bedrooms), pontificating male artists (the living room) and a demented dog made further crazy by my brothers' weekend torments (attic, kitchen, bedrooms, living room and yard).

Three floors down, in the dank and musty basement, was the mysterious world of my father's studio. Ten-foot paintings were propped against the staircase, acting as a flimsy railing. The smell of turpentine and oil paints drifted up through the ventilation system.

Tubes of paint were lined neatly along Plexiglas palettes, where he mixed colours for his sculptures and small triptychs.

The older children were allowed to work alongside my father in the studio, and so when my brothers visited on weekends they disappeared down into the basement for hours. At that point, my teenaged sisters were too wild and boy-crazy to care for our father's strange cave of creativity.

I can remember a great sense of unease while sitting with our dog, Buffer, at the top of the basement stairs, listening to the harried sounds of classical music and the occasional words of encouragement from my father about my brothers' work. Because both Buffer and I were barred from joining this club, we were all the more determined to creep down those stairs and spy on its members.

Buffer slipped down whenever someone left the door open. I often sat on the top two stairs, hidden behind the canvases, just to listen. But once I pushed too close trying to get a better look, and came crashing down along with one of the large-scale oil paintings. I believe it was of a French gravesite.

I spent a good deal of my youth in French cemeteries, peering into the open graves that my father found so inspirational while he sat on his little blue fold-out chair sketching, and envisioning the immense paintings that would eventually turn into an entire series. (Where was my mother? Writing maybe? Sitting huffily in the rental car? More likely, she was at our rented farmhouse in Flavigny, doing chores.)

You have never seen pure and simple joy until you spend a few minutes watching my father sketch. This can happen in his studio—now a small, house-like structure that takes up the entire square footage of my parents' backyard—or in a rental car parked in the French countryside during a torrential downpour. His work ethic is tremendous and his rapture is palpable. His love of art, both creating and appreciating it, is rivalled by only three other pursuits.

The first is food. An al fresco meal at a French café is the ultimate choice, but a can of Campbell's tomato soup will do in a pinch. The second is music, but only classical, and "Please don't turn off the car while the song is still playing." And the last is golf, which seems an odd pursuit to add to this mix, but he's strangely competitive in this area. This I know, as all of his children do, from my brief career as a caddy for him. The hours were long and the pay was terrible.

Of course, my father's pleasures extend beyond these four pillars. He also finds great happiness in his expanding family, which has multiplied several times so that it now includes nine grandchildren, who are all tiny carbon copies of my father. Good, strong genes, apparently, are why all of his grandchildren look uncannily like he did as a child.

I have not added to this brood myself, and I sometimes wonder if my children—yet unborn—will ever know their grandfather. And will he be able to identify my offspring in the crowd of all those other kids produced by my siblings?

Each of his children, and in turn his grandchildren, possesses an aptitude—if not exactly a talent—in visual art. (One nervous grandchild expressed an interest in becoming a landscape painter, as it was a profession free of danger and did not involve firearms—of which he is very scared.)

However, my brothers, with their early lessons in the musty basement studio, are the ones that shone. My eldest brother, Marsh, in particular, was a great draftsman and the only one among us to inherit my father's precise eye and the ability to create impossibly perfect lines. Marsh was my father's greatest achievement, and in the end, also his greatest failure.

Marsh was sensitive, too caring, crushed by worry and apprehension, but he was also pragmatic and organized. There was a constant battle between the two sides of his character.

He must have started drinking as a teenager in London, when he and my second brother, Aidan, still lived with their mother. He moved to Toronto after high school to attend what was then the Ontario College of Art, where he produced an impressive body of work, both in volume and sheer talent.

I've heard my father say that Marsh was simply waiting to make his name in the art world, waiting for our father's own impressive career to die (with him, I suppose) before arriving on the scene. It would be like Marsh, that patience and that fear of intruding, but I don't believe this was the case.

His talent deteriorated as steadily as his life. Instead of a signature, Marsh drew a caricature of himself to sign letters. It was a quick portrait of his black fringe, thick moustache and round glasses, but it was a perfect likeness. As his drinking grew heavier, this caricature changed. The glasses were askew, the moustache sparse and his mouth reduced to one simple line.

Through his drinking, he lost his girlfriend and then, much later, his job and, finally, in September 2001, his life. Not in a bar fight, or an accident. At thirty-six years of age, my brother died of alcoholism.

Throughout the year before my brother's death, my father lightly, and then strongly, suggested that Marsh check into a rehabilitation clinic. After a great struggle, the two of them visited a centre in Guelph, where the clinic facilitator looked at the yellowing whites of my brother's eyes and told him that his liver was failing and he'd be dead by the end of the year.

My brother refused to consider rehabilitation, and he and our father quarrelled in the car on the way home. After that, my father backed off for a while, but Marsh was constantly on his mind.

During this time, I was living in Toronto and my father made frequent trips to the city. We would meet at my apartment and then visit the galleries on Queen Street West, followed by a look at the latest

Art Gallery of Ontario show, and afterwards we would eat lunch at one of the little restaurants on Baldwin Street. Over the course of the meal, the conversation always led to my brother. These were sad and uncomfortable talks and I inevitably changed the subject.

We had one of these lunches on the day in late September that Marsh died, although we didn't hear about my brother's death until after six that evening. We ate at a corner table in a small Italian restaurant and we spoke about the recent terrorist attacks in New York and Washington.

"What do you think Marsh would say about this?" my father asked me. In recent days, my brother wasn't leaving his Etobicoke apartment. No one knew how he passed his time, but we did know that he was drinking.

"He's probably been watching those towers fall over and over on television all week," my father said.

"Maybe," I said, and changed the subject. Five hours later, my mother telephoned (always my mother on the phone) to tell me that my brother was dead.

Less than a day later, I am at my parents' home in Stratford. I sit in an armchair, staring out our front window, waiting for my father to return. He received the phone call while staying at a hotel in St. Catharines the night before, but he waits until morning to drive home. With a gripping horror, I believe that my father will die on the highway, as he drives with the terrible knowledge of my brother's death permeating the car. Even after he returns safely, but of course damaged, I can't shake this feeling. The concern I have for my father is compounded by a sorrow so thick I can taste it, and by a creeping, debilitating feeling of guilt. Over the next few days, flowers and baked goods arrive at the door and are left to rot where they rest. There is a new and heavy silence in the air. It's enough to say that life changed after that.

I leave for Toronto a week later. I want to stay at home with my father, but my mother ushers me out the door and onto the night train with no chance of saying goodbye to him.

I come home on weekends and lie around listlessly on the living room couches. I watch my father for signs (of what? I don't know). We sit at the table together one afternoon and he tells me, "Marsh was the most talented of all of my children." But I don't mind. Such is the lot of the dead, to be absolved of their siblings' envy.

A few months pass and I plan an uplifting trip to my father's favourite country. Together, my father and I will visit the art galleries in Paris, go to Lourdes (where he likes to draw the crutches left behind by cripples hoping for a miracle cure), and finally to Flavigny, where we'd lived the year that I was four. But France is actually quite dreary in February, and we both catch cold.

Six months later, when I need to make a decision about moving to Vancouver, I wonder if it's too soon to leave, as it is only a little more than a year since my brother's death. But I go, and from there I venture even further and get a job in Ukraine, a country where the phone lines are dodgy and a visit requires bribes, lies and an expensive visa. The distance helps.

As the years pass, I reserve my father-fretting for certain occasions, specifically when the scholarship is awarded in my brother's name at his alma mater. I would skip the ceremony just to avoid the stress, but thinking of my father there alone in the crowds of students, seeking out the scholarship recipient to congratulate him or her, is way worse.

I can't help worrying about my father; it is somehow innate and uncontrollable. But in the end, as natural order dictates, I still need him more than he needs me. Here is why I believe this is true:

When my contract with the Kyiv newspaper finished, in an effort to prolong the transition back to North America, I decided to return to Flavigny and stay there for several weeks. My father had made his annual pilgrimage to France, and although our dates only connected for a day, he'd agreed to meet my flight to Lyon so we could spend one night together in our former home.

It had been more than a year since I had last seen my dad, and in that time his hair had turned snow-white. He was thinner, too, dwarfed by a tweed suit-coat bought in another, heavier period of his life. But at seventy-one, he looked great. Healthy and red-faced, his eyes, bright blue, twinkled when he caught sight of me at the arrivals gate. I thought to myself, "No one in my life will ever be as happy to see me as my father."

He took the heavier of my two bags, and we walked through the cavernous space of the Lyon airport, past the train station and out into the parking lot to the rental car (a Peugeot, his favourite make).

He started the car and a symphony (Strauss, Beethoven maybe?) blared from the CD player. He reached forward to turn down the volume, as I always request when riding in his cars, but I told him to leave the music playing.

We had a three-hour ride ahead of us and only one day together before he returned to Canada. Tomorrow, he would have to turn around and do this drive again.

I had so much to tell my father about the last year, but as we pulled out of the parking lot and onto the autoroute, my mind was at rest. I was suddenly incredibly tired, and although I fought to stay awake, the fatigue was overwhelming. In that place between sleep and consciousness, it struck me that for the first time since I had left Canada, I felt safe. After months of struggle, heightened awareness and stress, I was able to relax. The symphony rose, reaching a crescendo, and just before I closed my eyes I knew that I had found my way home.

Fathers Know Best

by Pamela Wallin

M‍y father is comfortable with silence; he has no urge to make idle conversation. Don't get me wrong, he's very sociable, but truth be told, he generally prefers his own company—or that of Mother Nature.

You can ride with him in a car for hours, and his only engagement will consist of, "Did you see that?" Meaning, of course, a deer hiding in a bush two hundred metres away or a set of rabbit tracks in the snow, invisible to the human eye—at least any other human eye.

As a kid, I remember many quiet hours with my father. He didn't have a son, and so, as many young girls who idolize their dads do, I tried to play the part. As they'd say today, *we hung out*—often in his workshop.

He raised chinchillas there for a while, and then converted the place to reflect his near-obsession with hunting and fishing. He soundproofed the old shed so he could practise target shooting and display his rifles. As I think about it now, he probably had enough ammunition in there to blow us all to kingdom come.

I know what some of my city friends are thinking—so, as a point of clarification for those who didn't grow up on a farm or in a small prairie town, Dad was not some National Rifle Association fanatic. He was a passionate conservationist, an animal lover who was active in the Fish and Game League. He almost single-handedly built the wetlands project—a protected habitat for birds—just outside of town.

But he was also a provider, so our freezer was always filled with moose, deer, elk, ducks and geese, all felled by his hand.

Eventually I was allowed to participate in the preparatory ritual that took place in that old shop. The wall was lined with old coffee tins and jars and ice-cream pails, each filled with every conceivable shape and size of nail, screw or buckshot. And all organized so that he could lay his hand on just exactly what he wanted without even looking up. It would have put Martha Stewart to shame.

But what fascinated me the most were all those heavy little silver balls, a crucial ingredient in the lethal mixture that formed the innards of a shotgun shell. I would carefully measure the shot—the intended prey determined the size you should choose. Then, with a funnel, I'd fill the red cardboard cylinder. Carefully, with his hand on top of mine, we would pull the lever that magically folded and sealed the cardboard form into an actual shotgun shell.

My dad took me hunting once, and shooting that gopher was the first and last animal I've ever killed. It took the fun out of making shells and bullets, but I learned respect for guns and what they could do, and I share my father's view about the absurdity of the gun-registration laws in this country. Living on a farm and eating what you kill is a very different reality from that of the gun-wielding thugs and gang members on urban streets who hunt humans.

But I digress.

As I said, my father is a man of few words. Still, they are always carefully chosen and to the point.

I remember the much-dreaded conversation to break the news to my parents that I had been fired from the CBC in 1995. The story was about to hit the news pages—and the airwaves—and they needed to hear it from me first.

My mother, as mothers always do, commiserated, took my side and repeatedly denounced those who had done the deed as fools who would get their comeuppance one day.

The seriousness of said event had warranted Dad being dispatched to the basement to pick up the other phone. He waited patiently for a break in the conversation and then asked whether I was angry or sad. I paused for a moment to take my own emotional pulse and determined, not surprisingly, that I was angry. My father responded, somewhat cryptically, "Good. Now just make sure you keep it ice-cold, not red-hot."

I wasn't sure exactly what he meant, but after hanging up the phone it became so obvious. Red-hot anger is about getting even: it's about *them*. He was worried about *me*, and keeping things ice-cold just meant keeping my cool and staying focused on what was next, and not on what could not be undone. It was a million dollars worth of career counselling.

I've always turned to my father in troubled times, so I did it again several years later. Once again, we were in the car, driving to the cabin at the lake—the cabin he built and the place that to this day is my sanctuary and respite from the rigours of my particular real world.

Breaking the comfortable silence, I casually (I was in fact anything but casual but rather in the grip of panic and fear) asked my dad's opinion about some troubling medical symptoms. I had spent the last couple of months in a not-so-successful state of denial.

After years of working in the local hospital as the chief X-ray technician, he was the medical expert for friends and family. For years, he was really the second "doctor" in our town, working alongside old Doc Rollins, and he knew a symptom better than most doctors I've run across on either side of the border.

Somehow, subconsciously, I think I knew what was coming, but hearing it from him made it easier. And I'd have to believe it because he would never lie to me. As we made our way along that oh-so-familiar stretch of road, he listened. Quietly, looking straight ahead and without an ounce of panic in his voice, he said that it sounded like cancer to him and that I should get to a doctor as soon as possible.

It was inevitable, and in spite of my protestations, that Mom and Dad came to be with me for my surgery for colorectal cancer in Toronto. It was delayed for a few days as the hospital—also an international trauma centre—awaited the victims of 9/11. The sad truth, of course, is that there were no survivors. So, a few days later, the surgery went ahead.

Dad announced he'd be at the hospital every morning before 7 A.M., in time for shift change. The handover from the night shift to the day staff, he knew, was a dangerous time for patients. And so, true to his word, he arrived each and every morning of my complicated recovery, and more than once did battle with know-it-all interns and other experts who had forgotten to read my chart.

When it came time to make the decision about chemotherapy, it was again my father's words that guided me. I had wrestled with the decision for days—called doctors, friends, survivors and complete strangers to seek advice and insight. In fact, what I wanted was for someone else to make the decision about chemotherapy, because I simply did not know what to do.

Unfair as it was, I again called my folks. And again, my dad intervened with his particular wisdom.

After I'd laid out the case, both pro and con, he quietly asked, "How badly do you want to live?"

I shot back, "Of course I want to live—I've just come through surgery. I wrote my will, faced death—I'm coping with some bizarre kind of survivor's guilt in the aftermath of 9/11. Yes, I want to live!"

"No," he insisted, trying to clarify and calm. "Do you want to live so badly that you'll never cross the road, take a plane or take a risk ever again? You are not good at being sick, so don't be. Move on with living your life."

He paused for a moment and then added, "I'm your father. I love you. I hope I don't regret these words."

Many times since I decided against chemotherapy, I've tried to tell him that I hope he never regretted those words because I needed to hear them. I needed to be reminded that living cannot just be about fearing the alternative. His insight, his love, were healing and helpful. And I was also very, very lucky to have a couple of great doctors, and a surgeon who was deft and talented.

Recently, the tables were turned. My father was slated to go under the knife for a triple bypass and an aortic replacement. A little risky at the best of times, but for a man in his eighties who had just had a stroke, this was not going to be easy.

The lethally long waiting lists had forced a trip to unfamiliar turf—it meant a plane ride to the province next door. We survived the first phase, and as we sat in his hospital room, I couldn't cope with the predictable silence. I was annoyingly and uncharacteristically cheery about the gruelling procedure he was facing—and about its uncertain outcome. My dad, as you may have surmised, is more than a little stubborn. I was sure that he had made up his mind to survive, but this didn't preclude the awkward but necessary conversation about things like power of attorney, wills and when, or whether, he wanted a Do Not Resuscitate order.

Several years earlier, my sister and I had broached the inevitable and sat down with our parents to discuss wills, funerals, burial plots and under what circumstances they would want—excuse the blunt language—the plug pulled.

It was a little gruesome, but then again, my dad is the kind of guy who built a box to store his own cremated ashes out of the old kitchen cupboards because he didn't want all that good wood to go to waste! Always pragmatic, he decided, in the interim, to use it as a side table to hold the phone and the TV remote, because it's a waste to have it sitting in the basement just waiting. The funny thing is that the damn box represents quite a compromise. Mom wanted to be buried, with Dad at her side. Dad wanted his ashes scattered to the wind, over the places he loved to hunt and fish. So the deal was, Dad would give up some of the ashes to be placed with her on the promise we would do the right thing with the leftovers. Hence the box, which will contain some—but be clear, not all—of the ashes.

But again, I digress.

So, as I sat at the end of Dad's hospital bed, calmly discussing all the "what ifs," it was clear that my father had already thought through all the options: If he could not function, or if he were to be held captive by infirmity, then that would be no life—so, no heroics please.

And if he died on the operating table, he wanted us to know he was at peace. No tears, no drama, but a life lived well.

He did worry about my mother—his wife—being left on her own. He knew my sister and I and the grandkids would be fine. But he swore a blue streak about the new puppy Mom had just purchased—against his wishes. A dog lover, he felt they were past "parenting," and he worried about who would walk the dog or perform the myriad chores of a husband.

You see, a pet is my father's one vulnerability. The only time I ever saw my father cry when I was growing up was when our cocker spaniel, Bubbles, was dying. Unable to watch her suffer, he went across the street to the hospital to get something to put her down. That was one of life's important lessons, and without getting all Kahlil Gibran about it, if you love something, let it go.

Then came the next canine love of his life, Honey, for whom he built a booster seat so that she could see out when she and Dad took to the road in the truck. I'm sure he pointed out the deer and rabbit tracks to her too. They certainly were the talk of the town. When she died, Dad declared a moratorium on dogs. Apparently, my mother missed the meeting.

Conversations can take a strange turn while awaiting surgery—everything from dogs to death. As the clock ticked down, I remembered my moment of truth and how he had taken my hand, as he had in his shop so many years before, and guided me through.

A friend recently gave me a clipping from a magazine. It was the story of a man who, while taking a walk with his father, had encountered an elderly woman, accompanied by her dog, aided by a walking stick, winding her way down the road.

The men asked where she was going and she replied, "I'm already there."

Although they found the answer a little strange, they exchanged a few pleasantries, and parted. But the son felt compelled to ask the old woman another question, and so he doubled back and ran after her.

"What's the secret to a long and happy life?" he asked the old woman.

She paused, and finally answered, "Moments. Moments are all we get."

Living thousands of miles from my family now, each day I realize that our time, too, is measured in moments.

But it always has been.

In just a single moment, you can conquer a fear, feel an indescribable closeness, find peace of mind or remember how one man has saved your life, time and again.

The Contributors

Katherine Ashenburg has a ten-year attention span when it comes to careers. She has been an academic specializing in the Victorian novel, a CBC Radio producer, a *Globe and Mail* editor and a freelance writer. Her work has appeared in *The New York Times* travel section, *Toronto Life*, *The American Scholar*, and *Chatelaine*, among other publications. She is the author of *The Mourner's Dance: What We Do When People Die*, and *Going to Town: Architectural Walking Tours in Southern Ontario Towns*. Her third book, *Clean: An Unsanitized History of Washing Our Bodies*, will be published in fall 2007.

Margaret Atwood's father came from Nova Scotia, as did her mother. She herself spent much of her early childhood in northern Quebec and then Ontario, where her entomologist father was engaged in forest insect research. She began publishing in literary magazines in 1960; her first professionally published book was *The Circle Game* (1966), and her first published novel was *The Edible Woman* (1969). Since then, she has published more than thirty-five books—poetry, fiction and non-fiction—has had her work translated into upwards of thirty-five languages, and has won various literary prizes. Her most recent novel is *Oryx and Crake*, her most recent book of stories is *Moral Disorder* and her most recent volume of poetry is *The Door*, forthcoming in fall 2007.

Anita Rau Badami was born in India and moved to Canada in 1991. She earned a master's degree in English literature from the University of Calgary in 1995. Her graduate thesis became her first novel, *Tamarind Mem*, which was published worldwide in 1996. Her bestselling second novel, *The Hero's Walk*, won the regional Commonwealth Writers' Prize and Italy's Premio Berto, was named a *Washington Post* Best Book of 2001, and was longlisted for the International IMPAC Dublin Literary Award and the Orange Prize for Fiction and shortlisted for the Kiriyama Prize. As well, she is the recipient of the Marian Engel Award for a woman writer in mid-career. She published her third novel, *Can You Hear the Nightbird Call?*, in 2006. She lives in Montreal with her family.

Christie Blatchford, a journalist, has worked for *The Globe and Mail*, the *Toronto Star*, the *Toronto Sun*, the *National Post* and is now once again at *The Globe*, where she is a feature writer and columnist. She won a National Newspaper Award in 1999 for column writing. Born in Rouyn-Noranda, in northwestern Quebec, she moved to Toronto with her family when she was a teenager. Divorced, she has one brother and an English bull terrier. Currently, she is writing a book for Doubleday on Canadian soldiers.

Mary Anne Brinckman is editor-in-chief of *Green Living* magazine, editor of *Green Living Kids* and on the board of the Owl Children's Trust. She was a founding editor of *Toronto Life Gardens* and *Toronto Enviroguide* (now *Green Living*) magazines, and of the children's magazines *OWL* and *Chickadee*. She was also a garden designer, specializing in environmentally friendly gardens. Her gardens have been featured in magazines in Canada, England and the United States.

Nancy Dorrance, an email addict and closet romantic, inherited a love for reading and writing—but not arithmetic!—from her paternal grandmother, who was a rural schoolteacher and a stickler for grammar. Partly due to this nurturing influence, she has made her living from writing for the past twenty years, most recently in the

artment of Communications and Public Affairs at Queen's
University. She lives in Kingston, where she still sees her father regularly
and shares a home with her husband, Tom, and almost-grown son,
Jamie—who is living proof that miracles happen.

Jane Finlay-Young was born in England and immigrated to Canada in 1963.
Her first novel, *From Bruised Fell*, was published by Penguin Canada in
2000. She has recently rewritten a novel on behalf of a deceased friend.
Entitled *Watermelon Syrup*, it will be published in 2007 by Wilfrid Laurier
University Press. Her current project is a work of creative non-fiction about
Israel and her foray into Orthodox Judaism. She lives in Halifax.

Camilla Gibb is the author of three novels: *Mouthing the Words* (winner
of the City of Toronto Book Award), *The Petty Details of So-and-so's Life*
and, most recently, *Sweetness in the Belly* (longlisted for the 2007 IMPAC
Dublin Literary Award, shortlisted for The Giller Prize and winner of
Ontario's Trillium Award). She holds a Ph.D. in social anthropology from
Oxford University and has been writer-in-residence at the University of
Toronto and the University of Alberta.

Catherine Gildiner has a Ph.D. in psychology and was in private practice
for more than twenty-five years. She has written a bestselling thriller
about Darwin and Freud called *Seduction*, which has been published in
five countries and is slated to be a film. She is the author of the Trillium
Award–nominated childhood memoir *Too Close to the Falls*, which was
on bestseller lists in Canada and the United States for more than two
years. She is now preparing a sequel, *Tightrope*, which will cover her life
from the ages of fifteen to twenty-five, in the tumultuous sixties and
seventies. She is also a journalist who has written many humorous articles for newspapers and periodicals. She lives in downtown Toronto with
her husband. They have three grown sons.

Rebecca Godfrey is the author of the novel *The Torn Skirt*. Her most
recent book, *Under the Bridge: The True Story of the Murder of Reena Virk*,

received the 2006 British Columbia Award for Canadian Fiction and the Crime Writers of Canada Arthur Ellis Award. She lives in New York City.

Rachel Manley was born in Cornwall, England, grew up in Jamaica and now lives in Toronto. She is the author of *Drumblair—Memories of a Jamaican Childhood*, which won the Governor General's Literary Award for non-fiction in 1997, and *Slipstream: A Daughter Remembers*, a memoir of her father, Michael Manley, former prime minister of Jamaica.

Sandra Martin, a senior feature writer with *The Globe and Mail*, has won the Atkinson and Canadian Journalism Fellowships and multiple National Magazine Awards. She was the co-editor of the annual *Oberon Best Short Stories* and *Coming Attractions* anthologies from 1984 through 1986 and is the co-author of three books, including *Rupert Brooke in Canada* and *Card Tricks: Bankers, Boomers and the Explosion of Plastic Credit*, which was shortlisted for the Canadian Business Book Award in 1993. A past president of PEN Canada, she is the mother of a grown son and daughter. She lives in Toronto with her husband and her cat, Alice.

Lisa Moore is the author of two collections of short stories, *Degrees of Nakedness* and *Open*, and the novel *Alligator*, which, along with *Open*, was shortlisted for the Giller Prize. She has recently selected and introduced *The Penguin Book of Contemporary Canadian Women's Short Stories*. She attended the Nova Scotia College of Art and Design, and has written for radio and television as well as for *The Globe and Mail* and the *National Post*. Moore lives in St. John's, Newfoundland, with her husband and two children.

Sarah Murdoch lives in Toronto's Annex neighbourhood with her cat, Nora. She is the managing editor, features, of the *National Post*, where she has worked since 1999. Life index: Married: 2 (divorced: 1; widowed: 1); civil unions: 2; children: 0; cats: 10; fixed addresses: 22; full-time jobs: 16 (in journalism: 8; as a writer: 2; as an editor: 6).

ına Nemat was born in Tehran, Iran. After the Islamic Revolution of ɔ79, she was arrested, tortured, slated for execution and imprisoned for more than two years in Evin, a political prison in Tehran. She came to Canada in 1991. In 2005, she was a finalist in the CBC Literary Awards in the creative non-fiction category, and in 2006, she produced a documentary for CBC Radio. Her memoir, *Prisoner of Tehran*, was published by Penguin Canada in April 2007. She lives near Toronto with her husband and children.

P.K. Page / P.K. Irwin is a writer and artist. She was a scriptwriter for the National Film Board of Canada, has taught creative writing workshops and published more than a dozen books of poetry, travel writing, short stories and children's literature. She has had many of her poems set to music and wrote the libretto for a one-act opera. Her art is represented in the National Gallery of Canada, the Art Gallery of Ontario and private collections here and abroad. She has won numerous prizes, including a Governor General's Literary Award for poetry. She holds eight honorary degrees, is a Companion of the Order of Canada, a member of the Order of British Columbia and a Fellow of the Royal Society of Canada.

Emma Richler was born in England, the middle of five children of novelist Mordecai Richler and his wife, Florence. After the family returned to Canada in 1972, she attended a French convent school in Montreal and later studied French literature at the University of Toronto and the Université de Provence in Southern France. She trained in the theatre, studying at the Circle in the Square in New York City and acting at the Young People's Theatre, the Stratford Festival of Canada and at various venues in the United Kingdom, where she has performed on stage and in radio and television dramas. After deciding to give up acting for writing, she published the bestselling *Sister Crazy*, a collection of related short stories, in 2002 and her bestselling first novel, *Feed My Dear Dogs*, in 2005. She lives in London, England, where she is working on her third book.

Eden Robinson is a Haisla/Heiltsuk author who grew up in Kitimat, British Columbia. Her first book, *Traplines*, a collection of short stories, won the Winifred Holtby Memorial Prize and was a *New York Times* Notable Book of the Year in 1998. *Monkey Beach*, her first novel, was shortlisted for both The Giller Prize and the Governor General's Literary Award for fiction in 2000 and named a notable book by *The Globe and Mail*. Her most recent novel is *Blood Sports*. She currently splits her time between Kitamaat Village, Vancouver and Brantford, B.C.

Rebecca Snow has worked for the BBC and independent television companies as a documentary researcher and associate producer. She was born and raised in London, England, by a British father and a Canadian mother. Both journalists, her parents took her to explore far-flung corners of the world from a young age. She studied archaeology at university in England and Mexico and moved to Toronto in 2006. In her spare time, she writes for a Toronto lifestyle website, hosts a book club, is a keen blogger and reads about the ancient Maya. She dreams of being a museum curator.

Tina Srebotnjak, a writer and broadcaster, was the host of CBC's popular noon program *Midday*, and of TVOntario's book show, *Imprint*. She was born in Slovenia, and came to Canada when she was three. She lives in Toronto with her husband and daughter.

Susan Swan, a doctor's daughter, is a novelist who grew up in Midland, Ontario. Her fiction has been published in sixteen countries. Her last novel, *What Casanova Told Me*, was a finalist for the 2004 Canada and Caribbean regional Commonwealth Writers' Prize and named as one of *The Globe and Mail*'s top books of 2004. Her novel, *The Wives of Bath*, a finalist for the Trillium and Guardian fiction awards in 1993, was made into the film *Lost and Delirious*. Swan is also a humanities professor at York University and chair of the Writers' Union of Canada.

Emily Urquhart is a freelance writer whose work has appeared in *Chatelaine* and *The Globe and Mail*, among other publications. Her

⁄ career has included working as a reporter in Kyiv, Ukraine, an ⁄t-planner in Toronto and a temping chambermaid in Edinburgh, ⁄otland. All of these jobs were better than the summer she spent working as a waitress at Planet Hollywood in Dublin. She was born in Kitchener, Ontario, and has lived in three different provinces, including Newfoundland, where she moved in the fall of 2006 to begin a master's degree in folklore at Memorial University in St. John's.

Pamela Wallin is senior adviser to the Americas Society in New York City and is a corporate director for CTVglobemedia and Gluskin Sheff. She also serves on a Bank of Montreal advisory board and volunteers with many organizations. A journalist and entrepreneur, she was the first Canadian woman to co-anchor a nightly national television newscast and went on to serve as the Consul General of Canada in New York City. She has thirteen honorary degrees, is the author of three books, is a member of the Broadcasting Hall of Fame and has been twice recognized by Queen Elizabeth II for her public service.